WOMEN AND RELIGION IN ENGLAND 1500–1720

In the early modern period religious ideology reinforced the assumption that women were inferior to men. Nevertheless, Patricia Crawford argues 'women could both accept beliefs about their inferiority and transcend them'. She demonstrates the agency of women in religious change, and reveals the diversity and significance of religious experience and expression in women's lives.

Women and Religion in England 1500–1720 is an accessible and wide-ranging synthesis of the most recent scholarship on gender and religion. It also represents a distinctive contribution to research.

CHRISTIANITY AND SOCIETY IN THE MODERN WORLD
General editors: Hugh McLeod and Bob Scribner

This is a major series of social historical studies which explore the relationship between Christianity and its social context in the period since 1500. Recent exciting research in this field has greatly increased our understanding of how the changing face of Christianity as a historical religion during the period affected contemporary social attitudes, customs and behaviour. The books in this series draw this research together, providing new perspectives and interpretations on a fascinating area of social history and bringing it before a wider audience.

D1355487

CHRISTIANITY AND SOCIETY IN THE MODERN WORLD
General editors: Hugh McLeod and Bob Scribner

WOMEN AND RELIGION IN ENGLAND 1500–1720

Patricia Crawford

London and New York

First published 1993
First published in paperback 1996
by Routledge
11 New Fetter Lane, London EC4P 4EE

Simultaneously published in the USA and Canada
by Routledge
29 West 35th Street, New York, NY 10001

© 1993, 1996 Patricia Crawford

Typeset in Garamond by
Computerset, Harmondsworth, Middlesex
Printed in Great Britain by
T.J. Press (Padstow) Ltd, Padstow, Cornwall

British Library Cataloguing in Publication Data
A catalogue record for this book is available from the British Library

Library of Congress Cataloguing in Publication Data
A catalogue record for this book has been requested

ISBN 0-415-01697-5

Contents

CONTENTS

Part IV Restoration to toleration 1660–1720

Illustrations

Acknowledgements

Many people have helped me to write this book, and I thank them all. My thanks to librarians, especially at the Bodleian Library, the British Library, the Cambridge University Library and the University of Western Australia. I acknowledge the kindness of the trustees of Dr Williams's Library, London, for allowing me to quote from their manuscripts, and the library staff for their assistance; the librarian of the Angus Library, Regent's Park College, and the Principal, Barry White, for allowing me to consult and quote from manuscripts. My thanks also to the helpful staff of Friends' House Library, London, and especially Malcolm Thomas.

I acknowledge with gratitude the support of the University of Western Australia for study leave, and the Humanities Research Centre, Canberra, for a fellowship in 1986. And I warmly thank the office staff of the History Department – Dawn Barrett, Judy Bolton, Ingrid Buschmann and Muriel Mahony – for help with word processing.

The interest of my students in the University of Western Australia has provided me with support, and I thank especially Claire Walker and Josie Hill. Friends and relatives have assisted in various ways. I am grateful to them all, especially Ursula and Gerald Aylmer, and Mary and Ken Green who have befriended me in England over the years. Seminars at the Humanities Research Centre, ANU, in the feminism and the humanities year, at the AHMEME conferences, and at the University of Western Australia have provided valuable comments.

Living as I do in Western Australia, I am conscious of the kindness of friends who send me references, comments and their papers, enabling me to keep in touch with current work; special thanks to Val Drake, Ann Hughes, Sarah Jones, Anne Laurence, Phyllis Mack, Mary Prior and Keith Thomas. For allowing me to consult unpublished papers, I am grateful to Inez Alfors, Clive Field and Susan O'Brien; for discussion and comments, Patrick Collinson, Colin Davis, Gail Jones, John Morrill and Kevin Sharpe.

Bob Scribner suggested that I write the book, and he and Lois have been constant friends. Penny Boumelha, Sarah Jones, Anne Laurence, Jane Long, Hugh McLeod, John Morrill, and Bob Scribner I thank most warmly for reading the manuscript and making perceptive comments. In the Routledge editorial team, I am grateful to Claire L'Enfant, Louise Snell and Sarah-Jane Woolley for their encouraging support.

My greatest thanks are to Lyndal Roper, who has discussed with me the ideas about women in early modern Europe over a number of years, and has read and commented on the manuscript, and to Sara Mendelson who has been working with me on a social history of sixteenth- and seventeenth-century women in England. Sara had shared material and ideas for nearly a decade, and I deeply appreciate her careful reading of this entire book. None of these friends is responsible for mistaken views or errors. Finally, I acknowledge the support of my husband, over many years.

Patricia Crawford
February 1992

Abbreviations

BDBR	*Biographical Dictionary of British Radicals*
BL	British Library, London
Bodl.	Bodleian Library, Oxford
BQ	*Baptist Quarterly*
CSPD	*Calendar of State Papers Domestic*
CRS	*Catholic Record Society*
DNB	*Dictionary of National Biography*
DRO	Devon Record Office
DWL	Dr Williams's Library, London
EHR	*English Historical Review*
Eng. Exp.	English Experience, Amsterdam
ERL	English Recusant Literature
Foxe	*The Acts and Monuments of John Foxe*, ed. S. R. Cattley, 8 vols, 1939 edn
FHL	Friends' House Library, London
HMC	*Historical Manuscripts Commission Reports*
J. Eccles. H.	*Journal of Ecclesiastical History*
OED	*Oxford English Dictionary*
SCH	*Studies in Church History*
sig.	signature, or gathering of pages in an early printed book
Trans. R. H. S.	*Transactions of the Royal Historical Society*

Note concerning dates and spellings

The year has been taken to begin on 1 January, not 25 March as in the Old Style calendar.

Spellings and punctuation of original documents have been retained, but printers' errors have been corrected, and j substituted for i without comment.

The place of publication of books is London, unless otherwise indicated.

Introduction

Apprehending the divine: gender and the history of religion

There was a Father that came recently to England, whom I heard say that he would not for a thousand worlds be a woman, because he thought that a woman could not apprehend God! I answered nothing but only smiled, although I could have answered him by the experience I have of the contrary.[1]

A woman could not apprehend God: this man's assumptions were not a-typical of early modern English society, yet from the perspective of a woman, his views were ludicrously wide of the mark. Mary Ward, for it was she who smiled to herself, did not bother debating. She knew that she apprehended God and that nothing else mattered. Nevertheless, she also knew that she lived in a society in which religion, as well as all other aspects of social life, was influenced by ideas about the two sexes. So she did not argue, she only smiled.

This book focuses on women and their apprehensions of God in early modern England. Religious belief mattered to virtually everyone in that society, and many women's religious beliefs were of central import-ance in their lives. Women were generally assumed to be inferior to men, and religious ideology reinforced such beliefs. Nevertheless, it will be part of my purpose to show how women could both accept beliefs about their inferiority and transcend them. They were neither passive nor oppressed victims, but rather human agents, making their history within a social structure which was not of their making.

In this period of early modern history, from roughly the beginning of the sixteenth century to the early eighteenth century, certain major religious changes occurred. In 1500 there was one holy, Catholic church. By 1720 the established church was a Protestant one, and there were a variety of different Christian churches. The Reformation in the sixteenth century altered theology and institutions, arousing great passions. Religious disputes were a source of tension in seventeenth-

1

century England, especially during the Civil Wars and Interregnum. A further purpose of this book is therefore to discuss the effects of these changes and disputes upon women's religious practices and beliefs and to explore in turn women's part in bringing about religious change. Chronologically, the main focus is on the seventeenth century, and particularly on the revolutionary period, 1640–60.

Women's religious beliefs in the early modern period have been relatively little studied, although there is a vast general and specialist literature on the Reformation, religious change and Puritanism. A short book such as this raises some of the issues of women's history and religious history, and is designed both for general readers interested in the significance of gender in English society and for specialists in the early modern period and religious history. This introduction and chapter 1 provide some general introduction for those unfamiliar with early modern English history.

The sources for a study of women and religion are diffuse. Women created fewer records than did men, and since they were deemed to be of less social significance, this is reflected in the survival of evidence. There are more documents about the church as an institution and about the clergy, who were male, than about the laity. The known evidence can, and must, be re-read, but it is always a reading against the grain. There was a gender bias in the records, and this has coloured nearly all subsequent historical writing.

In this book I have concentrated on suggesting a new agenda for discussion, and on providing some indication of the findings which new approaches can offer. Since much of the evidence relating to women needs to be reinterpreted, detailed discussion of particular instances is necessary at some stages to illustrate the possibilities of a re-reading. Specific examples have the further advantage that they are far more suggestive than a series of general propositions.

In addition to discussing the role of religion in women's lives, and assessing their part in the English Reformation and subsequent religious changes, I have a third object. This is the most difficult: to show the significance of the male/female distinction in religious belief and the significance of gender in religious history. By gender I understand the socially constructed meaning of sexual difference. Gender is specific to a society and is subject to historical change. A study of religion should thus illuminate the social relations of the sexes.

God, the unknowable, was known in terms of human concepts, and, as we shall see, the relationship of the believer to the divine was usually referred to in metaphors of family life. Just as religious belief was understood in a gendered way, so belief in turn affected the ways in which men and women related to each other. It is crucial to analyse what may be termed 'the sexual politics of religion' in order to develop our understanding about the role of religion in early modern English society. Unless historians study questions about the politics of sex, of marriage and of the family, all of which involve questions of power between men and women, then they will fail to understand the wider systems of power in early modern society. Furthermore, if historians continue to write texts which purport to be universal, but which lack any awareness of gender, they participate in the perpetuation and legitimation of certain kinds of gender hierarchies in their own society.[2]

THE HISTORY OF RELIGION AND GENDER

The history of religion is of the ideas and beliefs by which people seek to apprehend the divine. In early modern England, practically everyone believed in a Christian God,[3] although there were major disagreements about the nature of God and the ways in which institutional worship was to be organised. Religion consisted of both private beliefs and public practices. Religious beliefs ordered people's views of the world.

Religion can be analysed in terms of the social functions which it performed, both for the individual and for society at large. It legitimated authority and enforced particular moral codes. More recently, anthropologists have focused on the study of religious beliefs as a system of cultural meanings.[4] Thus, the structure of beliefs can also be studied as a way of revealing the gender order. The beliefs of both men and women about the divine can be analysed in terms of ideologies which reflected and reinforced the dominant ideals of their society about the respective social positions of the two sexes. Religious symbols are, however, many-faceted, and these can be manipulated by individuals for complex and subtle purposes.[5] The symbolic significance of women's religious beliefs in early modern England awaits attention.

The historiography of the history of religion in England has been dominated by the work of Christian believers. This has been termed the vertical approach to religious history, a search for ancestry. By contrast, there is the horizontal approach which seeks to locate religion in a social context.[6] The social history of religion is less about the institutional church and ministers and more about the believers and how they found meaning for their lives and for death. The approach of the social historian to religious history, Bob Scribner has argued, should be one interested in 'popular religion' and 'religiousness' rather than in religion

3

defined through its doctrinal or ecclesiastical purity. While this should neither supersede nor detract from the value of the older genre of 'religious history', it should contribute to our understanding of the subject by relating it to the social context.[7] My approach is similar to Scribner's. In studying women and religious belief in early modern England, the focus is on the difficult and elusive subjects of women's religious practices and beliefs. The institutional church and theological disputes will be discussed in so far as they affected women's beliefs and the options open to them in worship. People's religious lives are far less documented than church history, and the task would be impossible without both the painstaking and careful work of denominational historians over the centuries, and, more recently, that of the social historians who have examined the archives of particular counties with questions about the religion of 'ordinary' people. Many gaps and questions remain, as will be indicated in the discussion which follows.

Not all social historians of religion are interested in women's religious experiences and beliefs. To study the faith of 'Everyman' or 'the common man' can be just that: sex-specific, about men only, without any acknowledgement of the female presence.[8] A feminist approach challenges some of the premises of these recent as well as the traditional historical accounts.[9] However, not all historians of women have studied female religious beliefs.[10] This may be because the subject appears unexciting: it seems as if the godly woman was the successfully socialised woman. But if we examine the lives of godly, pious women then we can see how belief could become an individual matter which women could transform into something of their own.

Furthermore, sociologists of religion have pointed out that religion did not always function in the interests of social control.[11] Religion could be a subversive force. Over the centuries, when various groups challenged the orthodox forms of Christian belief and established order, they usually did so in terms of a reinterpretation of the teachings of Christ. Most of these movements, which were labelled heretical, involved a disproportionate number of women. Yet although these heresies may have been similar in theology, each was worked out in a specific social context, and the conflicts reveal part of the process by which sexual identities and religious beliefs were defined. Radical religion, such as was found in religious sects particularly during the period of the English Civil Wars and the Commonwealth, provided an opportunity for social criticism and subversion of the established order.

The role of radical religion in the 1640s and 1650s as a force undermining the established order has been widely discussed by historians. The effect of puritan belief on traditional political ideas and on social attitudes has been central to the work of Max Weber, R. H. Tawney, and most recently, Christopher Hill. Hill argued that the radical questioning of the established society was so significant that it amounted to a revolution in ideas and attitudes.[12] Current revisionist scholarship questions the whole idea of a mid-century revolution. Hill, so his critics have argued, over-estimated the significance of the radical challenge. J. C. Davis, in his recent book, argued that the Ranters, a group which Hill identified as some of the most radical revolutionaries, were not a significant group, but rather a figment of contemporary imagination and wishful thinking on the part of historians. [13] The status of the events between 1640 and 1660 – a revolution or not ? – is currently under debate.[14]

While the relationship between religious belief and radical social action has been of central significance in debates about the changes in English society in the period from 1500 to 1720, a discussion of women's role in the 1640s and 1650s has not always been adduced in the debates. Like Joan Kelly's question 'did women have a Renaissance?', the question 'did women have a revolution?' has not usually been asked.[15] Yet if it is argued that radicalism involved a challenge to conventional norms of belief and behaviour, then women's participation in religious movements especially during the 1640s and 1650s has enormous signficance for an assessment of the revolutionary nature of those years. It would be ironic if, at a time when the whole concept of these years as an English Revolution is under attack, it were found that for women there was indeed an English revolution![16]

Yet the radicalism was limited. The radicals only challenged parts of the social order of society, and certainly not its gender order.[17] In a justly famous article in 1958, Keith Thomas examined the effect of the sects on family life. Although a belief in the equality of all before God led to a concept of equality between men and women, Thomas concluded that in the long run the experience of the sects was not of great significance for the history of women's emancipation. The restoration of Anglicanism in 1660 and subsequent suspicion of religious enthusiasm suppressed women in areas where they had been active.[18] Nevertheless, it will be argued here that the opportunity for participation in radical religious activity, and to express ideas individually and collectively with greater freedom than ever before, did have long-term significance for women's position in English society.

A further question to be considered is how social change affects religious belief. Historians have long debated the social consequences of changes in faith. Weber's thesis was that the Protestant Reformation had a profound effect upon the economic development of western Europe and a new attitude to the accumulation of capital and to work.[19] Subsequently, the effects of Protestant social thought upon attitudes to the poor and to marriage and family life have likewise been debated.[20] Less examined has been the reverse process, namely the effect of social and economic change on religious belief. Society was undergoing rapid change in the sixteenth and seventeenth centuries because of the price rise and population growth.[21] Rulers sought to control potential disorder by emphasising the need to obey authority. Social and economic change affected the family and household. The ways in which people thought about domestic relations – those between husbands, wives, fathers, mothers, parents, and children – influenced in turn their understanding of the nature of 'God the Father' and the church as 'the bride of Christ'.

Thus questions about the social history of religion take us to issues of central significance for our understanding of gender and belief in early modern England.

BELIEFS ABOUT WOMEN IN EARLY MODERN ENGLAND

To natural sexual differences all societies ascribe social meaning. These meanings differ across cultures and over time. In early modern England everyone believed that men and women had separate social functions because God had made men and women differently. Their very natures were God-given. Anyone who tried to alter the roles of men and women was deemed both unnatural (against Nature) and ungodly (threatening God's plan). Thus the gender order was powerfully supported by religion.

Christianity affected early modern society's ideas about the functioning of the female body. According to the stories of the creation in Genesis, God created Eve second, after he had created Adam. She was a contingent being, made specifically for Adam. Because woman was the first to sin, God decreed that her punishments would be pain in childbirth and subjection to her husband.[22] The Old Testament interpreted the female biological functions of menstruation and childbirth as polluted and polluting. According to Leviticus, copulation with a menstruating woman should be punished with death. After giving birth, a woman was to be ritually cleansed by a priest. Although the medieval church had sought to treat the churching ceremony as a thanksgiving,

Keith Thomas has argued that for the people at large it remained a purification ritual closely linked to the Jewish one.[23]

Medical understanding of the female body reflected Biblical ideas about the female as a contingent being. According to Galenic medicine, her temperament was cold and moist whereas man's was hot and dry. While he could keep his body healthy by exercise, woman, with a more sedentary life-style and a different constitution, could not, and needed to menstruate in order to rid her body of ill humours. Dire consequences attached to the failure of a woman to menstruate, including green-sickness, mother-fits, and even suicidal fancies. Menstruation was necessary for health.[24]

Ideas about conception were also influenced by ideas of female inferiority. One theory suggested that the sperm was the active agent, shaping the child from the passive matter of the female. At the beginning of the seventeenth century, it was widely believed that a child was conceived by simultaneous orgasm, so female sexual pleasure had a recognised place in a marriage.[25] Churchmen acknowledged that sexual pleasure was necessary for conception, and endeavoured to teach the laity that sexuality should be confined to marriage. Later in the seventeenth century, the discovery of sperm under the microscope led to theories of the preformation of the child in the sperm or the ova which rendered female sexual pleasure irrelevant to the process of conception.[26]

The Catholic church in 1500 was strongly aware of the importance of sexuality in people's lives and attempted to define approved sexual behaviour and to regulate people's conduct through the confessional and the church courts. The celibate clergy were deeply suspicious of woman as a temptation. As Archbishop Longland advised his clergy, 'Everywhere the company of women is to be avoided lest their beauty cleave to your heart.'[27] Virginity and chastity were preferred states of being. However, for those who lacked the gift of continence, marriage was ordained by God, and sexuality had a place there. Although the preference for virginity and celibacy was rejected by the Protestants, they like the Catholics attempted to prescribe rules for sexual conduct, which they shaped in harmony with the common medical assumptions about human sexuality. For example, both Catholic and Protestant divines explained that the birth of monsters indicated God's displeasure at the transgression of rules. The Bible told everyone that if a husband and wife had sexual relations at the time of her menstruation, a monstrous child would be born.[28]

The sexual division of labour in early modern England was explained in religious terms. From the time of the creation, God had appointed men and women to different labour: 'when Adam delved and Eve span' was a description of separate spheres before the Fall.[29] Man was expected to work to provide for his family, while a woman was responsible for caring for children and the household. 'The office of the husbande is to go abroad in matters of profite, of the wyfe, to tarry at home.'[30]

> As huswives keepe home, and be stirrers about,
> so speedeth their winnings, the yeere thorow out.[31]

The household was the most important economic unit, hence it was difficult for a woman to survive outside it. Wages for men and women were fixed at different levels. Thus even if women did engage in paid labour outside the home, their restricted choices of occupation and their lower pay were reminders of the constraints of gender as well as a practical barrier against independent survival.[32]

The symbolism of woman as nurturer was also important. Women cooked, and men ate. In cultural terms, the symbol of a woman came to mean the one who provided nurture, while man was the recipient of nurture. Women were 'nursing mothers', literally and symbolically. They were more concerned than were men with the religious significance of food. Taken together, as Caroline Walker Bynum has shown, the phenomena such as devotion to the eucharist, fasting, and lactation miracles all indicate the religious significance of food.[33]

Certain virtues had come to seem sex-specific. Man was strong and brave, woman was weak but tender-hearted. Then, as even on occasions now, to speak of a quality as masculine was to praise it. (Elizabeth I is still described by historians as 'the most masculine of all the female sovereigns of history', and Margaret Thatcher was referred to as 'the only man' among the Western political leaders.[34]) A Catholic writer preferred 'a woman with a masculine soule' rather than one with 'a tender eye that is soft to teares'.[35]

Justice and law were to reflect God's will. The Bible made wifely subordination a divine injunction, and the assumptions of English common law were in harmony with God's purpose. A married woman was described as a feme covert. She owned no property of her own and her husband answered for her.[36] Nevertheless, while this was the case in theory, in practice married women were allowed some legal and financial rights.[37] In some criminal cases married women might be deemed under their husbands' authority, and therefore they were likely to be charged as accessories rather than instigators of a crime, but in other cases they were required to answer for themselves. In practice, the criminal courts may have been more lenient towards the female sex.[38]

Politics and public administration of the law were defined as male business. Yet even here, there were contradictions, as the accession of two female monarchs during the Tudor period demonstrated. All subjects owed allegiance and obedience to their monarch, yet women were not expected to exercise authority over men. To be a good woman and a good ruler was to be a contradiction, and thus Mary and Elizabeth placed their male councillors and their subjects generally in an awkward position in both secular and religious matters.[39] In the smaller worlds of the towns and villages, an ordinary woman's pursuit of her proper business as a godly wife and mother might take her into the public sphere, as we shall see. The significant point at the outset is that men had claimed the public sphere, both secular and religious, as their domain. Any intrusion by a female was potentially a source of resentment and resistance.

Religious beliefs and practices thus both reflected and reinforced ideas about difference of sex in English society. It is important to remember that even in times of great change and upheaval such as during the Civil Wars and Interregnum, when many traditional ideas were questioned, assumptions about the two sexes remained virtually unchallenged. The Ranters talked of sexual freedom, but when men advocated liberty they were, as Christopher Hill has pointed out, talking of a greater license for men than for the women who were still responsible for the children.[40] There was no reason, however, why the basic ideas about men's and women's earthly roles should have shifted during the period of the English Revolution. All the medical assumptions remained in place about the different natures of the two sexes. Movements to purify and reform religious belief intensified emphasis upon the Bible rather than diminished it. Divines continued to use the Bible, and especially the Pauline epistles, to legitimate particular views of women.[41] From the beginning to the end of the early modern period, from the archbishops of Canterbury to the pastors of separatist congregations, men were agreed: woman was created to be subject to man. As John Bunyan put it later in the seventeenth century, 'Women, therefore, whenever they would perk it and lord it over their husbands, ought to remember that both by creation and transgression they are made to be in subjection to their husbands.'[42] Christianity was itself a significant ideology justifying female subordination.

Contemporaries agreed that religion was necessary for women and also good for them. However, there were attempts to define the ways in which women might relate to the divine. If ideology were all, then the godly woman might appear to be the successfully socialised woman. However, it will be argued in chapter 4 that a regime of piety legitimated an area of activity for women. Religion was something which could provide women with a space of their own. It could also sometimes serve a woman as her best alibi for incursions into the male domain. Authorised to take their beliefs seriously, some women embarked on independent religious activity, as will be shown in part III.

The influence of the stereotypes of the good woman upon individual women and their lives is a difficult question. Certainly, ideals and practices differed.[43] Although ideals were modified during the early modern period, the essential elements of inferiority, passivity and dependence remained constant and the negative construction of female biology had an effect at every social level.[44] Nevertheless, contemporaries recognised that in reality some women were able, intelligent, and more capable than men. Some women also recognised that they were not so incapable as ideology represented them. As Mary Ward wrote early in the seventeenth century, it was a lie to present women as inferior in all things:

> I would to God that all men understood this verity, that women, if they will, may be perfect, and if they would not make us believe we can do nothing and that we are 'but women', we might do great matters.[45]

Religion was not a matter of learning, she said, but of knowledge, 'true knowledge which you all may have if you love and seek it'.[46] Women's own search for meaning in life and for comfort from sorrow influenced their approach to religion. Through faith they attained great spirituality. Because religious belief was something of which everybody approved, women were permitted to take their beliefs seriously, and to make of them something of their own. Perhaps because religion was so important in women's lives, it has been the most widely studied aspect of women's lives in early modern England.[47]

GENDER AND THE LANGUAGE OF RELIGIOUS DEBATE

No one could talk about religion in early modern England without using gendered language and metaphors. Historians are familiar with the discussion about the nature of God in terms of anthropomorphic images. God was the father, Christ the son. Less examined have been the religious metaphors and imagery reflecting difference of sex, and the implications of these ideas for an understanding of religion as another gendered domain in early modern society. Since no one could talk of God, the unknowable, in other than familiar human terms, so it was impossible to discuss religious belief without reference to contemporary understandings of gender difference.

Given the fundamental assumptions about the different roles of males and females in early modern England, it is not surprising that when the organisation of the institutional church was discussed, when theology was debated, and when people practised their Christian faith, the same assumptions affected their understanding of the boundaries between the sacred and the profane and the rituals to be performed. Theology affected social life, because the metaphors in which the relationship of the believer to God was symbolised had as much to say about social relations as about the divine.[48] Edmund Morgan, in his study of the Puritan family in New England, was one of the first to comment on the significance of female metaphors for religious discussion. In a brilliant chapter entitled 'Puritan Tribalism' he inquired 'whether the natural relationships between husband and wife and between parents and children did not influence the way Puritans thought about God and the church'.[49] However, by assuming that domestic relations were 'natural' rather than socially constructed, he precluded examination of questions of gender. Barker-Benfield, in a study of Anne Hutchinson in 1972, explored further the significance of theological difference for gender relations.[50] In other areas of historical study, the significance of gender in religious faith has been the subject of some exciting studies of Christianity, particularly by Caroline Walker Bynum. Walker examined the role of the female metaphor of maternity in thirteenth-century Cistercian thought. The symbol of Christ as a lactating woman made the spirituality of that period more androgynous and susceptible to female influence.[51]

It has been suggested that the sixteenth-century Reformation and Counter-Reformation emphasised hierarchy and authority in the churches. Christ in might and majesty was worshipped rather than the suffering sorrowing Christ. This emphasis upon qualities associated with masculinity rather than weakness and femininity had implications for gender relations in society. The work of Natalie Davis, Lyndal Roper and others on sixteenth-century France and Germany has drawn attention to much of the ambiguity and contradiction of social thought about women's roles at a time of religious change.[52] There was similar ambiguity and contradiction in England. If the concept of God became more masculine, the effects on men and women should be considered. It could be argued that a more masculine deity provoked a more gendered response: a more masculine God emphasised the feminine, the weaker, passive and dependent characteristics of the believer. The more the masculine attributes of God were emphasised, the more the human worshipper was forced to awareness of his or her own sexual being. Thus a woman confronted with a masculine God of power could relate to him in a feminine way. On the other hand, her apparently 'natural' experience of pain in childbirth which had allowed her to associate with the suffering of the crucified Christ in the medieval period was no longer so significant when there was less focus upon Christ's sufferings. Protestants had little place in their theology for bodily pain.

Preachers used familiar words and concepts to teach their congregations about the nature of the divine. Through sermons, homilies and general advice books they sought to make people good Christians. In translating the Bible or in discussing the relationship between believers and God, divines used language and metaphors from customary daily relationships. Metaphors for God were invariably masculine. Everyone spoke of God as Father and as Son. Even the Holy Ghost was referred to with the masculine pronoun. Hausted, for example, wrote in 1636 of the coming of the Holy Spirt as '*hee* shall leape in thee' (my italic).[53] The masculinity of the Father was reflected in the iconography. God was usually depicted as 'an Old Man, with a great beard', 'a grave, ancient, holy old man', or a 'Venerable old man sitting in a chaire, with a severe aspect, wrinkled forehead, circumflext eie-browes, great white curled beard'.[54] In St Edmund's church, Salisbury, he was pictured as an old man measuring the world with a pair of compasses and raising Eve from the side of Adam.[55] A boy from Yarmouth was in trouble in a case before the Court of High Commission in 1634 because he referred to such a picture of God as 'an old fool in heaven with a white beard'.[56] Although preachers cautioned people against taking ideas literally, trying to counter the speculations of those who said that if God was a man, he must have had a tailor or a shoemaker, it is clear that the theological points were not understood by everyone.[57] Most people thought of the deity as male-gendered.

All the imagery of Christ was of a handsome, young man. One minister, Nathaniel Ranew, encouraged meditation on Christ as 'a most glorious and delicious Object',

> her Beloved the Lord Christ, his pure Colours, white and Red, his
> most rare features and exact proportions of every part, his Head,

Locks, Eyes, Cheeks, Lips, Hands, Legs, and all his glorious perfections and then adds to sum up all, that he is altogether lovely.

Mary Penington dreamt of Christ as a 'lovely young man'.[58]

The church, on the other hand, was female. The true church was the ideal bride, wife, or mother, while the false was a whore. The spouse and mother were only two of several metaphors employed to discuss the relationship between God and humanity; those of parent and child, king and subject, master and servant were also frequently invoked. The gender implications of all these differed. The metaphor of wife to husband conveyed intimacy and passion. For this reason, perhaps, the relationship of wife to husband was the most significant one invoked to express people's longing and desire for union with God. Such a metaphor had as much to say about the nature of a wife as about God: a good wife, as we have seen, was loving, obedient, subordinate and passive. Theologically, Calvin's concept of an active God, seeking to save his elect, emphasised the human being as a receiver of grace, and such a passive position again was associated with femaleness.

Metaphors of weddings, marriage and brides were commonly deployed to symbolise the relationship of an individual, or of the whole church to God. A Catholic mother referred to her son's martyrdom, 'rejoicing at his death by marriage, by which his soul was happily and eternally espoused to the Lamb'.[59] Charles I, on the day of his execution, which he called his second marriage day, said that 'before night I hope to be espoused to my blessed Jesus'.[60] In spiritual matters, men could become as female, passive and dependent.

The true church was discussed through the metaphor of human marriage as 'the bride of Christ'. Preachers amplified the concept in their sermons. Just as the bride, ideally, was to be chaste and pure, decked out for one alone, so too the church was to remain pure for Christ. Furthermore, since sexuality had a recognised and important role in human marriage, so one way of talking about closeness to God was to use the language and metaphors of sexual union. As the bride longed for the closest embrace with her husband, in which the two became as one, so the church longed to be one with Christ. Men of very different theological persuasions employed the concept of the church as the spouse of Christ. 'Christ hath a Spouse', wrote John Taylor.[61] A Baptist church in 1648 wrote of themselves as 'a Church and Spouse of Christ Jesus'.[62] In turn, a wife was dependent on her husband, just as the church was totally dependent on Christ, for 'they have nothing but through him'.[63]

Given that sexuality was central to human marriage – it was widely believed that no children could be conceived without mutual sexual pleasure – when divines discussed the church as 'the bride' or 'the spouse' their vocabulary had sexual overtones. The verb 'to know', for example, was one used for male sexual intercourse; to know a woman was to penetrate her sexually.[64] St Paul's expression of longing for oneness with Christ was translated into words with a sexual meaning, 'to know, even as I am known'. The metaphor of the spouse thus also reflected a positive attitude to human sexuality, within existing sexual and social contraints.

The use of female metaphors in religious discussion could place all men in an ambiguous situation in relationship to God. Other relationships, such as parent and child, master and servant, king and subject, and lord and tenant were all familiar through daily life. Men could remember their childhood dependence. As Stephen Marshall explained to the House of Commons in 1645, just as the church was to Christ 'his Love, his Dove, his Fair one, his Spouse, his Jewell', so the church was mother to the believer. 'And to themselves likewise, it is their Mother, in whose womb they have laine, whose breasts they have sucked.'[65] John Bastwick used the same metaphor: as a mother bore children, whom she nurtured with her own breasts, so the 'mother church' nurtured the 'new borne truth' with 'the sincere milke of the word'.[66] In this metaphor of the believer as a child, dependence was emphasised, but both male and female could retain their sexual identity, so men did not lose their superiority. In some instances the preacher even expressed yearning for infancy at his mother's breast. John Mayer warned that no man could attain the kingdom of heaven unless he was following Christ and 'resting in the bosome of the church his mother'.[67] Women were, of course, comfortable with the metaphor because they too had received a mother's nurture: 'I desire ye Word', wrote Mary Cary, 'even as that babe doth ye breast, which can take nothing else for its nourishment'.[68]

Contemporary views of maternity coloured the discussion of the church as mother.[69] A barren wife and a barren church were condemned: 'a barren wombe in it self is a curse, a fruitfull one a blessing: and so is it with a barren and a fruitfull Church'.[70] Likewise, true maternity was biological; step-mothers were suspected and feared. The Barrowists in Elizabeth's reign disavowed the legitimacy of the Church of England: 'that she never was the Lord's wife, nor he her husband; but that she is at the best a murthering step-mother'.[71]

Men could find themselves both giving and receiving service and deference in the secular sphere, but only in the religious sphere were they placed in the female role of obedience, passivity and dependence. On the other hand, women of very different theological persuasions unambiguously rejoiced in the language of marriage for their relationship to God. Mary Rich, countess of Warwick, was 'mightely comforted under my worldly trobles to consider that my maker was my husband'.[72] Mary Churchman was at a sermon around 1678 when she felt the Lord shine over her: 'Oh then I saw the Lord Jesus become my Husband!' Later she referred to 'the days of his espousals when I followed him in the wilderness'.[73] The New England poet Anne Bradstreet concluded one of her poems about spiritual pilgrimage with a plea to Christ: 'Come deare bridegrome Come away.'[74] Women could unequivocally rejoice in the marriage relationship with Christ, as did Mary Cary to whom Christ appeared 'as a Husband, taking me with nothing, but giving me all ye Treasures of Heaven and Earth'.[75] Margaret Clitheroe, a Catholic martyr in Queen Elizabeth's reign, was seen by her confessor as a woman 'prepared as Thy loving spouse to so gracious a marriage day'.[76]

Even more direct was the sexual language of a woman visionary about her experiences of union with God. On 8 September 1679 Anne Bathurst wrote of her longing for night, 'yt I might ly in his Arms as I had done ye night before'. She desired the kisses of Christ's mouth, but reminded herself that this was more than Isaiah had desired, which was that God would touch his lips with a coal from his altar: 'but god has touched me with fire from his Lips, a pledge of his love . . . O Jesus, I am thine, thou hast ravished me. . . . O the sweetness & full Satisfaction'.[77] While in the context to be 'ravished' suggests being carried away by force, another meaning was sexual. On 12 September she referred to herself as 'a spouse betrothed'.[78] Bathurst also saw herself in other relationships to the Trinity, including that of child to the father, but the language of most of her writings was sexual and ecstatic.[79]

The false church was most usually symbolised by the female metaphor of 'the whore'. The whore tempted men to illicit and dangerous sex. She brought forth no healthy, lawful children, but was said to be infertile or to spawn monsters. Her infected milk poisoned rather than nourished. The most important feature of this metaphor for an understanding of gender relations was that men could condemn whores unreservedly. They could confidently scorn the woman for illicit sexuality, separating themselves from her by their condemnation. Women were less comfortable about this metaphor. To be labelled a whore was a risk they all ran. For a woman to call another 'whore' publicly was actionable in the church courts.[80] However, the public debate about female sexual honesty brought the sexual reputation of all women into question. According to some contemporary wisdom, all were potentially whores. Women were sexual beings, weak by nature and liable to the temptation of the devil.

Every church was described by its enemies as a 'whore' at some stage during the early modern period. Protestants regularly referred to the Catholic church as such after the 1540s. John Bale, in 1543, condemned the 'whorishe mother the church of antichrist the strompet of babylon, the rose coloured harlot' and in 1627 Christopher Lever referred to 'that Romish strumpet' with 'so venimous a breast'.[81] 'Rome is the Babylonish Harlot', said the Baptist Thomas Grantham.[82] Anti-Catholic propagandists of the 1680s multiplied abuse of the Catholic church as 'a foul, filthy, old withered harlot . . . the great Strumpet of all Strumpets, the Mother of Whoredom'.[83] But Protestants used the term 'whore' against each other as well as against the Catholics when they argued over the nature of the true church. In the 1630s Bishop Cosin was accused of imitating 'the whore of Babylon, the church of Rome'.[84] A Quaker in the 1650s called the established church 'an harlot' (in a work entitled *The skirts of the whore discovered*) while a Baptist at the same date described the payment of tithes to the established church as 'the whore kept up'.[85] The church of the radical Richard Coppins was branded by one enemy as 'the Whore of Babylon, the Strumpet of Antichrist'.[86] Robert Read, in 1656, said that the Lord would not meet the rulers of England because they had failed to walk with him, 'yeelding to the Harlot Iezabell'.[87] Whores were, as men told each other, expensive to maintain. In the 1660s the Protestant church was described as poorly dressed, while the Catholic church walked 'like a Queen mounted on her gawdy choppines, curiously dressed, all be-jewelled, bespangled, powdered, painted, perfumed'.[88] Further, the outward show disguised inner corruption: idolatry was 'an old, foul, filthy and withered Harlot . . . [who] doth paint, and deck, and tire her self with gold, pearle, stone'.[89]

Just as every woman had the potential to change from a chaste virgin to a whore, so every church was in danger of altering from the bride of Christ to a strumpet. In 1593, critics alleged that by retaining the Catholic hierarchy and the canon law, the Anglican church was committing Christ's beloved spouse 'unto the direction of the Mystresse of the Stewes, and inforcing her to liue after the orders of a Brothel house'.[90] The Book of Discipline published in 1621 warned that novelties in worship 'hath changed the comely countenance of Christs Spouse . . . into the Antichristian complexion of that whore of Babel'.[91] Heresy wore a female face to divines of the early modern period. As Henry Ainsworth said, Solomon warned us of a heretic 'under the figure of a foolish woman'.[92]

Divines used Biblical concepts about the natural female function of menstruation to symbolise profanation in worship. In Isaiah, the coverings of images which were defiled were to be thrown away 'as a menstruous cloth'. Ezekiel 18.18 stated that it was 'one of the properties of a good man, not to lie with a menstruous woman'. Sometimes men used the concept of menstruation to convey their loathing and disgust. For example, where Isaiah had discounted man's own righteousness 'as filthy rags', the marginal annotation of the Genevan Bible explained that this was '(as some read) like the menstruous clothes of a woman', or, as another recollected, as 'a menstruous rag'. The image which one Jacobean dramatist chose to picture the foulness of the soul of Pope Alexander VI was a menstrual one:

> Thy soule foule beast is like a menstrous cloath, Polluted with unpardonable sinnes.[93]

Evidence of women using menstrual metaphors with such aversion has yet to be located.

Contrasted with men's gendered metaphors about God and the church, women's images and metaphors related more to their natural female functions – pregnancy, parturition and lactation. Women spoke of Christ within them as both lover and baby. The separatist Joan Robbins was widely believed to be pregnant, literally, with Christ.[94] Men spoke of Christ within them, but in 1649 Elizabeth Poole wrote of a message from God as 'the Babe Jesus in mee'.[95]

The social meanings ascribed to difference of sex were thus fundamental to religious thought and debate in the early modern period. It was impossible for men and women to talk of their beliefs about God without reference to a set of ideas about female inferiority and weakness. When, in practice, women stepped outside the clearly defined boundaries which had been drawn, they challenged fundamental axioms of social life in ways which men found socially subversive and deeply threatening to their sexuality. Masculine identity and self-confidence depended upon the maintenance of the established gender codes of behaviour. If women attempted to behave independently, they subverted the gender order, and threatened men's sense of identity at the most fundamental sexual level.

Part I

Religious changes
1500–1640

1

The Reformation

Our very reformation of Religion, seems to be begun and carried
on by Women.

Bathsua Makin, 1673[1]

THE PLACE OF WOMEN IN RELIGIOUS LIFE AT THE BEGINNING OF THE SIXTEENTH CENTURY

Until the 1960s, very few Reformation historians devoted much attention to women. Some of the subsequent studies provided some useful
biographical information, but little else.[2] Even the social history of the
Reformation, which ought to have been more concerned with the female
half of the 'ordinary' people, did not necessarily include women.[3]
Indeed, although the great discovery of Reformation studies in the 1970s
was 'the common man', the obvious maleness of this person was ignored
until the work of Lyndal Roper showed how gendered a concept this
was.[4] Wiesner, Roper and other feminist scholars are making women
more visible in the European Reformation.[5] Among the social historians
of the English Reformation there have been varying degrees of sensitivity to questions of gender.[6]

Historians have found it difficult to judge the importance of religion
in the lives of ordinary men and women in England at the beginning of
the sixteenth century. There is evidence both of piety, and of criticism of
the church. In the sixteenth century, the Reformation in England – or
rather, since it was no single event, the reformations – led to changes in
theology which in turn altered the nature of the institutional church.
Inevitably, lay beliefs were fundamentally affected.

Women were prominent in medieval religious life. To be female was
no obstacle to the highest vocation, monasticism.[7] Women as well as

21

men entered religious orders. During the later medieval period, there were some 138 nunneries in England, over half of which belonged to the Benedictine order, and a quarter to the Cistercian.[8] Some nuns were attracted to orders with a strict ascetic rule, others to those serving through practical charity, such as nursing the sick in hospitals.[9] Although all women in orders depended upon a priest for spiritual direction and the mass, the authority exercised by individual women as abbesses and prioresses was considerable.

By the early sixteenth century, the number of nuns in England was depleted to around 2,000, and in 1536, at the dissolution of the monasteries, there were an estimated 1,600 nuns living in various orders.[10] Assessments of the reasons for this decline in numbers have usually focused on what were perceived to be the failings of individuals to live up to the monastic ideals. For example, Margaret Bowker, in her study of the diocese of Lincoln during the episcopate of John Longland, argues that many women had fallen away from their vocation. In the 1520s Longland directed one group of nuns to abandon their fancy veils and to wear their head-linen 'playn without rolle'. At another nunnery he told the sisters to live 'in a scarcer manner' and without so many servants. But these incidents could be reinterpreted as conflicts between the bishop and the nuns over the nature of conventual life and the authority of the bishop. Longland's attempts to impose a new prioress to reform the abuses of the Benedictine community at Elstow prompted a walk-out. The nuns resented the bishop's imposition of a prioress, contrary to their rule, and complained that the new prioress 'makes every faute a deadly syne'.[11] It is difficult to assess the spiritual strength of monasticism. Much of the evidence about corruption was collected from the hostile observations of Henry VIII's visitors who were seeking reasons to justify the dissolutions of 1536 and 1539. Evidence from Yorkshire, where there were twenty-four religious houses for women, suggests that there was still considerable spiritual life in the convents. Nunneries had no difficulty in recruiting young women to the cloister.[12]

Lay women expressed their religious beliefs in various ways. Some pious women, like pious laymen, chose to live a religious life outside a formal religious order. A few became anchorites, enclosing themselves in four walls and devoting their lives to contemplation, with intercession as their special work.[13] Anchorites were expected to give advice to others, and in the early fourteenth century Margery Kempe consulted the famous mystic, Julian of Norwich.[14] In Europe, lay devotion outside religious orders was also expressed in communities known as beguinages. These communities were especially attractive to women in

Europe, but in England, Norwich seems to have been the only city where a community of lay women lived together under vows of chastity and devotion to God.[15]

Many people chose a life of piety which involved a quest for personal holiness. Certain forms of piety were specific to women. Since women were responsible for household routines, self-denial was relatively easy for them to organise, and was socially acceptable because it reinforced medieval views of appropriate womanly behaviour. Although the most famous ascetics were male, women were prominent as penitents and ascetics.[16] Other women chose to devote themselves to the poor, and some of the parish fraternities which women joined were dedicated to mutual charitable help as well as communal prayers for the dead and living.[17] A study of popular devotion in France has shown how the laity, through individual patterns of prayer to the Virgin and saints, linked their everyday aspirations to the divine. Thus although women could not be priests, they could attend the Mass, and participate through their private prayers and devotion.[18] By the end of the medieval period there was a strong tradition of female lay piety in England. There were individual mystics such as Julian of Norwich and Margery Kempe, although it would be difficult to establish whether their names were known to women early in the sixteenth century. Some of Margery's writings were published by Wynken de Worde in 1502 which may have brought her work before a new audience.[19]

Studies of popular belief during the medieval period have shown how women's Christian beliefs had private and public significance. In the private sphere of the household, parents, especially mothers, had a role in socialising their children as Christians. Religion was present in everyday life, from the blessing of food to requests for divine aid. Acts of charity, even when secretly performed, took women into public life. Pilgrimages had a role in the devotional life of the laity in the twelfth and thirteenth centuries. Finucane's analysis of 1,933 miracles performed for pilgrims to shrines in England showed that 39 per cent of those who visited were women, of whom 86 per cent were of the lowest social classes. That is, poorer women valued the divine aid accessible through shrines more than did any other section of the female community.[20] Later, Protestantism offered this social group no substitute form of devotion.

The institutional church had considerable influence on women's religious lives, and most women turned to their priests for the administration of the sacraments which were linked with the rites of passage of baptism, marriage and burial. In turn, women supported the church in various ways. Among the wealthier aristocratic levels of society, ladies gave endowments. They expressed their piety through personal regimes of devotion, reading manuals of prayers and attending public worship.[21] Their devotion to the Virgin and female saints provided a feminine influence upon religion. In some parishes, a few women even served as churchwardens. For example, in the parish of Morebath in Devon, they kept their accounts as 'maydyn wardyns' until the guild disappeared at the Reformation. A few women presented churchwardens' accounts up to 1572.[22]

The Catholic church offered a series of rituals to help and comfort women. Mothers attended for the ceremony of churching after the birth of their babies. Women recited prayers, often using the prompt of rosary beads. They prayed in the church at the stations of the cross. They lit candles for the Virgin Mary, for the saints, and for the dead. The church buildings were beautiful, a contrast to the homes of poor countrywomen. Frequently they were illuminated through coloured glass, and walls were decorated. Bequests by wealthier women showed female devotion to the fabric of the church, which undoubtedly enhanced the interior. Examples abound. In 1496 a widow, Margaret a Dene, bequeathed vestments, an altar cloth, and two tunicles of purple velvet to the church at Rickmansworth.[23] A 1517 inventory in Reading listed various embroidered cloths given by women.[24] Images carved in stone or wood were sometimes dressed in rich coloured fabrics: an inventory of St Mary's, Cambridge, of 1511 included 'a Coote of tawney damask for our lady'.[25] The sacred relics which the church treasured afforded help in trouble. For example, a woman could borrow the girdle of a saint when she was in labour.[26] As various historians have shown, the role of the Catholic church was important in offering supernatural aid for various problems of daily life in the early modern period. The church also channelled charitable relief. Women had less property to dispose of than men, but they gave poor relief through charitable bequests to the church and its hospitals. The vitality and importance of faith and charity in neighbourly and social obligations gave the church a central place in the community.[27]

Priests advised married women about their marital conduct, including sexuality. Priests could be mediators, or an alternative source of authority to whom a wife could turn. Through the confession, priests sought to establish certain norms of marital conduct, particularly of sexual behaviour. Tentler has suggested that the general view of the clergy, although that of individual confessors might differ, was that husband and wife each owed the other sexual pleasure, and that each should satisfy the other lest they fall into worse sins.[28] From the eleventh century, priests themselves were forbidden to marry, and celibacy came to seem fundamental to the exercise of any sacred functions in the church. However, priests were widely suspected of attempting the chastity of their female parishioners, and popular anticlericalism attacked the sexual morality of the clergy.

The Catholic church viewed men and women differently. Men controlled the institutional church and men dispensed the sacraments. The boundary between the most sacred parts of worship and the female sex was firmly drawn. Virginity was preferable to marriage. Woman's nature was sexual, and she represented a constant danger to herself as well as to men because her sexuality inclined her to sin. A woman was polluted during menstruation and by childbirth. Furthermore, her nature rendered her particularly vulnerable to the wiles of the devil. Just as Eve had fallen, and with her the whole human race, so women represented a continuing danger after the Fall. In the sixteenth and seventeenth centuries, prosecutions for the crime of witchcraft in England and Europe were sex-related to women.[29]

Further alarm was caused by the presence of women among the Lollard heretics in early Tudor England. At the end of the fourteenth century, the English medieval church had been threatened by the criticisms of John Wycliffe and his followers, who became known as Lollards. Later, Protestants claimed Wycliffe and his followers among the ancestors of the Protestant Reformation. Among the Lollard teachings which were similar to those of later Protestants were the importance of the Bible and of preaching.[30] Wycliffe reduced the distinction between the clergy and the laity, which offered encouragement to women, whose sex debarred them the priesthood. There was a strong female presence among the Lollards, but as Margaret Aston, in her studies of Lollardy, has observed, historians have shown a surprising lack of interest in the role of women in the movement. She found fascinating evidence which showed not only that women were preachers in the formative stage of the movement but also that claims were being made that women were capable of priesthood. There were even rumours that women offered the sacrament to believers.[31] From the earliest days of Christianity, the church fathers had commented adversely upon the attraction of women to heresy.[32] Female support for the Cathar and Waldensian heresies of the fourteenth and fifteenth centuries in Europe was marked, and there were women preachers.[33] During the fifteenth century, the Lollards were persecuted. Dickens has argued that many humbler adherents remained undiscovered, especially in the

Chilterns.[34] However, Derek Plumb has since discovered that Lollards were present at all levels of rural society.[35]

Women's role in religious heresy was revealed in the trials of the early sixteenth century.[36] Some women influenced families: in 1522 Thomas Hernsted confessed that his wife had taught him 'the *Paternoster, Ave Maria,* and *Credo,* in Englishe'.[37] Other women played a role in their neighbourhoods: in Burford, Alice Colins, the wife of Richard, 'was a famous woman among them, and had a good memory, and could recite much of the Scriptures, and other good books'. She taught not only her daughter, but also a conventicle of men.[38] There is evidence in heresy trials of women reading books: Anne Watts confessed that she had hidden an English translation of a treatise about the sacrament in a ditch.[39] Other women criticised current Catholic practices. Mistress Cotismore spoke scornfully to her servant of several devotional practices: 'that when women go to offer to images or saints, they did it to show their new gay gear: that images were but carpenter's chips; and that folks go on pilgrimages more for the green way, than for any devotion'.[40]

The spiritual condition of the Catholic church in England prior to the Reformation has, of course, been much debated.[41] Protestants, whose case depended upon a view of a corrupt and unreformed church, stressed its inadequacies. Catholics, who saw the origins of the Protestant heresy in the sordid matrimonial difficulties of Henry VIII, argued that the church was spiritually satisfying to the majority of the population. For women, it may be agreed, there were both strengths and weaknesses in the institutional help they were offered for their faith prior to the Reformation. Despite many misogynist traditions, the Catholic church allowed women a place in its worship, and participation in its spiritual life. As mystics during the medieval period, women had pronounced spiritual truths of central importance to their society. Further, the church had tolerated a range of beliefs which gave women help in their daily lives. The Catholic religion offered faith and hope, and a range of approaches to the divine.

THE HENRICIAN REFORMATION, 1530–47

The Reformation dominates the history and historiography of sixteenth-century England and Europe. Luther's doctrine of salvation by faith alone meant that a priest as an intermediary was no longer needed, and monasticism was no better a way of life than any other. The good Christian needed to study the Bible and hear preachers expound the word rather than engage in good works and devotional rituals. In England, there was no single reformation, but rather a series of reformations. Initially, the Henrician Reformation of the 1530s separated the English church from the rest of the Catholic church, and opened the way for changes in belief which altered theology and the nature of the church. Although many of the institutions of the pre-Reformation church remained – convocation, the church courts, even the buildings themselves – the face of belief and of worship altered during Henry's and subsequent reigns. By the end of the sixteenth century, the English Church was a Protestant one. Catholics in England struggled to sustain their faith and to win converts, while within the Church the more extreme Protestants, the 'godly' or 'Puritans' as they were often called, sought further reformation.

Recent debate about the sixteenth-century Reformation in England has made relatively little explicit comment about women's participation. Major discussion has focused around themes such as the extent to which the Reformation was imposed from above, and the role of the populace familiar with the teachings of the Lollards and early Protestants.[42] The outcome of this debate affects ideas about women's part in the religious changes and the effects of alterations in belief on their lives. If historians favour the view that the Reformation was primarily an act of state imposed from above, then they will perceive women's agency in the Protestant Reformation as limited. They will see women as part of a resisting populace, struggling to keep their faith alive. Other historians will see these women as part of the conservative and uneducated mass of the population in the sixteenth century, resisting change. However, any assumption that the masses were unthinking about their faith is not supported by studies of popular belief.[43] On the other hand, if historians interpret the Reformation as a spiritual movement, begun from below by people dissatisfied with the Catholic church, then women ought to play an important part in the discussion. The question has not been posed directly by historians such as Delumeau, who discuss whether the Reformation created a new and more pious kind of Christian.[44]

The Henrician Reformation was neither simply a divorce case nor a popular movement. Through legislation in Parliament in the 1530s the church in England was separated from that of the rest of Christendom. The acceptance of these changes depended not just on members of Parliament but on the population generally. Initially, there was relatively limited alteration in doctrine, for King Henry VIII was conservative. But the general interest in religious debate could not be restricted, and the break with Rome allowed the expression of Protestant views. Previously, Protestant books and English translations of the Bible had been secretly printed or smuggled into England by merchants with European contacts. As printing in England developed, literacy increased. Many Protestant books were smuggled into England from abroad. Testimonies in the heresy trials of the early sixteenth century show that people had read religious books, and discussed the tenets of their faith. For example, in the trials between 1518 and 1521 in Lincoln, a man and his two daughters were informed against 'for being present and hearkening unto Richard Bennet, reading the epistle of St James in English'.[45] Access to the Bible increased when the King's Injunction of 1536 directed that an English translation be placed in every parish church.[46] Among the population at large, there was both hostility to and support for the religious changes, with regional variations.

Among the powerful patrons of the new faith were some ladies at the court of Henry VIII, and in particular, his queen, Anne. Anne was a patron of evangelical bishops, reforming clergy, and Protestant writers. She was active in promoting Christian education and scholarship. Anne read and discussed Protestant literature and especially the Bible with other educated women at court. Her contemporaries believed that she influenced Henry's plans for the dissolution of the monasteries, and saw her as a key figure in the reforming group around the King.[47] Other ladies of gentry status participated in the religious debates of Henry's reign and were among the defenders of the Catholic faith. Margaret Roper, the daughter of Sir Thomas More, for example, was highly educated and won renown for her translation of religious works from Greek and Latin. Her version of Erasmus's Latin commentary on the Paternoster was published. Elaine Beilin has shown how her family, and particularly her father, influenced Margaret's views. By containing her humanist scholarship within the family circle, and using her learning to support conventional ideals, she gained her father's approval.[48]

The first female martyr to the conservative cause was a young woman, Elizabeth Barton, who was of lower social status, a servant before she made her profession as a nun.[49] She was 16 years old when an illness precipitated trance, visions and prophecies. She entered a convent and was protected by powerful individuals, including Warham, the Archbishop of Canterbury, and some of the Kentish nobility. Towards the end of the 1520s she began to prophesy that no good would come to the King or realm should he cast aside Catherine to marry Anne Boleyn. Initially, Henry entertained a wide variety of opinion, but by 1533 his attitude had hardened. 'The Nun', as she was known, was identified as a rallying point for opposition to the King. She was proceeded against without trial, by an act of attainder, and executed in 1534. Her story has been told in hagiographic terms,[50] and more recently as part of the Reformation story. Elton has shown how Cromwell used her to bring her monastic supporters under control and to discredit the Catholic cause; after Warham died, Cromwell publicised Barton's confession of fraud to make her a symbol of superstition and spiritual corruption.[51] The historical problem of fraudulence is a real one: since the publication of the story of Benedetta Carlini, an Italian nun who counterfeited her visions, we are sensitive to the possibility of deception, and our own predelictions encourage scepticism.[52] Yet the discovery of the cheating by the lesbian nun was contemporary, and the only evidence of Elizabeth Barton's faking was her own confession, which was both ambiguous and possibly exacted under torture.[53] Reputable contemporaries attested to the veracity of Barton's sickness, cure and visions, while others doubted. Historians have been divided; some deny her martyrdom, while others regard her as an hysteric.[54]

Elizabeth Barton is better understood in the context of a long tradition of women visionaries,[55] which will be discussed further in chapter 5, than as an example of female hysteria. She was a political prophet whose voice was heeded, and who was destroyed because her words were feared. The amount of energy devoted to undermining Barton's credibility indicated the importance of her prophecies. Bishop Capon preached a sermon at St Paul's Cross and again in Canterbury in which he denounced her for faking her visions and implied that she was guilty of immorality. It is significant that the charges against her were sexualised, for it shows that her antagonists hoped to undermine her spiritual credibility by destroying her reputation as a virtuous woman. Later Protestants amplified stories of Barton's sinful life; John Ponet wrote of the 'baudry practised . . . with Monks fryers and priestes under color of strayt nunnishe lyfe'.[56] Capon carpingly observed that Barton enjoyed the pleasure of an audience, of having her words taken seriously, but only through the medium of prophecy could an ordinary servant girl have been heeded in the 1520s.[57] Beyond the interpretation of her as hysterical and dishonest, her story raises useful general questions of sexuality and rank. In another case of prophecy during Henry's reign, a 12-year-old girl who experienced trances and visions in 1516 was more fortunate than Barton. She was of gentle birth, and disappeared from the world when she professed religion.[58]

The Henrician Reformation affected monks and nuns differently. When the lesser and then the greater monasteries were dissolved in 1536 and 1539 and the monks and nuns were pensioned off, women fared worse than men. While a number of men were able to obtain ecclesiastical promotion, women of course could not. A study of the Lincoln diocese showed that those who received pensions of £2 or less lived in penury. Only 6 per cent of men were on this stipend or less, but 60 per cent of the women were. Marriage was legal after 1549, and 19 per cent of the Lincoln ex-nuns married. A few joined together to keep house.[59]

Among the populace at large, women were not merely passive observers of the upheavals. Urban women defended the religious orders in the 1530s. In Exeter, for example, they appeared with pitchforks to protect St Nicholas's priory.[60] In other places, women as well as men were outraged when the words of the service were translated into English, and protested that the new services which replaced the Mass were 'but like a Christmas game'.[61]

In the Henrician period, women were less likely than men to be executed for heresy.[62] Nevertheless, Anne Askew, a young gentlewoman who left her Catholic husband for the sake of her faith, was one of the first and best-known martyrs for the Protestant faith in England. She was burned in the reign of Henry VIII when she was 25 years of age. Unusually, her own record of her trial survived. Through her words, which were printed by the Protestant John Bale after her death, a clear picture of her courage and faith emerges.[63] Recent feminist scholarship has analysed Askew's autobiographical testimony to show how her private beliefs took her into public conflict. Under examination, she was perfectly capable of alluding to the 'weak woman' stereotype, but her actions belied her words, and she was a skilful and courageous antagonist. Whereas John Bale praised her as a feeble woman made strong by God, her own autobiography reveals that she saw herself as a defender of the faith, a teacher, a visionary, and a fighter, the spiritual equal of any man.[64]

The motives of individuals, in espousing or rejecting the new faith, have been interpreted in terms of a conflict between youth and age. Susan Brigden has shown how young people especially may have been attracted to the Reformed faith for reasons ranging from genuine delight in hearing Scripture expounded to pleasure in image-breaking and the traditional protest of youth against age.[65] Some of this behaviour may relate more to the radicalism of young men rather than young women. Certainly women were among the older generation who condemned their sons' heresies. When Julius Palmer's widowed mother learnt that her son had espoused the new Protestant faith, she rejected him harshly:

*The manner of burning Anne Askew, Iohn Lacels, Iohn Adams, &
Nicolas Belenian, with certane of y^e counsell fitting in Smithfield.*

Figure 1. The execution of Anne Askew. From Robert Crowley's *Confutation of
Nicolas Shaxton, 1548* (Mansell Collection).

'If thou be at that point,' saith she, 'I require thee to depart from
my house and out of my sight, and never take me more for thy
mother hereafter. As for money and goods I have none of thine,
thy father bequeathed nought for heretics: faggots I have to burn
thee.'[66]

But no explanation of religious affiliation on the lines of age, gender or
region suffices. Women and men were influenced by spiritual
considerations.

THE EDWARDIAN REFORMATION, THE MARIAN
REACTION AND THE ELIZABETHAN SETTLEMENT
1547–1603

When Edward VI came to the throne in 1547 England was exposed to
more Protestant influences. Because Edward was a minor, policy was
largely directed by two men – Edward Seymour, Duke of Somerset, and

John Dudley, Duke of Northumberland – both of whom supported a reform of religion. Parliament enacted further alterations in the direction of Protestantism. In 1549 the first English Prayer book was issued in English, and reissued in an even more Protestant form in 1552. New doctrines were introduced. The sacraments were reduced to two, namely baptism and the Lord's Supper. The 1549 Prayer Book allowed for a belief in the real presence, but in the 1552 Prayer Book the eucharistic doctrine was pure memorialism. The laity were offered the communion in both kinds; for the first time, the male priesthood were not the only Christians to receive the wine as well as the bread. The doctrine of salvation by faith alone further altered the relationship between the clergy and the laity. There was no longer any special priesthood set apart to perform the rites and rituals. In theory, there was an equality of all believers. Priests were to be ministers of the word, to teach the people about salvation. Furthermore, they were permitted to marry, and a number of the most prominent Protestant ministers did so, including the Archbishop of Canterbury, Thomas Cranmer.[67] The doctrine of Purgatory was declared unscriptural, so there was no longer any point in saying masses for the souls of the dead, and the chantries were dissolved.

Edward reigned for only six years, but at the time of his death Protestantism had gained support in many parts of England, chiefly in London and the south. In explaining the conversions to Protestantism, historians have considered various factors. Lollard inheritance was one. The influence of Protestant books was another, and it has been observed that particular areas of England – namely East Anglia and London – were exposed to new ideas by merchants' contacts with European reformed ideas. Influential Protestant ladies as well as gentlemen protected reformist writers, printers and publishers. Catherine Brandon, Dowager Duchess of Suffolk and Mary Fitzroy, Duchess of Richmond, provided employment for reformers and probably financial support for their publications.[68] Furthermore, by Edward's reign the years of anti-papal propaganda, of translation of texts into English, and of alteration of doctrines had had an effect, and both the pace of religious change and the level of discussion accelerated during this period. Inevitably, the views which some people developed were labelled heretical. One of the most prominent of those tried in Edward's reign was Joan Bocher who was burnt in 1550 for believing that Christ was not incarnate of the Virgin Mary. Her words to her ecclesiastical antagonists before her death indicate a shrewd awareness of the situation:

It is a goodly matter to consider your ignorance. It was not long ago since you burned Anne Ascue for a piece of bread, and yet came yourselves soon after to believe and profess the same doctrine for which you burned her. And now forsooth you will needs burn me for a piece of flesh, and in the end you will come to believe this also, when you have read the Scriptures, and understand them.[69]

Her views and actions, John Davis suggests, showed a mixture of indigenous heresy and the movement for reform.[70]

Rulers had a great influence upon national institutional religious belief. When Mary succeeded her step-brother Edward she sought to restore Catholicism. Her first difficulty was that by the Henrician statutes still in force at her accession, she was the supreme head of the church, a position which she believed belonged to the Pope. Her religious aspirations have not been treated very sympathetically by a Protestant nationalist historiography. Historians have labelled her 'Bloody Mary' although the persecutions of her reign were not so savage as those in the Netherlands at a slightly later date.[71] Yet in bringing to England some of the ideas of the Catholic reformers in Europe, Mary restored a more vital Catholicism and renewed the faith of many of the laity. The survival of Catholicism in England owed much to her work.[72]

Women's reactions to the religious changes instigated by Mary varied. Many conformed, but others resisted. Troubled by conscience, some women consulted the reformers about their dilemmas: should they attend the mass or not? Rose Hickman stayed away from the mass, but asked advice of imprisoned bishops about the baptism of her child. Like other wealthy and more extreme Protestant families who preferred exile in Europe to Catholicism in England, Rose Hickman and her husband fled soon after and found refuge in the Calvinist city of Antwerp.[73] Other leading Protestants remained in England, where some were tried for heresy, and publicly burned. There were fifty-five women among the nearly three hundred Protestants who were martyred for their beliefs.[74] Others died in prison.

The stories of the Protestant martyrs were immortalised by John Foxe in his *Acts and Monuments*. First published in English in 1563, the book was reprinted many times, illustrated, and was second in popularity only to the Bible.[75] Foxe's work provides an invaluable record of the stories about women's defence of the Protestant faith. Martyrdom was usually less likely for them than for men. Since they did not occupy public offices, the government was less concerned about their compliance. Besides, less was expected of women generally. Nevertheless, when women were questioned for heresy, although the ecclesiastical authorities may have tried persuasion, in the end they were prepared to torture and to execute women who refused to recant. In fact, resistance was probably regarded as a more heinous offence in a woman, from whom compliance with male authority was naturally expected. As the Bishop's Chancellor told Elizabeth Young, a Protestant bookseller of over 40 years of age, 'It is necessary for thee to believe, and that is enough.'[76] Furthermore, a woman's capacity to withstand the pain of martyrdom was viewed as evidence of guilt, for it was the devil who gave her the strength. She had an affinity with the witch, whose body bore the Devil's marks which were insensible to the pain of pricking.[77]

On the whole, the women martyred during Mary's reign seem to have been poor. Dickens suggested that they were widows, assuming that independent female action was incompatible with matrimony, but Warnicke's work shows that only ten of the fifty-five were poor widows, and twenty-eight of the fifty-five were married.[78] Many of the women's statements show both a strong religious faith and a recognition of the social limitations to which they were subject. Alice Driver mocked her university-educated antagonists:

> You be not able to resist the Spirit of God in me, a poor woman. I was an honest poor man's daughter, never brought up in the University, as you have been, but I have driven the plough before my father many a time (I thank God).[79]

Foxe recorded John Bradford's story of an early woman martyr who exhorted other women to be steadfast in their faith for 'ye were redeemed with as dear a price as men. For although ye were made of the rib of man, yet be you all of his flesh: so that also, in the case and trial of your faith towards God, ye ought to be as strong.'[80]

In defying the ecclesiastical authorities, women jeopardised their reputations as good women. Ecclesiastical authorities abused Elizabeth Young, who claimed the right to exercise her own judgement and to risk all for the sake of her conscience, as 'Thou rebel whore and traitor heretic'.[81] One writer in Elizabeth I's reign said that Joan Bocher was 'openly reported to have been dishonest of her body with base fellows'.[82] Women who defied authority were deemed to be 'masterless women' and therefore whores, because a woman who was outside authority was a wanton woman.

Among those who suffered during Mary's reign, the wives of the bishops and clergy have frequently been overlooked. Since the Catholic church required a celibate clergy, bishops and priests who had married were suspended, and subsequently required to put away their wives. Mary Prior's study of the bishops' wives shows their resourceful and courageous responses to adversity, while the wives of the lower clergy await their historian.[83] The Catholic view of clerical marriage defined it as 'incest and worse than adultery', especially for former monks.[84] Nuns who married were even more censured than priests. They were required to resume their monastic garb, but no financial support was provided for them to do so. Some were forced to undergo public penance.[85] Just as the term 'priest's whore' was used of clergy wives, so the term 'incest' was commonly used to refer to any sexual relationship with a nun. One writer assumed that Christ's reaction would be the same as that of any other jealous male faced with female infidelity; when Christ saw a virgin 'that hath dedicated . . . her selfe unto his holinesse to lye with another man, oh howe is he stirred up to wrathe and indignation?'[86]

The accession of Elizabeth led to further changes in religious policy. By the Acts of Supremacy and Uniformity of 1559, the church was established as a Protestant one with the Queen as the Supreme Governor. The Prayer Book was a compromise between the two Edwardian versions. Communion in both kinds continued, and clerical marriage was permitted, although Elizabeth herself retained a preference for celibacy among the clergy, especially the bishops. A story, which was probably spurious, told of Elizabeth drawing attention to the anomalous social position of the wife of Archbishop Parker, whose hospitality she had just enjoyed: 'Madam I may not call you, and Mrs [mistress] I am ashamed to call you, so as I know not what to call you, but yet I do thank you.'[87]

Contemporary assumptions about gender affected the position of monarch as religious leader. Both Mary's and Elizabeth's religious opponents attacked their position as female rulers. 'Ah, Lord God!', wrote Thomas Becon, attacking Mary Tudor,

> heretofore in the time of thy blessing, thou gavest to the realm of England a man to reign over it . . . thou gavest unto us his son to be our king . . . whose death was the beginning, and is now still the continuance of all our sorrows, griefs and miseries. For in the stead of that virtuous prince thou hast set to rule over us a woman, whom nature hath formed to be in subjection unto man, and whom thou by thine holy apostle commandest to keep silence, and not to speak in the congregation. Ah, Lord! to take away the empire from a man, and to give it unto a woman, seemeth to be an evident token of thine anger toward us Englishmen.[88]

The Scottish reformer, John Knox, published a tract entitled *The first blast of the trumpet against the monstrous regiment of women* against the right of a woman to rule.[89] Its appearance was ill-timed, for Mary Tudor had just died, and her Protestant stepsister Elizabeth had succeeded her. Catholics deployed similar arguments against female rulers, to the embarrassment of the Protestants. Catholic polemicists concentrated on attacking Elizabeth's exercise of spiritual authority. Using all the arguments which the Protestants themselves had deployed against Mary, which were the basic conventional arguments about women exercising authority over men, Catholic writers mocked the Anglican church. A female spiritual head was impossible, as Archbishop Heath explained to the Parliament in 1559: 'her highnes, beyinge a woman by birth and nature, is not qualyfied by God's worde to feed the flock of Chryst'.[90] The Jesuit Robert Parsons argued that the logical consequence of female headship would be female government throughout the church: why should Queen Elizabeth not appoint a woman as her Vicar-General? Just as Henry VIII had appointed Thomas Cromwell, so Elizabeth might choose Lady Cromwell. There was no need for Parsons to elaborate the point: it seemed so self-evidently ridiculous and absurd that no further reasoning was necessary. Absurd, but perfectly possible. Indeed, he could not see 'why the feminine sex may not have conspired togeather to haue put downe men for a time, and to haue taken the gouernment of the church for themselves'. Since only the 'novelty and indecency of the the thinge' was against it, if the Protestants had swallowed the absurdity of a Queen's ecclesiastical primacy, why not a female deputy?[91] The threat of female authority was the nub of the argument, which was not confined to academic debate. A Catholic martyr, Thomas Felton, cited the unauthorised female headship to discredit the Anglican church: he had 'never read that God ordained a woman should be supreme head of the Church'.[92] In so far as the Protestants had used arguments against female rule in the reign of Mary Tudor, they were correspondingly embarrassed by the arguments of their opponents in the reign of Elizabeth.

Women were active participants in the religious changes of the sixteenth century, and many were strong supporters of the reformed faith. Yet the Protestant church established under Edward and Elizabeth was less open to a female element in worship than was the Catholic church. Protestant reformers were deeply troubled by Catholic veneration of the Virgin, particularly given the widespread popular belief in her power over Christ: 'they call [the Virgin] a Ladie, a Godesse, a queene whom Christ her sonne obeyeth in heauen, a mediatresse'.[93]

Protestant teachings against the exaltation of Mary led to some popular denigration. In 1605 a glover in Buckinghamshire was in trouble for affirming 'that the virgin Marie was the instrument of the devill'.[94] Catholics criticised those who gave her 'no higher a stile, than of Mal, Gods maid', and wrested Scriptural texts to prove that Christ 'slighted and rebuked her'.[95] The Protestant reformers had a fine line to tread, for they sought to give Mary due honour without encouraging exalted views of her power. In general, they preferred to discourage veneration of Mary. Thus, in 1645, the Westminster Assembly of Divines resolved against calling the Virgin Mary 'Blessed'.[96] During the Elizabethan period, the campaign against idolatry led to the defacing and destruction of statues and altar screens depicting the virgin and female saints, many of which had been erected between 1450 and 1530. The reformers removed a female presence from the churches leaving a masculine Trinity and an all-male ministry. However, too much should not be made of this, for the pace of change was slow and uneven.[97]

Certainly women had more spiritual influence in the Protestant household than they did in that of their Catholic counterparts. Many became literate, great readers of the Scriptures. But the benefits of Protestantism should not be exaggerated. Protestantism has been said to encourage individualism, but no one has suggested that it did so for women. In fact, the Protestant teachings about marriage and the family strongly supported patriarchal authority.

2

The social teachings of the Protestant church: women, marriage and the family

Ye wives, be ye in subjection to obey your own husbands. To obey is another thing than to control or command; which yet they may do to their children, and to their family; but as for their husbands, them must they obey, and cease from commanding, and perform subjection. . . . *Let women be subject to their husbands, as to the Lord: for the husband is the head of the woman, as Christ is the Head of the church.* Here you understand that God hath commanded that ye should acknowledge the authority of the husband, and refer to him the honour of obedience.

An Homily on the State of Matrimony, 1562.[1]

In the reigns of Edward and Elizabeth, Protestant leaders tried to persuade women that they would benefit by accepting the new faith. They claimed that Catholics denigrated women, especially married women who were deemed inferior to virgins. The implications of Protestant social thought for the position of women are contentious. Since the nineteenth century, when Karl Marx popularised the claim that a civilization could be measured by the degree of emancipation which it allowed to women, there has been additional heat in this debate as different churches have urged their claims to be the most enlightened on the basis of their policies towards women.[2] Several issues are involved in the debate. The first is whether Protestant teaching about marriage differed from Catholic. If it was not so very different, then was it new to England in the early modern period? Second, and more importantly, what were the implications of this religious ideology for the position of women? This latter question has been hotly debated since the sixteenth century, as Protestants have argued that their faith was better for women, and Catholics have disputed their claim. This chapter

examines Protestant teachings about women, the family and the household, and then addresses these questions in turn.

The main sources of Protestant ideals are found in catechisms,
homilies, domestic advice books, and in sermons, particularly funeral
sermons for women. The 1562 Homily on the state of matrimony was
widely read throughout the Elizabethan period. Thomas Becon's catechism of the mid-sixteenth century was one of the earliest of the
Protestant advice books in English, and by the early seventeenth
century a growing literature of domestic advice was available.[3]
Preachers were encouraged to print their sermons to reach a wider
audience. Of the domestic advisers, the clergyman William Gouge was
probably the most influential. His treatise, *Domesticall Duties,* published in 1622, covered the subject in the most exhaustive and systematic
manner. Also widely cited were William Perkins, and John Dod and
Robert Cleaver.[4] It is important to note that there was no single
Protestant or even Puritan view of marriage and family life, and that
domestic ideals were widely debated by contemporaries. Furthermore,
although the Reformers discussed revision of the canon law relating to
marriage, the proposed changes were never enacted, and the Protestant
church continued to administer a version of the Catholic canons relating
to marriage and separation.[5]

The most significant Protestant teachings about marriage and the
family are generally well known: marriage was an honourable estate, not
a poor substitute for celibacy. The ideal relationship between husband
and wife was one of mutual love. While parents should approve their
children's choices of marriage partners, they should not force marriages
upon them. Ideally, the couple should be of similar age, the husband
slightly older, and of similar social status. Companionate marriage was
the ideal, with husband and wife sharing spiritual and family concerns
in loving harmony. Christian duty required obedience on the part of the
wife, but wife-beating was increasingly discouraged. On the other hand,
as Becon explained, husbands were not appointed heads that they
should reign over their wives likes lords, 'or bridle them like horses, or
make them to crouch down like dogs, or to tumble before them in the
mire like swine'.[6] Thus, the archetypal good woman was a godly matron,
obeying her husband, caring for her children and servants, and spend-
ing her spare time in private devotion. From the 1530s at least,
Protestants argued that celibacy was no longer a special virtue: 'Christ
aloweth mariage in all men and in all tymes.'[7] Marriage was instituted by
God, and marriage and child-bearing were women's appointed
purposes.

The general view among historians now is that these views were not especially new. Kathleen Davies, in an important article, concluded from her comparison of Catholic and Protestant doctrines of marriage that there was not really a great difference between them.[8] Margo Todd has argued persuasively that both Catholics and Protestants shared a common Erasmian humanist influence.[9] Patrick Collinson, in the most recent review of the literature on the Puritan family, has suggested that Christopher Hill was probably right to see a slow change in cultural ideals of the family from the fourteenth century onwards. Nothing very dramatic occurred in the sixteenth century as a consequence of the Protestant Reformation. Nevertheless, Collinson concluded that the Protestant doctrine and practice of marriage offered an 'ideal type', understood in Weberian terms, whose features were emulated in subsequent generations: 'It was here that the family as we know it experienced its birth.'[10]

Thus the social teachings of the Protestant churches concerning family life are still considered to be an issue of significance for historians. It is generally agreed that the Protestant Reformation did affect family relationships, although the precise nature of this influence is debated. Lawrence Stone has asserted that Protestantism was a major factor in the shift of emphasis to the nuclear family, in which ties of affection were strong, but Ralph Houlbrooke has argued that families did not change over the period 1450–1700.[11] I would argue that there were changes, but they were less dramatic than Stone has argued, and more significant than Houlbrooke allows. The most important develpments were the increased authority of the husband and father in the family and an alteration of views about human sexuality.

Change in ideas about the family inevitably had consequences for the position of women. Because contemporaries assumed that marriage and maternity were the natural female condition, Protestant divines and subsequent commentators have asserted that Protestant teachings about women improved their position. There have been notes of caution. Schücking suggested that the Puritan emphasis upon individualism devalued women and accelerated the separation of the two sexes.[12] Morgan pointed out that if the Puritans emphasised spiritual companionship in marriage, they did little to educate women to fulfil their role in the partnership.[13] Feminist writers such as Wiesner and Roper on the European Reformation, and Warnicke and Willen on the English Reformation have taken even more critical views of the alleged benefits of Protestantism.[14] Still, the argument about whether Protestantism or Catholicism was 'better' for women continues, and

Protestant ideals of marriage continue to be adduced as though they were evidence of women's improved status.

Furthermore, the discussion about whether the Protestant or Catholic church was better for women suggests that women made religious choices on the basis of their perceptions about the social situation of women. Nothing could be further from the truth. Women's reasons for their choice of beliefs were complex. Like men, they were influenced by their families of origin, by the families into which they married, by their places of residence, and the ideas to which they were exposed. Women made choices, which were influenced by their gender, and gender in turn helped determine the nature of their activity within a particular faith. Furthermore, male religious leaders were ambivalent about female choices. For all their talk of individualism and equality, priests and ministers of both the Protestant and Catholic churches believed in female inferiority and subordination. This point needs emphasis because the debate about which of these churches was 'better' for women has sometimes obscured the essentially patriarchal nature of both.

Catholic and Protestant beliefs affected women's social roles and the gender order in society. Women's proper sphere was believed to be the household and family. Yet Protestant writers criticised the Catholic church for confining women to uneducated domesticity. Foxe recorded the views of Catholic clergy in Queen Mary's reign, one of whom told a woman 'It is more fit for thee to meddle with thy distaff, than to meddle with the Scriptures', and another who told a woman not to meddle with matters such as the high altar and the body of Christ, saying 'Keep thy work, and meddle with what thou has to do. It is no woman's matter.'[15] In 1614 the Puritan divine John Dod attacked the Jesuits who 'straightly tie the woman to the wheele and spindle', debarring them 'from all conference touching the word of God, as absurd and far unbeseeming their sexe'.[16] Even so, a feature of much of the Protestant writing against the Catholics was that it was directed to persons of the masculine gender. George Gifford, an anti-papal polemicist of the 1580s, addressed himself to 'the simple unlearned man' and the 'poore plowman', but not to women.[17]

Yet for all their criticisms of Catholic attempts to confine women to uneducated domesticity, Protestants themselves were just as prone to do the same. Protestants believed that there was a rigid division between the two sexes; men were designed for sacred functions, women for domesticity. The good woman, said Robert Wilkinson in a sermon in 1607, is compared to a snail, 'not only for her silence and continuall keeping of her house' but also for the commendable timorousness of her

41

nature.[18] The snail was a popular image of the good woman: in 1632 another clergyman commended the woman who might well have been given for her emblem 'the snaile with her house on her backe'.[19] But while Wilkinson believed that it was praiseworthy when a woman instructed her children and gave good counsel to her husband, it was intolerable 'when women shall take upon them . . . to build Churches . . . for her hands, (saith Solomon) must handle the spindle or the cradle, but neither the Altar nor the Temple'.[20] These metaphors of spindle and cradle to symbolise female activity recur through the debates about women's proper role in religious life. Minding the distaff and washing dishes were other phrases used to symbolise woman's proper sphere of household duties. This attempt to confine them was not unnoticed by women: 'Vain man is apt to think', observed Hannah Wolley tartly in the later seventeenth century, that 'we were meerly intended for the World's propagation, and to keep its humane inhabitants sweet and clean.'[21]

The cult of domesticity was restrictive for wives and mothers, but the husband and father of the family, on the other hand, multiplied his public roles. The Protestant Reformation enhanced his power at home when he became the priest, or even the bishop in his household. As Hugh Latimer preached in a sermon,

> Every man must be in his own house, according to St Augustine's mind, a bishop, not alonely giving good ensample, but teaching according to it, rebuking and punishing vice.[22]

A man was responsible for the godly conduct of the family under his governance. In his absence, a wife might say family prayers.[23] But, as we shall see, not even the radical Protestant divines thought that a woman should exercise sacred power.

The Protestant reformers changed some of the boundaries between the good and the bad, the sacred and the profane which affected understandings of male and female sexuality. Sexuality was to be expressed only in marriage, that is, between husband and wife and at certain times of the church and female calendars. Prior to the Reformation, however, the church believed that men's powerful sexual impulses needed to be accommodated, and so the existence of brothels had been condoned. The Reformers viewed such tolerance of sin as a consequence of the doctrine of a celibate priesthood. They closed the brothels in most of the European cities, where they had control, including those in England in 1546.[24] Ending legally sanctioned prostitution, as Lyndal Roper has shown in a fascinating article, had contradictory and ambiguous effects for women. In declaring that there were to be no more prostitutes, the reformers did not change their ideas about female sexuality: they still believed that women were sexual beings with needs and desires, and that they tempted men. All women's social conduct came under scrutiny. Any women, even if they were in business or trading, who received men at their houses, were regarded as whores. Furthermore, as we shall see, more responsibility for moral standards shifted to the male head of the household. Consequently, the behaviour of the females in his household reflected even more upon his reputation as a godly man. The Protestant Reformation enhanced men's need to control women and power to do so.[25] The Reformation changed some emphases, but the fundamental assumptions about women's natures remained unaltered. The primacy of male desire remained constant.

A 'double standard' of sexual morality always operated. While some divines did try to insist that extra-marital sexual activity was equally sinful on the part of both husbands and wives, in practice the equality was never established.[26] The Elizabethan Homily 'against whoredom' thundered against the widespread view that illicit sexuality was 'a pastime, a dalliance, and but a touch of youth'.[27] However, women were much more likely to be punished for illicit sexual activity than men. They were cited to the church courts in the sixteenth century, or, increasingly, into the secular courts during the seventeenth century, where their pregnancies rendered them liable to physical punishment and confinement to a house of correction.[28] The London Bridewell authorities attempted to stop organised prostitution in the capital in the later 1570s, prosecuting brothel keepers and clients as well as prostitutes, but they soon found that social pressures were too hard to resist. Confronted with a wealthy offender who was 'a man of callyng in a company of most worship, and hath a good wife and great famely', the governors found it easier to let him off with a fine and an admonition to reform. By the end of the Elizabethan period, the governors had abandoned the attempt to discipline clients, and the campaign for reform focused on the punishment of prostitutes.[29] Similarly, in the 1650s, the attempt to enforce a similar standard of sexual morality on husbands and wives was unsuccessful.[30] In part, the double standard persisted because everyone believed that there were fundamental differences between men's and women's sexual natures. Further justifications, such as that female illicit sexuality disrupted family inheritance, depended on the socially constructed idea of inheritance, namely, that it depended on biological paternity.

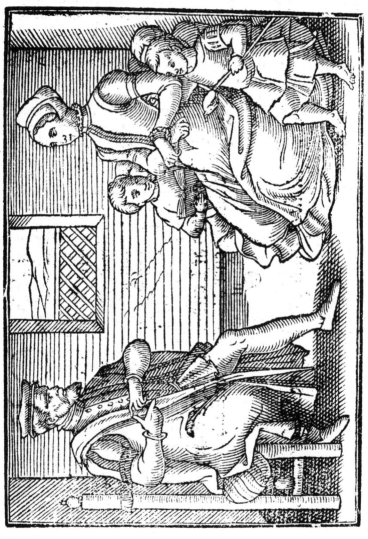

Figure 2. A husband's authority was enhanced after the Reformation. From *The Whole Book of Psalms in Four Parts, 1563* (Mansell Collection).

The reformers had different views of the relationship between body and spirit from those of the Catholics, which again had implications for their thinking about women. The Protestant view about the presence of Christ in the eucharist was that he was present in spirit, not in the body, and the separation between the spirit and the flesh created problems for Protestant men, as they wrestled with their own corporeality. Much of their distaste for the flesh was projected upon women, who were equated with nature and the uncultivated.[31]

Some of the conflicting views of sexuality and celibacy can be seen in the debate on clerical marriage. The Protestants deployed a range of arguments to justify the marriage of priests. First, marriage had been instituted by God in the Garden of Eden, and blessed by the presence of Christ at the marriage of Cana. Second, they pointed out that celibacy was a recent institution and led to abuses and whoredom. The Catholics attacked clerical marriage as polluting to the priest: 'For the Pope rekeneth it fylthy, and not seemely, that a Priest should with his holy handes touch a womans body, and with the same handes to consecrate ye holy sacrament.' The Protestant Becon argued that this was to make a whore's flesh clean, 'and the fleshe of an honest and a good woman so uncleane, that the Priest must bee burned for handeling of it'.[32] In Mary's reign, when priests were required to put away their wives, John Poynet again insisted that it was no uncleanness for a married priest to lie with his own wife. Rather, the marriage bed was 'an undefiled bed/ a pure/ a clean/ and an unspotted bedde/ as a spirituall manne . . . may lie in'.[33] Poynet attacked the claim of Cardinal Joannes Cremenses 'that it was exceadynge great abhominacion, for a preest to aryse frome a whores side (for so he called preestes lawfull wyves) and immediatly to goe to make gods body'.[34]

Protestants did not believe that male marital sexuality was incompatible with the exercise of the priestly function, but they were sure that woman's sexual nature disqualified her from all sacred offices. In some Protestant churches women might preach or speak, but the only church office ever open to women, even in the sects, was that of deaconess in some separatist congregations. Even the office of deaconess, which involved relief of the sick and the poor, required celibacy.[35] In one seventeenth-century Baptist church where the qualifications for a deaconess were spelt out, the woman was to be a widow, over 60 years old, and promise never to remarry.[36] In the fifteenth century, Sir John Fortescue had argued that a woman could not exercise the semi-sacred function of touching for 'the King's Evil' since it was 'inconsistent with a woman's nature' and a gift from heaven to kings alone. Nevertheless, in the sixteenth century both Mary and Elizabeth did successfully cure by their touch.[37]

Protestant emphasis on the value of marriage for women was based on some misunderstanding of the Catholic doctrine of virginity. Clarissa Atkinson has shown that by the late medieval period this was understood less as a physiological than as a spiritual state. Widows were admitted to nunneries, and many wives found that they could express their spirituality without entering a religious order. There was little approval for celibacy, especially for women, among early modern Protestants, but they built on a Catholic tradition in seeing married women as capable of the highest spiritual rewards.[38]

Protestants were especially fearful of monasticism. They denigrated the sexual morality of monks and nuns, and condemned their avarice and gluttony. They scorned the contemplative life as idle and useless, and in particular, regarded the dedication of a woman's life to the ideal of celibate chastity as a denial of the purpose for which she was made. The reformer Hugh Latimer criticised even widows who entered monasteries: they might have done much more good by maintaining servants and relieving the poor.[39] Later in the 1630s, when a family of Arminian Anglicans, the Ferrars, set up a community with ascetic ideals at Little Gidding, they were suspected by others of being crypto-Papists. 'Oh the stupid and blind devotion of these people', wrote the anonymous author of *The Arminian Nunnery*, 'for Men and Women in health of able and active bodies and parts to have no particular Callings . . . as if diligence in our particular lawful callings were no part of our service to God.'[40] Two of the Ferrar women who were in their thirties sought to make vows of chastity, but Bishop Williams 'admonish'd very fatherly, that they knew not what they were about . . . Let the younger Women marry was the best Advice, that they might not be led into Temptation.'[41] At the end of the seventeenth century, Mary Astell's plans for establishing a female 'Monastery' or 'Religious Retirement' were thwarted by fears that it was too like a Catholic nunnery.[42] Thus the Reformation closed off one mode of religious expression for women. In England, there was no lawful avenue for an unmarried woman with a religious vocation. Among the minority of wealthier Catholics, families still tried to send daughters to convents abroad. Although this was an option only for the few, the significance of monasticism for Catholic women was great, out of proportion to the numbers involved. Catholic Englishwomen founded new religious orders; the most famous of these women was Mary Ward, who established the Institute of the Blessed Virgin. Protestant writers remained deeply critical of what they believed was unquestioning obedience exacted by the nuns' clerical superiors. Ironically, in practice Protestants themselves favoured similar unconditional obedience from wives to husbands.

Since Protestants regarded celibacy as unnatural, they viewed all unmarried women with disfavour. The lot of the unmarried woman, or spinster, as the term came to be, was worse under Protestantism. She had no special social role. Compulsory marriage and child-bearing and, it could even be argued, a destiny of breeding and cleaning was that which the Protestant church attempted to enforce upon women. Unmarried women were distanced from opportunities to express their spirituality after the monasteries were closed. The household was their proper sphere of activity. Although the Protestants argued that female status as a wife and mother was enhanced after the Reformation, their attitudes to the Virgin Mary devalued maternity. A popular and widespread belief among Catholics was that Mary was a powerful intercessor with Christ because a son could deny his mother nothing.[43] This belief was strictly heretical, but it attested to the high esteem of maternity in Catholic popular culture. In 1603 William Perkins attacked the belief that 'his Mother must be the Queene of Heauen, and by the right of a Mother command him there'. Christians should honour Mary but not transform her and the saints into 'detestable idols'. They should not worship Mary under the terms of 'a Ladie, a Goddesse, a queene, whome Christ her sonne obeyeth in heauen, a mediatresse'.[44] The Protestants who denigrated worship of Mary also undermined respect for her. 'What a cruell harted gentlewoman our Ladie is', mocked Barnaby Rich, for not forgiving sins which Christ had forgiven.[45]

The social teachings of Protestant divines were, in fact, full of ambiguity and contradiction for women. The ministers taught women that they had souls to save, but their predestinarian theology limited the scope for individual action. A Protestant minister would encourage a woman to defy her father and her husband for the sake of her true Protestant faith, and offer the examples of the female martyrs for Protestantism for emulation, but in practice the divines disliked wifely disobedience. Ministers especially disliked women who defied them. Even though theologians stressed the value of women learning to read so that they could understand the basic tenets of their faith, the clergy always sought to confine the texts which women should study. While education for girls received a stimulus as basic schooling expanded, and the female literacy rate probably increased faster that that of the general male population, girls' education was limited compared with that offered to boys of the same social level.[46]

'A LITTLE CHURCH, A LITTLE COMMONWEALTH':[47]
HOUSEHOLD, FAMILY AND THE REFORMATION

Religious change was only one of a number of factors focusing attention on the household in the sixteenth century. Population growth, rising prices and agricultural change increased the number of people unemployed and in poverty. Successive Tudor governments, fearful of potential disorder, sought to deal with the problems of idleness and vagrancy by statutes aimed at putting all the able-bodied to work and allowing relief to those who were incapable. As a basic economic unit in society, the household had a central role, for there people could both be placed in work and subject to authority.[48]

The problem of the unmarried unemployed was addressed in the Elizabethan Statute of Artificers of 1563, which directed that they be placed in service.[49] The series of statutes for the relief of the poor insisted that the able-bodied should work and only those incapable should have relief. Parish officials exercised control over the behaviour of those in need through their distribution of poor relief. Of special concern were unmarried women who lived outside patriarchal control. Efforts were concentrated on making independent women subject to the authority of a household. Girls who wished 'to keep house by themselves' were objects of suspicion to parish officials.[50] Typically, a woman without employment 'found masterless' in 1616 was ordered to the House of Correction for a whipping.[51]

Economic life for single women was increasingly difficult in the early modern period, although the medieval period was no 'golden age' for single or any other women.[52] Wiesner's study of working women in Germany shows that as specialisation of crafts and traders increased, so training was needed. At the same time, men in the guilds felt the effects of increased competition. Not all journeymen would be able to set up as independent masters, and they resented women competitors. Furthermore, as they remained as workers in the households of masters, they felt degraded by working alongside women.[53] Thus even in the household economy, women's position suffered. Alice Clark has shown how women in England were excluded from participation in the guilds.[54] The development of new industries – by-employments, Joan Thirsk has called them – took place outside the control of cities and towns, and focused on households rather than guilds.[55] Women workers participated there as members of households and families rather than as independent agents. Thus even the new economic opportunities for women had the effect of increasing their dependence on households and on the masters who controlled them.

Religious ideology which dignified the well-ordered family and household as a microcosm of God's plan for the world was one of the forces strengthening patriarchal control. As we have seen, both Protestant and Catholic divines emphasised the woman's duty of obedience. But just as contemporaries considered questions of the extent of obedience to the prince, so they deliberated about the limits of wifely obedience.

A central problem in Tudor and Stuart society was that of authority. Parallel to the rule of the prince in the kingdom was the rule of the patriarch at home.[56] The focus on men, husbands, fathers and masters as the source of authority and control in households was problematic in practice. First, preachers such as Gouge who emphasised the duty of wifely obedience were challenged by the women in the congregation as 'an hater of women'.[57] The sense of debate is present in much of the ideal literature about wifely obedience. An anonymous author in 1608 who said that a wife should govern the household 'to the honour of her husband, like the moon who takes her light from the sun, taking all her light from him', defended himself against feared objections: 'Can this be counted slauerie, or servill suiection?' The answer was that there must be degrees in all things, for just as the subject who obeyed his prince was not slavish, nor was the obedient wife. There was no use in a wife striving with her husband, just as there was no use in 'the horse (pardon mee good wiues to use so base a similitude) the horse (I say) [striving] with him that hath the bridle and is able to sit fast'.[58] The animal imagery was significant, and the reiteration of the basic points – 'neither yet is it a vile estate whereunto the wife is thus subiected', 'I haue meant no servil subiection or dutie, but dutie with a kind of equalitie' – betrayed an unease that obedience could be slavery.[59]

Second, it is clear that the family was not a 'private' world, contrasted with a public one, but rather a meeting point between the public and private. The household was public in the sense that the government used it to enforce public order. In return, the church preached obedience. Although both church and state upheld patriarchal authority, they did not abrogate concern with the family and household. Susan Amussen has pointed out that early modern people were accustomed to see social institutions in parallel ways, so disorder in the family was of concern to both church and state. Disobedient wives, children or servants would not respect wider authority.[60] Gouge's oft-quoted comment encapsulated this truth: the family was 'a little Church, a little Commonwealth'. Granted that women 'were not admitted to any publike function in church or commonwealth', this did not mean that they had no public calling at all: rather, said Gouge, 'a conscionable performance of household duties, in regard to the end and fruit thereof, may be accounted a publike worke'.[61]

For masters of families there were tensions and divided interests. In reality, they knew that as individuals they were vulnerable to the challenges of their subordinates. Wives' sexual infidelity, real or rumoured, exposed husbands to the ridicule of the village community, to gossip and even to public shame.[62] Disobedience of wives, children and servants likewise subjected men to public rebuke. For example, if their wives, children or servants refused to comply with the established faith, the courts summoned heads of household to answer for their families' nonconformity.[63] Some members of Parliament resisted attempts to make husbands responsible for their wives' religious opinions. MPs acknowledged that they were often powerless to change their wives' religious opinions. So, while in theory men supported the patriarchal power of the state, recognising that they shared a common interest in it, men argued as individuals that the household was their private sphere, one where the state could not interfere.

The household was thus a public as well as a private place. In the sixteenth century, the boundary between work and home was not a rigid one. Much work could be done at home, including the business of administering justice and affairs of state. The royal household was paralleled on a smaller scale in the households of the officers of the crown and even of justices of the peace. Given that men both recognised women's influence in the household and were suspicious of its value (the example of Eve's influence over Adam was constantly before them), they feared lest women should extend their influence into the public sphere via their husbands. During the Elizabethan period, this anxiety was exacerbated with the lawful presence of wives in the households of bishops and clergy. A private legislative draft in 1575 proposed to limit female interference: the wives of bishops should be confined to works of charity and the management of maid-servants, 'And not to intrude themselves into the worldly affairs of any such seat of government as now far otherwise at this present is reported to be by the said matrons'.[64]

The Reformation changed the status of the priest. He too could be a head of household. Ministers, as heads of household, were subject to public surveillance. They began to see themselves as models for other families, as ideals. Stories of godly families were celebrated in funeral sermons and subsequently published as godly lives for emulation.[65] The minister's family was very much in the public eye. But by the same token, the minister's control was subject to scrutiny. If there were misdemeanours, then his parishioners were scandalised. Even in separatist congregations, ministers were accountable, as the example of English exiles in Johnson's congregation in Amsterdam shows. In 1604 Johnson's church complained about his wife's style of dress, which they believed was above the minister's station.[66] And if ministers were unable to claim that their households were their private domains, no more could other masters of families. When ministers took on themselves to rebuke the sins of their parishioners, they came into conflict with masters who considered themselves absolute and resented their interference. Censures by the clergy undermined the control and reputation of other men.[67]

Gouge's first parallel between the family and social institutions was with the church. The parallel worked the other way too, for the church was discussed in the metaphor of a family. Although the church was frequently represented as the bride and the spouse of Christ, in its social organisation it was seen as a family, with the clergy as fathers in God.[68] Parishioners were children begotten in God, as Bunyan claimed later in the seventeenth century.[69] The laity were no more free to choose their spiritual leaders than their social fathers: the Injunctions of 1559 ordered that people should attend their own parish church, and not go gadding abroad.[70] Furthermore, Protestant ministers saw themselves in familial roles not just as fathers but as husbands too. For example, Samuel Clarke commended Mrs Margaret Corbet because she 'kept close to the publick Ministry where she lived' and did not 'separate from the Ministry of a godly Pastor *and Husband*' (my italic).[71] For a minister to claim paternal authority over his parishioners was not new, but to assert husbandly power brought him into competition with men in his congregation who were heads of household and husbands themselves.

The Protestant Reformation had altered the status of the priest. He was no longer set apart from the laity in a celibate state. In theory, clergy and laity were equal before God, but in practice, differences between clergy and laity, layman and laywoman remained. While some of the highest clergy remained celibate, such as Archbishop Whitgift in the later sixteenth century and Archbishop Laud in the 1640s, many ministers were married. This altered their relationship with their parishioners. While in the past, in practice the laity recognised that priests were sexual beings with their own desires, the Reformation legitimated the ministers' sexuality. Clerical sexual sins were probably viewed more seriously by the laity. Sometimes the minister was already married, when a congregation was troubled at rumours of sexual scandal. In one parish in the 1640s, women gossiped about stories of a minister's apparently insatiable sexual desire for his own wife.[72] In this instance a woman's responses to her minister's sexuality varied, depending on whether she was parishioner, maid-servant, or wife. The explicit recognition in Protestant churches that a minister was a man thus added a new element of sexual tension to congregational politics.

Religious duty raised another conflict of authority. If the husband were an unbeliever, or of a different faith, whom was a wife to obey? Initially, theologians stressed the equality of all believers before God. Individuals were responsible for their own salvation. Potentially, the role of the individual conscience was enlarged, and most divines agreed that a wife should place obedience to God and the true church above her duty to her husband. Such was John Bale's view, who commended Anne Askew for leaving her husband for the sake of her faith and reverting to her maiden name. By saying that she was 'a Saint canonized in Christ's blood', Bale was conferring the status of martyr upon her.[73] Thomas Becon, who condemned the wife who could 'grow up into such arrogancy, pride, and haughtiness of mind' as to despise her husband, even if he were simple, nevertheless said that if a husband should command a wife to commit idolatry, 'and to defile herself with image-service . . . to play the harlot', she should forsake him and suffer death if necessary.[74] The issue of female conscience continued to plague the divines. In 1634 Gouge published four pages in his *Domesticall duties* advising against the marriages of people of different faiths, pages which had been suppressed in earlier editions.[75] The extent of obedience to authority was of central concern in England up to the Civil Wars, and religion gave scope for defiance.

The religious changes of the sixteenth century were thus only one of many factors influencing the patterns of authority within the family. Men who ruled were so concerned about disorder around 1600 that they used religious belief as a prop for the authority of male heads of household.

3

Anglicans, Puritans and Catholics 1558–1640

ANGLICANS AND PURITANS

In the 1550s, Margaret Ellis was in trouble for her faith: because she had not been to confession, nor taken the sacrament at Easter, nor borne a candle at Candlemas day, nor received ashes on Ash Wednesday, she was imprisoned.[1] Her refusal to perform certain actions identified her religious adherence as Protestant. A decade later her religious behaviour would have been the norm.

Historians are uncertain how far Protestantism had advanced by the beginning of Elizabeth's reign. Haigh has discussed the difficulty of converting a reluctant laity, and Scarisbrick has argued that the laity acquiesced in the religious changes but they neither initiated nor promoted them.[2] Local studies are increasing our knowledge of the progress of the Reformation, and it seems clear that there were marked regional differences.[3] As we shall see, Catholicism certainly survived in many areas, but Protestantism had a wide popular following.

During the Elizabethan period the Anglican church took shape and a generation grew up who had known no other. The parish clergy tried to instruct their congregations in the saving tenets of the faith. They battled with resistance, ignorance and superstition, as the records of the archdiaconal courts reveal. Women were among those presented for ignorance. For example, one woman confessed that she knew nothing about Christ, although 'by our dear Lady sure it is some good thing, or it should never have been put in the Creed'.[4] Women were also among those prosecuted for disorderly conduct at worship. One, told by a churchwarden to be quiet in church, 'sayd she woulde talke and aske him no leave'.[5] Others were prosecuted in the church courts for behaviour which signalised more extreme Protestant beliefs, such as objecting to vestments as a sign of popery. Such behaviour, while essentially no different from that of men, was more offensive because it flouted contemporary expectations of female obedience and conformity.

Elizabethan prosecutions also offer insight into Catholic resistance to the new Anglican faith. Some refused to come to church 'because there is neither priest, altar, nor Sacrifice'.[6] Women were presented for superstitious practices but on many occasions these were Catholic survivals. For example, in 1580 four women in York were accused of placing lighted candles about the body of a dead woman.[7] Women objected that the church's ceremonies were no longer efficacious, that 'the Baptism is not as it hath been', and that 'those that be now married are not right married'.[8] Hostility to the clergy and clerical marriage led to trouble for other women: one was presented in 1580 because she had said that she did not like the ministers, their wives, or godly religion. Many people were hostile to the sacrament of the Lord's Supper. In Chester, one woman and six men refused to communicate in 1578 'oneles they have singing breads or wafer breade'.[9] In 1582 Matilda Watson received the communion bread but 'did convey the same forth of her mouth into her handkerchief'.[10] Bishops' Visitation articles enquired about unlawful worship, such as praying with beads, auricular confession and wearing of crosses, and women were prosecuted for offences.[11] As historians analyse these regional records, we are gaining a clearer picture of the acceptance and resistance to the new church and the different responses of the two sexes.

A few public protests about religious issues were recorded. In May 1566 Bishop Grindal wrote to Sir William Cecil about a disturbance at St Giles Cripplegate. Grindal had suspended a lecturer, one Bartlett, and sixty women came and made suit for him, and left only at the request of another suspended reader, Mr Philpot. A month later, Grindal sent for a warrant to support him against 'a womannyshe brabble' in a church in London.[12] A crowd of two or three hundred women supported ministers who were sent out of London for their hostility to wearing vestments: they greeted them on London Bridge with provisions, and exhorted the men 'to stand fast' in their doctrine.[13]

Other incidents reveal individual women entertaining beliefs which were unacceptable to other stricter Protestants. In 1629 Henry Sherfield, a lawyer, challenged a woman in his parish church who bowed to a church window depicting God as an old man. She told him that she was reverencing God, there 'in the window'. Later Sherfield smashed the window, an act for which he was prosecuted in the court of Star Chamber.[14]

Yet the majority of women were probably content with the Anglican church. From the mid-sixteenth century to the outbreak of the Civil Wars, there were women who worshipped happily in the Anglican church, finding comfort and assurance in its services and the ministrations of its priests. The liturgical responses in which the congregation participated were greater in the Anglican church than in the Catholic. By the 1620s and 1630s, the laity were attending church more regularly, and participating more usually in annual communion than they had been during the Elizabethan period.[15]

A specifically female service which allows us to assess female support was the ceremony of churching after a woman had given birth.[16] The bishops tried to enforce churching through articles of enquiry to the clergy followed by episcopal visitations. In 1619, for example, Bishop Andrewes enquired among other things whether all women were churched after the birth of their children.[17] Certainly there were always some who objected. In the Elizabethan period, archdiaconal records reveal a mixture of motives for refusal. In 1597, Jane Minors of Barking, for example, was slow in having her child baptised. She came to be churched after four or five hours in the tavern, and then went out again, saying that churching 'was a ceremony'.[18] The Barrowists objected because the ceremony was unwarranted by Scripture.[19] In Shrewsbury in the 1620s Katherine Chidley, later famous for a public defence of Independency which she published in 1641, objected to being churched: 'before the mother dare goe abroad, shee must have their blessing, that the Sun shall not smite her by day, nor the Moone by night'. In addition to the unscriptural nature of the ceremony, Chidley resented the clergy's demand for payment.[20] Her comment merits serious consideration, for it was one of the few written statements on churching by a woman for the entire century. Furthermore, there is evidence from Bristol that separatist women objected to the ceremony. Baptist women went to lie-in at the house of Mrs Dorothy Hazzard, to avoid churching.[21] Nevertheless, the work of Jeremy Boulton on one London parish of the 1630s has established that there was a high correlation between the number of baptisms and the number of churchings in Southwark, suggesting that 93 per cent of the mothers accepted the ceremony.[22]

The strength of attachment to another Anglican ceremony, that of marriage, was demonstrated during the Interregnum, when marriages became the responsibility of the civil magistrate rather than the clergy. Many couples still tried to involve the Anglican clergy in this rite of passage.[23] All this suggests that the Anglican church had secured a measure of popular acceptance, and that its survival during the Civil Wars owed much to the devotion of the laity.

To be female was still, under Protestantism, to be incapable of administering any of the sacraments. The Catholic church allowed anyone, including women, to baptise in an emergency, but Calvin, with a theology of predestination, thought that an infant who died before baptism was not excluded from the kingdom of heaven. He instructed that since baptism was part of the public ministry, no women or men in general should administer the rite.[24] Initially, the Anglican church followed Catholic practice, and allowed both midwives and laity to baptise a child privately in case of necessity.[25] James I successfully insisted that any private baptisms should be conducted by lawful ministers only.[26] This restricted women's role in the Anglican church. There are hints that some people still viewed the natural function of menstruation as polluting. An Anglican minister was complained of during the 1640s for refusing to administer communion to a woman at 'the time of her natural courses'.[27] But even if ministers implied that female presence could pollute the sacred space, there is no indication that their view was resented by the majority of women, or that it alienated them from the church. Many women were devoted to the institution and its fabric, and sought to beautify and domesticate it in ways open to them. They made gifts to the church, such as altar cloths.[28] Some also endowed ministers.[29] One function which women were always allowed to exercise in the church was cleaning. Right through the early modern period, irrespective of theological differences, there were always poor women sweeping the building and washing the linen.[30]

At the other end of the social scale, well-educated women devoted time and energy to furthering the Protestant cause. The Cooke sisters translated important texts for the service of Anglicanism. Lady Anne Bacon, who translated the standard edition of Jewel's Apology in 1564, won renown for her translation. She used her religious work to justify her education in European languages.[31] The improved education of girls was of concern to other women during the early modern period. Bathsua Makin, tutor to the Princess Elizabeth in the reign of Charles I, pleaded for sound education to make women religious.[32] Some wealthy women, usually widows, were patrons of ministers. For example, the widowed Lady Joan Barrington exercised a powerful influence on the religious affairs of her locality, as the correspondence addressed to her between 1628 and 1632 reveals.[33] The role of piety in the lives of these more prosperous women and the significance of the model they created of the godly household will be discussed later in part II. Here, the purpose is to show women's influence on religious changes.

The Elizabethan settlement was not acceptable to all Protestants. From the first, those who came to be known as Puritans wanted a further reformation. The term Puritan has a complex and rich historiography, and although some historians doubt whether it can be used before 1640, it seems a useful term for distinguishing those who wanted change in the church in a Protestant direction.[34] While the Puritan clergy and influential Puritan laymen concentrated their efforts for reform of the church on convocation and Parliament, women who were dissatisfied were not expected to engage in public controversy. Although a few women, as we shall see, separated from the Anglican church and formed new churches, the majority of those who were discontented turned their attention to their families, households and neighbourhoods, and to their own personal religion. Personal faith informed lifestyles, and the good Puritan, like the good Anglican woman, tried to live a pious, godly life. For the most part, Puritans were from the middling ranks of society but no sociological studies have succeeded in distinguishing the social characteristics which divided Puritans and Anglicans.[35] Separatists, however, both men and women, tended to be of lower social status.

Disputes within the Anglican church were exacerbated with the rise of a party known as the Arminians in the reign of James I. Favouring an amendment of the rigid Calvinist doctrine of predestination, they polarised the church in the reign of Charles I.[36] In matters of worship the Arminians favoured sacramentalism over preaching, and under the direction of Charles I and Laud, subsequently Archbishop of Canterbury, the clergy were required to restore order in worship.[37] Among the requirements in episcopal visitations were that men and women continue to sit separately, that altars be railed at the east end of the church, and that the congregation express reverence during the service by bowing at the name of Jesus and standing for the Creed. In 1630 a gentlewoman who sat quietly while others stood for the singing of the Nicene creed was abused by Bishop Cosin who urged her to stand, pulled her by the sleeve and tore it, 'with these reproachful words, "Can you not stand, ye lazie sows?"'[38] Charles supported the Laudian clergy's efforts. He too sought to see women in their proper place in church, and wanted the seats of women moved out of the chancel.[39]

CATHOLICS

The Elizabethan settlement was unacceptable to Catholics, for although the Anglican church was designed to encompass everyone, and many Catholics did intermittently attend its services, the reformist forces in the Catholic church abroad were not content to see England in a state of heresy. In 1570 the Pope excommunicated Elizabeth and absolved her subjects from obedience. Later, the king of Spain undertook to unseat her. Meanwhile, missionary priests arrived to reconvert the heretics and to strengthen the faith of English Catholics. The laity's responses to these Counter-Reformation initiatives varied.

The history of Catholicism has been dominated by the heroic struggles and martyrdoms of the Catholic missionary priests, and this has overshadowed the heroism of some of the laity, especially of women. The stories of women who devoted their efforts to the maintenance of their faith, and even died for it, were available to contemporaries in highly engaging narratives. The names of the martyrs Margaret Clitheroe and Anne Line were well known to contemporaries. Sister Hanlon and others have written the history of the heroism of individual women.[40] Aveling has written of nuns, and Scarisbrick has emphasised the importance of women's traditional role in Catholic households.[41] Although Bossy believes that the Catholic community was a matriarchy from the early days until about 1620, he does not develop his insight about the centrality of gender to Catholic history.[42] A. L. Rowse recognises women's contribution to the survival of Catholicism, but argues, unsympathetically, that Catholicism was easier for them to maintain than for men: they did not have to go to prison.[43] While it is true that the courts were initially reluctant to imprison wives, many women were gaoled. More interesting than an argument about degrees of suffering is to see how women were able to use their gender and social situations in order to secure their object, the defence of Catholicism. The major study of women recusants in the period 1558–1640 is that by Marie Rowlands.[44]

After the Act of Uniformity of 1559 the penalty of a fine was levied on those who refused to attend the Anglican church.[45] The term recusant was applied to all those who refused to comply with legislation supporting the Anglican church. There were many people who remained Catholic but who avoided recusancy, in some cases by occasional attendance at services. This was more common for men than for women. In many Catholic families, male relatives complied with the legislation which preserved the family property while Catholic women stayed away from church. The motives of the two sexes have been variously explained, but many historians agree that women may have felt a deeper commitment to their faith.[46] Unmarried women and widows were all indicted, fined and imprisoned, as were men. The case of a married woman, a feme covert, was more difficult, since the government believed that a household's religious conformity was the responsibility of a husband. Many members of Parliament had recusant female relatives, and knew that in practice they could not enforce Anglicanism, even if they wished to do so. Thus although some married women were imprisoned, the penalties were usually less severe than on the unmarried. In the Elizabethan period, men complained of the imprisonment of their wives.[47] After the 1610 Act for the Administration of the Oath of Allegiance and the Reformation of Married Women Recusants, the oath was tendered and a number of women were imprisoned. For example, in 1612 Sir Francis Stoner's wife, daughter, sister, and daughter's servant were all imprisoned for their refusal to take the oath.[48]

After 1620, prosecutions of married women for recusancy declined, leaving the problem unresolved. The government concentrated on priests and gentlemen. Later, during the Interregnum, Parliament passed an Act against recusants in 1657 directing that a man whose wife was a Catholic was to suffer the confiscation of two-thirds of his estate. MPs still resented the state's intrusion into a family's religious life.[49] Further, they objected, as husbands, to taking responsibility for their wives' religious views: 'if my wife turn Papist I shall suffer sequestration of two parts [of three] of my estate'.[50] Sometimes, wives worshipped as Catholics with their husbands' approval, but others professed their faith in defiance of husbands and fathers. Lady Tasborough, who made her profession to the order of Augustinian canonesses at the Louvain in 1622, so enraged her father when she refused to renounce her religion that he evicted her from his house. It was her grandmother who gave her a portion and helped her to go abroad.[51] Elizabeth Cary, Lady Falkland, converted in defiance of her husband. Lord Falkland, who sought a career in the service of King Charles, was seriously embarrassed by his wife's Catholicism. He refused to support her and reduced her to a beggarly state.[52] In addition to suffering legal penalties, women who chose to worship as Catholics risked their reputations as good women, for they were defying established authority.

Why did some women either adhere or convert to Catholicism? While their decision to support Catholicism was influenced by many factors, including family of origin, marriage, social situation, and their neighbourhoods, their own individual choice and conscience played a major role. This can be documented from the statements of a number of educated women, but in addition the records of the ecclesiastical courts show that questions of conscience were not confined to those of gentry status. In proceedings against recusants at York in 1576, women at the social level of tradesmen's wives considered doctrinal issues important enough to keep them from conformity. They said that the Anglican church was not a proper church, there were no priests, and the sacrament was not properly consecrated.[53] Their actions ranged from taking their children to priests for baptism to spitting out the communion bread.[54]

During the Elizabethan period, the situation of Catholics became increasingly difficult with the arrival of the missionary priests from 1572 onwards. Between 1558 and 1660, 1,740 English priests were ordained abroad; most of them visited England, even if briefly. Their presence, and the Spanish threat, provoked harsher legislation against recusancy. Many Catholic women risked their lives to protect the priests and to foster the faith. Since the public world was very dangerous for professing Catholics, the private world of the household became extremely important, the only place in fact where the faith could be practised. Everyone agreed that the household was women's domain, and their role was correspondingly important. However, few households were large enough to hide a resident priest, and after 1580 even the gentry were forced to rely upon noble Catholic households for their priests.[55] Thus, a wide infrastructure was needed so that priests could work in England, and women of lower social status were vital to that network.[56] In Newcastle in 1615, for example, the faithful knew that the seminary priest William Southerne said mass at a widow's house. She was obviously of low social status for she sold 'some small commodities in her shop, as Ropes, Red herrings and some salt fishes, and many small trifles'. Nevertheless, upstairs in a red chest were 'the hosts in great number in a painted box, books, paternosters or beads'.[57] Catholic women of wealthier status organised their households to provide safety for the priests. This required first of all that their households be made up of loyal Catholics. Dorothy Lawson, a prominent gentlewoman of the early seventeenth century, took care to provide Catholic servants.[58]

Many wealthier Catholic women ensured that their households were instructed in the faith. Being responsible for the education of young children, women had the opportunity to influence them. One of Anne Wigmore's daughters, Winefrid, became a nun, and one of her sons entered the English College at Rome. Her son said that 'my mother was always a Catholic, and most strict in enforcing Catholic discipline in her family'.[59] Nearly a quarter of those who entered the College said that their mothers had influenced their conversion and vocation, sometimes against the wishes of their Protestant fathers.[60] The records of admissions of men and women to other religious orders abroad show that maternal persuasion was influential. In 1600 John Smyth said that in his youth, he had been a schismatic, like his father and grandfather,

> But it is most true that, moved by the instructions and holy life of my mother, I believed from my tenderest years that the Catholic religion was the best, and was afterwards, as I think, induced by her counsels and example to embrace it.[61]

Smyth's mother also provided the means of his reconciliation to Catholicism by introducing him to a priest. Rather different was the case of Margaret Plowden who professed at St Monica's convent of English Augustinians in 1625. Margaret was the youngest child of Catholic parents; her mother had 'made a promise to God, that if one of her daughters would be religious she would willingly give her to God'. Margaret's mother brought her over to the convent when she was 12 years old, and five years later she professed.[62]

Since women were responsible for household routines, they were in a position to arrange for masses to be said, and to hide the church vessels and vestments.[63] Secrecy was not always necessary. The Dowager Lady Montague, who lived at Battle Abbey in the 1590s, took advantage of her social position which made the justices reluctant to present her for recusancy. She walked abroad openly with her beads. Although as many as 120 people attended mass in her house, about half of whom communicated, Lady Montague actually endured little persecution for matters of religion 'other than that she was once accused to the pretended Bishop of Canterbury, her house twice searched, and her Priest once taken, and imprisoned'.[64] Because of her social position, she was an important link in the network which enabled priests to arrive in England and move around. But such activities were not confined to the wealthy, and all over England there were Catholic women contributing in their separate ways to the survival of their faith.

When people needed priests, either to be reconciled or to receive the last rites, women were frequently the ones who located them. For example, Dorothy Lawson found a priest at her dying husband's request, and a lay sister was instrumental in bringing Benedictine priests to converts in the 1620s.[65] When the pursuivants arrived in search of priests, women were usually the ones at home, and they exploited the conventional feminine roles of weakness and ignorance in courageous attempts to protect the priests.[66] If priests were imprisoned, women servants could visit them more easily without arousing suspicion. For example, when Morgan, a priest, was imprisoned in Newgate in 1584, Margerie Throckmorton confessed that he was a priest. Lady Throckmorton sent her servant Joane Morley to warn Morgan. Lady Throckmorton told Joane that she should not scruple to deny on oath that Morgan was a priest. This incident also demonstrated the determination of Lady Throckmorton, who counselled that the oath could be taken with a good conscience, for 'our Englishe books where upon they should be sworne were but the bookes of heretiques and of no force before god'.[67] Margaret Ward was executed in 1588 for helping a priest to escape by supplying him with a rope.[68]

Some Catholic women were powerful agents for conversions. In less danger than priests, women could move around easily, and gain entry to the houses of others without arousing suspicion. When Sir Richard Wenman was absent abroad, Elizabeth Vaux converted his wife to Catholicism.[69] Women could work on their own households, too. On her marriage in 1597, Dorothy Lawson set about the task of converting the household with such dexterity that her husband 'between jest and earnest, tould her, his family was become Papists ere he perceived it'.[70] Lawson also worked away among her neighbours, especially during her widowhood.[71] A lay sister of Mary Ward's Institute also influenced a wide range of people in the 1620s. She taught children and endeavoured 'to instruct the simple and vulgar sort', and she tended and served the poor, especially the sick. Where she was instrumental in conversions, she observed that she never gained one person alone, but always more.[72] Ursula Middleton, wife of Henry Fermor, used her skill in surgery to save the souls of children. She had a wide practice in surgery, so when children were brought to her with rickets, and she found that they were not christened, 'she wou'd carry the Children up with som excuse & there in the Chappel desire the Priest to Christen them, or els baptise them herself'.[73] Less spectacular than the activities of the missionary priests, women's work for Catholicism was unobtrusive and constant.

Catholic women risked punishment for their religious work. They acted in the conviction that what they were doing was significant both in their present lives and in the life to come: 'Happy are they that suffer persecution', wrote Dorothy Lawson, 'for theirs is the kingdome of heaven.'[74] Some were imprisoned and died in gaol. The best-known examples of women suffering for their faith were the martyrs, Margaret Clitheroe, Margaret Ward and Anne Line. Clitheroe was the Catholic wife of a Protestant butcher in York. She refused to plead to the charges against her, probably because she feared implicating others, including her children and servants. She suffered the terrifying death of being pressed to death with stones.[75] The martyr Margaret Ward was a Cheshire gentleman's daughter. When in London in the service of a lady, she organised the escape of a secular priest, William Watson, from Bridewell. Imprisoned and tortured, Ward was offered the Queen's pardon if she would recant. Ward avowed her actions, arguing that her compassion was part of any woman's true nature:

> that as to what she had done in favouring the priest's escape, she believed the Queen herself, if she had the bowels of a woman, would have done as much, if she had known the ill-treatment he underwent.[76]

Anne Line, the other female Catholic martyr in Elizabeth's reign, was a convert. She was disinherited by her father because of her faith. Married to a Catholic, she sheltered priests for some time until she was arrested in 1601. When asked to plead to the charge of sheltering a priest, she declared 'My Lords, nothing grieves me but that I could not receive a thousand more'. Anne Line was hanged in 1601.[77] Three other women were under sentence of death in prison at Elizabeth's death but were subsequently pardoned.[78]

The example of these female martyrs demonstrates that although the household was important for Catholicism's survival, women were not confined to domestic roles. Their faith took them outside their homes into the community at large and into public conflict.[79] Such a life could seem even more worthy than the conventional highest ideal, the religious life. The gentlewoman Anne Vaux believed that she could do more for Catholicism by ministering to the needs of the Jesuits in England, than by entering a convent abroad. She devoted her life to helping the Jesuit English mission from the mid-1580s to her death.[80] Around 1635 she was reported to be keeping a school where 'the sons of divers persons of quality' were brought up under the tutelage of the Jesuits.[81]

Catholic women seeking a more intense spiritual life joined monasteries. After the Reformation, it was not possible to enter a Catholic religious order in England, so after 1598 women went abroad to fulfil their vocation in the conventional way. Motives were scrutinised at admission to the convents, and tested during a period of novitiate. Mary Ward's statement in her autobiography was not expansive: she wrote that when she was between 15 and 16 years old, 'it pleased our loving Lord to inspire me with a desire to lead a religious life'.[82]

Although hostile Protestant propaganda negated the value of monastic spirituality, from 1598 onwards English Catholic women established

some forty convents abroad.[83] Most orders were devoted to the contemplative life. The Counter-Reformation church wanted all female
religious houses to be strictly enclosed, but one Englishwoman, Mary
Ward, believed that a more active piety was needed, because 'the very
distressed condition of England, our native land, is greatly in need of
spiritual workers'.[84] Mary Ward (1585–1645) first joined the Poor
Clares, but she received in a vision the direction to found an order of
nuns, the Institute of the Blessed Virgin Mary, on the model of the
Jesuits. In 1617 two houses at St Omer and Liège had seventy women or
so in each; by 1631 some 500 women had entered. Ward believed that
women were as capable as men of the higher forms of education and
spirituality. She recognised that women faced difficulties because of
their limited education, so her order was devoted to the work of
education and active work for the faith.[85] Her goals included the
salvation of others, so her Institute was responsible directly to the Pope,
was not enclosed, and its nuns wore only semi-religious dress.[86] Mary
Ward's educational aims dictated such a lifestyle as the most suitable,
but her contemporaries found her and her religious order deeply
threatening. Men's comments indicate that women with independence
and autonomy, even if nuns, were sexually suspect: 'because they would
walk abroad at pleasure and return to their convent when they please,
his Holiness [the Pope] hath utterly denied them any such grace, so that
before long they may hand out their sign Burdello [brothel]', wrote one
critic.[87] They sauntered around, wrote another, 'as if they had been so
many Beeches, and the others so many Dogges that followed after'.[88] In
1631 Urban VII issued a Bull of Suppression. Subsequently, Mary Ward
pursued her educational goals in a less ambitious order.[89] The Institute
functioned in England on a small scale through the support of the
Catholic gentry community.[90] Of the forty convents established abroad
before 1789, seventeen or so were hers.

Protestant leaders always feared that women would succumb to the
wiles of the priests. Since women were thought to be more liable to error
because of their weaker constitutions, Protestants suspected that women might give easy credence to stories of faked miracles: people were
'overmuch seduced . . . by these and suchlike popish devices'.[91]
Legislation against beads, images and Catholic books all attest to
Protestant fears of reconversion. However, there was no way of legislat-
ing against certain dangers, and when Charles I married Henrietta
Maria of France, Catholic worship was openly permitted at court. The
Queen was a powerful personality who exposed her husband and her
courtiers to Catholic European culture. A number of conversions at

court were attributed to her influence.[92] Interestingly, her contemporaries were in no doubt about her powerful role in promoting Catholicism. In 1642 there were rumours that Parliament would impeach her, and in subsequent treaty negotiations, the Parliamentarians sought to restrict the religious freedom of any spouse of a monarch.[93]

By the seventeenth century, the majority of adults alive in England had never known a time in which Catholicism was the religion practised. They had not grown up with the Mass or other Catholic services. Catholicism's survival therefore depended upon the maintenance of faith in those who were already Catholic, and the efforts of those with wealth and social status to maintain the priesthood. Women's role was considerable. Furthermore, as the Catholic church was in crisis in England at this time, the surviving stories of their activities formed a powerful mythology. These accounts showed women as strong, capable, energetic and humorous, while subject to the authority of the church. They contributed a positive image of womanhood to other Catholics in early modern England.[94]

MARTYRS

Gender influenced the form of prosecutions for heresy of both Protestants and Catholics. It may be useful to discuss the phenemonon of martyrdom with reference to women during the whole of the sixteenth century. The fact that fewer women than men were burned was in part because women were not officers of the church, whose public compliance was necessary. This, thought Anne Line, was an unfortunate limitation. She longed for martyrdom and envied priests and others who 'seemed to be in a fairer way to that happy end'.[95] The courts, believing that women were weak and easily misled, were unwilling to make martyrs of them, and sought to persuade them to abjure rather than to secure their conviction. However, when it came to a trial, women were still expected both to answer for themselves and to reply in terms of conventional Christian faith. While the possibility of martyrdom was never something which affected the majority of women, who concentrated on their personal and household religion and left the public debate of religion to others, a few women did die for their beliefs.

Contemporary wisdom expected less of women than of men. Women were not expected to be skilled in theology, nor were they educated for debate, and some women really felt that they could not participate in theological argument in the trials for heresy. Others, however, exploited the convention of female incapacity to advantage. For example, when

Figure 3. Foxe listed eight women among the twenty-two conventiclers arrested in Colchester in 1557 and sent to London. From *Foxe's Book of Martyrs, 1632* (Mansell Collection).

the Protestant Elizabeth Young was before the ecclesiastical court for heresy, she refused to debate the question of clerical marriage, saying 'I am no divine'.[96] Margaret Clitheroe, the Catholic martyr, used the same argument at her trial: 'I am no divine, neither can answer you to these hard questions'. In debate she pleaded ignorance of books of divinity: 'I have no learning to read them'.[97]

Women could accept the conventional belief in female weakness, but find strength in the Lord. Their faith gave them power. Margaret Clitheroe's belief 'overruled all worldly fears and natural inclination in her'. She thought that a man who advised caution over the admission of children and servants to the secret services was cowardly, and she rejected 'such timorous Catholics'.[98] The awesome trials for heresy that the martyrs faced provided them with an opportunity to testify to their strong and clear Christian beliefs for which they were prepared to die. Father Mush said that Clitheroe showed 'her graces *in her frailty*' (my italic), and was strengthened by her 'confidence . . . in so just and godly a cause'.[99]

At their trials, women claimed the right as believers to speak publicly of the things of God. Alice Davis, one of the Marian martyrs, rejected the social barriers which separated her from her university-educated antagonists:

> You be not able to resist the Spirit of God in me, a poor woman. I was an honest poor man's daughter, never brought up in the University, as you have been, but I have driven the plough before my father many a time (I thank God).[100]

Inevitably, the sexual reputation of the martyrs was attacked. Margaret Clitheroe's accusers alleged that it was 'not for religion that thou harbourest priests, but for harlotry', and they preached against her sexual reputation after her death.[101] The martyr herself was anxious to demonstrate that she was a modest woman, like any other. When Clitheroe was sentenced to be stripped naked before she was pressed to death, her confessor reported that she 'was ashamed on their behalfs to have such shameful words uttered in that audience as to strip me naked, and press me to death among men, which methought for womanhood they might have concealed'.[102]

In discussing female martyrs, subsequent writers discoursed on the power of the Lord who had taken the weakest of his instruments to manifest his glory. For example, Thomas Hall, a Protestant divine, wrote in 1658 of how 'God doth great things usually by weake meanes. He can make weake women instrumental to spread the

Gospel.'[103] Male writers frequently used this metaphor of weakness magnifying the power of the Lord, but we know in the case of Anne Askew, since we have her own autobiographical writings, that this was not how she appeared to herself. In the recorded statements of the women before the courts, we have hints that women other than Askew saw themselves as powerful in their faith.

Martyrdom was an awesome fate. Most seventeenth-century Protestant women greatly revered the Marian martyrs. But not everyone subsequently empathised with them. Later in the seventeenth century, Hannah Ellis, a Baptist, observed of the Marian martyrs generally that 'they were as wise yt keept themselues out of ye fire and kept there Conscience to themselues'.[104]

CONCLUSION: GENDER AND RELIGION

Obedience to the 'true' church could involve conflict over women's proper roles. Throughout the period, both Protestant and Catholic divines were vexed over what they came to see as the 'problem' of women's place in the church. Believing that God had ordained women to inferiority and subordination, the ministers and priests also recognised that women were individuals with souls to save.

The wife of an unbelieving husband presented a special difficulty to casuists. In the sixteenth and early seventeenth centuries, most divines believed that religious duty should come first, so they argued that a wife should obey God rather than her husband. Catholic casuists supported Catholic wives of Protestant husbands, arguing that it was morally right for wives to maintain priests without their husbands' knowledge. Catholic priests argued that this apparent dishonesty was really in the best interests of their husbands, because the maintenance of true religion, and priests, was part of husbands' duties. The church did not want to make life too difficult for a wife, so it was allowed that if a husband ordered the preparation of a feast at a time of fast, a wife was excused if she obeyed.

Protestant divines also condoned wifely disobedience for the sake of the true religion.[105] They were more worried, however, about the power of Catholic wives over their husbands. Protestant divines recognised that, although Scripture declared that woman was weak and inferior, in practice wives had persuasive powers which men found hard to resist. The Protestant husband of a Catholic wife was at special risk. The dangers were spelled out when overtures were made for the Spanish Infanta to marry Henry, the elder son of King James, in 1605. Sir

Charles Cornwallis, ambassador to Spain, argued that the risk was greater to England, because it was harder for a husband to change a wife's opinion than a wife to influence a husband. 'From the time of Adam (whoe had the firste taste of the force of a womans perswasions) untill this daye, many more wilbe found perswaded by their wiues, then wiues by their Husbands.'[106] More conventionally, in the later seventeenth century Protestants generally thought that it was unwise to marry daughters to Catholic husbands: 'it wil be very hard for one of the weaker sex perpetually to resist'.[107]

The Protestant and Catholic churches had contradictory views of women. Both churches believed that women should be subject to male authority, yet both believed that she was an individual responsible for her own religious behaviour. Although Protestant reformers taught that God had predestined each individual to salvation or damnation, they still expected her to live a godly life, obeying God rather than man. During the sixteenth and seventeenth centuries, many women tried to negotiate these contradictions, arguing one side or the other as it suited their purposes. In the sixteenth century, there were women who were prepared to place duty to their consciences above life itself. As the Catholic Margaret Ward said, 'she was willing to lay down not one life only, but many, if she had them, rather than betray her conscience'.[108] It was all a question of which was the true faith, and that a woman had to decide for herself. Christian beliefs could lead some women to abandon the established church as they sought a more immediate experience of union with God.

Part II

Women's religious beliefs and spirituality 1500–1720

4

Piety and spirituality

THE 'NATURAL' RELIGIOSITY OF WOMEN

Although contemporaries believed that women were weaker and inferior to men, they recognised that women were religious. This female religiosity seemed relatively unproblematic. As the preacher Richard Sibbes explained, because women were in frequent danger of death in child-birth, they were 'forced to nearer communion with God'.[1] Cotton Mather in Boston later echoed his sentiments, showing how suffering had turned women to God.

> It seems that the Curse in the difficulties both of Subjection and Child-bearing, which the Female Sex is doom'd unto, hath been turn'd into a Blessing.[2]

By the eighteenth century men said that religion was good for women, and performed a valuable function in keeping them virtuous.[3]

In similar vein, some sociologists have discussed the function of religious belief in terms of social control, as a means of persuading individuals to observe the laws and conventions of their societies. Marxists have discussed religion as a legitimating mechanism by which the dominant group in a society provided compensation to a subordinate group for their suffering. Women, on this argument, were a subordinate group who experienced the sorrows of childbirth and children's deaths but who found satisfaction in religious belief. Here the Marxist analysis meshes with that of the functionalists, who argue that religious belief serves the individual as well as the society at large.[4] These approaches help explain the social function which religion performed for women, but they make the godly woman appear to be the successfully socialised woman. As such, pious women would require rather less discussion than other unconventional individuals.[5]

More recently, historians have acknowledged a problem in explaining female religiosity. Interestingly, they have assumed rather than argued that female piety was different from male piety, but they have not problematised male beliefs to the same degree. Lawrence Stone has depicted aristocratic women as driven to religion by their 'idle and frustrated lives . . . in the man's world of a great country house', and Richard Greaves wrote of women's 'more real or induced spiritual neuroses'.[6]

Opportunities for religious experiences were structured by society and affected by gender, as they had been at earlier periods.[7] Men of a deeply religious nature could enter the church as priests or ministers. Until the dissolution of the monasteries, women as well as men could join religious orders, but thereafter the monastic life was restricted to those who could join orders abroad. The majority of women and men expressed their piety in daily life, but increasingly the demands of urban life on men were incompatible with hours of devotion. Women, especially those of the middling and upper ranks, had more time than did their male counterparts for piety. Furthermore, their lives as married women were more contingent upon the decisions of others than were men's. Part of the explanation for female religiosity, as Sara Mendelson suggests, may have been the inadequacies of wedlock; a heavenly spouse was more satisfactory than an earthly one.[8] More cautiously, Keith Thomas has suggested that 'it is possible indeed to hold for the seventeenth century a theory of the greater natural religiosity of women', for not only were they conscious of the imminence of death because of their experiences in childbirth, many had more time for piety.[9]

Here it will be argued that far from being 'natural', female religiosity was socially produced. Furthermore, because their lives were different from men's, women's spirituality had certain distinctive emphases. Denied many other avenues of self-expression, women could express themselves through their religious devotions. Through piety, women could find a meaning in life and develop their spirituality which gave many deep satisfaction. However, personal piety and asceticism could lead some women beyond socially sanctioned behaviour to more intense forms of religious expression: to mysticism, trancing, visions and prophecies. All these more extreme forms of religious belief were dangerous, because contemporaries questioned the sources of women's supernatural power: from God or the devil? More straightforwardly, personal faith was a source of strength in varying degrees, and for some women it provided a justification for social and political action. Faith legitimated protest as well as providing consolation. Finally, women did not confine themselves to Christianity for divine aid. For some domestic tasks, for sickness and health, and for the crises to which their female nature subjected them, such as childbirth and the deaths of children, they turned to beliefs which their contemporaries classified as magical.

This chapter is less concerned with the question of the social effects of religious belief than in the subjective experiences of the believers. Recognising that religion has a different importance for subordinate compared with dominant social groups, I will focus upon women as a subordinate group and discuss their beliefs and what these meant for them. In this context I am arguing that women were a group with some common experiences despite their differences of social status, and theological beliefs.

THE PRACTICE OF PIETY

A regime of godliness, devotion or religious discipline was known as piety. While there were common elements in male and female piety, there were also distinctive forms of feminine piety which were affected more by social level than by theological differences. Piety was especially important for women, because there were few other avenues through which they could legitimately express their faith. Women could not become priests, ministers or theologians. They did not sit in Parliaments which debated religion, nor did they make or administer the policies of the church. After the Reformation, when only those Catholic women who could afford to travel abroad could express their spirituality through a monastic life, lay piety was an accepted and approved area of activity for both Protestant and Catholic women. While piety could degenerate into an end in itself, it could also lead to deep spirituality.

In theory, women were not expected to debate religion. The controversial parts of religion were for educated men. Theological niceties were points which men had marked out as their own territory. As a sixteenth-century French author explained, 'Women must not apply their minds to curious questions of theology & the secret matters of divinity, the knowledge of which belongs to prelates, rectors and doctors.'[10] In practice, there was some inconsistency here, as the example of the sixteenth-century female martyrs demonstrated, for when women came before the ecclesiastical authorities for questioning, they were required to give an account of their faith. But although men agreed that religious controversy was not suitable for women, no one ever said that about piety.

In the later sixteenth and seventeenth centuries piety in its intenser forms is usually associated with the more extreme form of Protestantism known as Puritanism. The signficance of Puritanism in early modern England has been one of the most debated questions of twentieth-century historiography.[11] Recent scholarship suggests that the differences between Anglicans and Puritans were matters of degree and emphasis; both shared a common culture. Margo Todd has shown how both Protestant and Catholic social thinking developed from a reformist tradition stemming from Erasmus, and diverged only after the Council of Trent in the later sixteenth century.[12] Thus, to associate piety exclusively with Puritanism would be a mistake. Although some studies of piety have ignored women, there have recently been some interesting and suggestive analyses.[13] Despite differences in faith between Protestant, Puritan, and Catholic women, their patterns of piety had many features in common. The social level of the female believer was a significant determinant of her pattern of piety. Women of the middling and upper ranks had more time to spare for devotion. Better educated than poorer women, they read devotional books.

The pathway to piety was well known and has been relatively well documented. Protestant ministers encouraged individuals to examine their daily lives and consciences and so developed the habit of diary-keeping among the literate. Individuals who spent time alone in piety developed introspective skills and a personal spiritual life. Diaries, spiritual autobiographies and meditations can be analysed to reveal women's sense of identity.

Godliness could begin at an early age. 'Pietie throve with her even from infancie' was a not uncommon observation.[14] 'She came not from her Nurses arms, without some knowledge of the principles of the christian religion', was said of Lady Letice, Viscountess Falkland.[15] Mary Walker, a minister's daughter, was described by her father as a pious child who loved her books, read the psalms, and had divers Scriptures by heart. She died at the age of 6, but even at that early age she had wrestled with temptation: 'She told one of the Maids that the Devil tempted her to Play at Prayers; but she had pray'd against him, and that he did not trouble her so much since.'[16]

In many cases, women came to faith by a religious conversion. Usually, conversion came during adolescence. Some autobiographical accounts focus on the woman's spiritual quest. Mary Rich described her conversion, which occurred when she was 21 years of age, as a dramatic alteration: 'I was so much changed to myself that I hardly knew myself, and would say with that converted person, "I am not I"'.[17] Sometimes, if she had grown up in a godly family, a woman worried because she lacked that dramatic moment. Elizabeth Angier 'was often in feares about the main work' because she had neither revelation nor 'shakings and convulsions . . . that others have met with'.[18]

Ministers and priests were important in women's devotional lives. Protestant women's narratives of their spiritual lives testify to the preacher's role as inspiration, comforter and counsellor. In many cases, a sermon acted as a trigger to a more intense search for salvation. In 1655 Katherine Gell, aged about 20, heard a sermon by 'Mr Marshall' – presumably the famous Puritan preacher, Stephen Marshall – which led to her seeking a better way.[19] Faced with spiritual doubts, a woman or girl might consult a minister in person, or submit her case to him in writing. Katherine Gell consulted the well-known minister Richard Baxter about her own situation. In Gell's case, the minister was unknown to her, although she was familiar with his writings, but he was widely known as a sympathetic correspondent to distressed individuals.[20] Catholic women remained sensitive to the advice of their confessors. Both Margaret Clitheroe and Dorothy Lawson allowed their priests to direct their spiritual lives. Lawson was a widow, but Clitheroe defied her husband, who was a Protestant, with the support of Father John Mush.[21] In some cases, no doubt, a psychological dependence on the spiritual director developed.[22] Yet the relationship was not entirely one way, and male clergy showed themselves dependent on their female followers for approbation and support. Wealthier women often provided financial as well as emotional support to ministers. Widows gave benefices and gifts, and bequeathed money in their wills. A York parish recorded a widow's bequest of £40 towards the minister's maintenance as a pious work, by which 'being dead, she yet speaketh'.[23] Susan Wabuda has shown how the provision of hospitality to travelling preachers was formalised in London in the 1590s, as individual women took on the role of 'Shunamites' and offered housing and food for Paul's Cross preachers.[24] Even the poorest woman could take comfort from her meagre offering by remembering the Biblical story of the widow's mite.

The female ritual of piety had both a public and a private face. Public attendance at church services was required. The Protestant reformers emphasised the duty of hearing sermons. From sermons came a sound knowledge of the Word of God. People thought that sermons would win converts back from Catholicism. For example, when Mary Gunther, who had been brought up as a Catholic until she was 14, came under the care of the Countess of Leicester, the Countess took away her 'Popish boks and beads' and insisted that she attend two sermons every

Sunday, 'for the encrease of the source of knowledge of God, which is the onely Hammer of Popery'.[25] Some godly women attended extra sermons or lectures, and perhaps took notes for further discussion at a subsequent time. Elizabeth Juxon allegedly heard nine sermons a week.[26] By the end of the seventeenth century, women probably outnumbered men in many congregations. Certainly by the later eighteenth century there were complaints that 'the business of worshipping God is, for the most part, left to the women'.[27]

Receiving the sacrament of the Lord's Supper was generally less important in Anglican devotion before the Civil Wars than hearing sermons, but even so, taking the sacrament was an important part of the godly routine. In many places the Lord's Supper was celebrated only three or four times per annum. Lady Mary Vere was ardent for frequent communion, 'Saying that she durst not neglect, no not any one opportunity that was offered for the enjoying of this sacred Ordinance'.[28] Lady Anne Waller, who died in 1662, tried to receive the sacrament monthly, and prepared carefully beforehand.[29] Later in the seventeenth century, sacramentalism was more emphasised than preaching in the Anglican church, and monthly attendance was more usual. In 1682 a woman's funeral sermon commended her for never missing communion. The preacher said that this display was not 'an affected Out-side' but an example of very real piety.[30]

Some godly women hankered for what they referred to as 'pure' or 'good ordinances', objecting to what they saw as corruption in worship. Anna Temple, for example, in 1641, longed to see idolatry and superstition rooted out, and 'gods ordinances set up in purity & power'.[31] Mary Cary, in 1649, wrote of the comfort and joy which she found in the sacrament, 'ye spiritual Food of my Soule unto eternall Life. . . . O this Soule refreshing, Soule assuring Ordinance'.[32]

For Catholic women, the sacrament of the Mass was a vital and necessary part of their faith. From the time of the Elizabethan settlement increasingly heavy penalties attached to the saying and hearing of the Mass. After 1585 when it was treason merely to be a priest in England, women were crucial in providing cover and secrecy for the missionaries. Very often it was women who looked after the 'church stuff' – vestments, chalices and such – for use in the services. When officers seized Margaret Clitheroe's goods, they 'thought so much Church stuff had not been in a whole county as they found with her'.[33]

Piety also involved a regime of private devotion. Indeed, since no-one was supposed to know about the prayers, religious meditations, or godly activities of the truly pious woman, it was a secret life. This created a tension, because godliness was also to be an example for emulation. Funeral sermons for godly women frequently drew attention to their private devotion. For example, John Mayer praised Mrs Lucy Thornton in 1639 for her secrecy: the 'singular, pious, and charitable acts done by her in so great closenes, were hidden from my knowledge'.[34]

While prayers, meditation, and the reading of devotional books, the instruction of children and servants and the relief of the poor all kept a godly woman largely at home, nevertheless her piety was subject to public scrutiny. A private, indeed a secret mass was a matter for public concern, especially at times of crisis, such as the 1580s. The church authorities were also concerned about unauthorised meetings for prayer and discussions, or prophesyings. In Essex between 1582 and 1584 the ecclesiastical authorities prosecuted several lay people who attended such meetings as frequenters of 'secret conventicles'.[35]

The practice of piety involved the godly woman of the middling and upper ranks of society in a daily ritual. Poorer women may also have had daily rituals, but since this regime was unobserved by the literate, and was undocumented by the women themselves, the records of female piety were restricted to the higher social levels. From the diaries, the published lives of women and funeral sermons of more prosperous women, we can see how they spent their days.

Godly women spent hours in prayer and devotion, both public and private. Lady Anne Halkett divided the day into three, allowing five hours for devotion.[36] Reading godly books was important, and women's rate of literacy increased faster during this period than did that of men, albeit a smaller proportion of the female population could read. [37] Protestant women read their Bibles, usually in a systematic fashion. Katherine Brettargh, who died in 1601, read eight chapters of the Bible as well as other religious books every day of her life.[38] Elizabeth Poley entreated Sir Symonds D'Ewes to buy for her several godly books including a Bible with marginal notes and large print 'for her weake Eyes' and Perkins's *Cases of conscience*.[39] Elizabeth Brooke was 'an indefatigable Reader' of godly books and commentaries.[40] Lady Mary Langham, who died in 1662, read the Scriptures through once each year.[41] Some highly educated women even translated devotional texts from Latin to help their sex to a better understanding of their faith.[42] Daily devotion varied with a woman's level of education. Susannah, Countess of Suffolk, for example, loved George Herbert's devotional poems, *The Temple*, [43] while at the other end of the social scale, Elizabeth Moore, a very poor woman who depended upon charity, comforted herself with 'evidences of salvation'. Although Mrs Moore was poor, her spiritual message was printed after her death, and remembered by the dying Lady Mary Langham who asked her husband to read 'Mistris Moores Evidences for Salvation'.[44] Devotional works were dedicated to wealthier women patrons by religious writers.[45]

Many godly books were directed to a specifically female readership.[46] Of these the best known may have been Thomas Bentley's three volumes, *The monument of matrones*, containing prayers by women as well as those for them in special circumstances, such as childbirth. Bentley's collection reinforced many stereotypes of woman by offering prayers for her 'sobernes, silence and shamefastnes, and chastitie' which once lost, 'she is no more a maid but a strumpet in the sight of God'. At her churching, 'thy most defiled and polluted hand-maid' was to remember that 'our giltie and polluted nature, like the fowle menstruous cloth of a woman, is washed by the blood of thy sonne'.[47] How much of literate women's devotional life was influenced by such works, and to what extent they uttered their own extemporaneous silent prayers are impossible to determine.

Reading played a part in the devotional life of educated Catholic as well as Protestant women. Thomas à Kempis's work, *The Imitation of Christ*, went through many translations and editions in the seventeenth century, and appealed to both Protestant and Catholic women.[48] Catholic theologians published devotional treatises especially for a female audience. For example, Molina's *Treatise of mental prayer* was translated in 1617 and dedicated to Mother Mary Wiseman, Prioress of the English Monastery. Molina included a method for saying the rosary which divided the mysteries into the days of the week. The believer was urged to imagine herself present at each mystery: 'Mental prayer consists in taking pains.'[49] Several manuals were specifically devoted to the use of rosary beads as aids to meditation. John Bucke's treatise of the use of the beads was compiled 'for the benefit of unlearned' and dedicated to Anne Lady Hungerford.[50] Another, published in 1576 in response to the request of the sister of an English monk, stated that 'there be many good women in England that honour our Lady, but good bookes to stirre up devotion in them are scarse'. The devotional reading of pious Catholic women included lives of saints which offered a range of female models. The life of St Aldegonde promoted an active Christianity: true devotion consisted in doing rather than saying and weeping.[51] Several Catholic writiers translated devotional treatises and other religious works which they dedicated to the ladies who were their patrons. The translator of Francis de Sales's *Treatise of the love of God* dedicated his work to Lady Elizabeth Dormer whom he referred to as

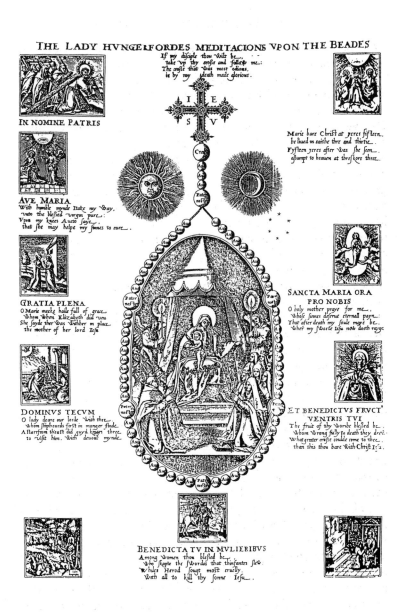

Figure 4. Rosary beads were an aid to Catholic devotion. *The Lady Hunger-forde's Meditacions Upon the Beades,* from John Bucke's *Instructions, 1589* (British Library, London).

his patroness. A Jesuit translator referred to the great affection for mental prayer and 'Bountifulness & Piety' of Elizabeth, Viscountess Wallingford, and another translator acknowledged the perfection of Lady Elizabeth Herbert in the art of prayer.[52]

Diaries allow glimpses of Protestant women's spiritual lives. For example, one diary, probably by Anne Bathurst, contains entries about prayers, of which the following are fairly typical examples: 18 October 1680, 'went to my closet where all my devotions this day have bin full of incomparable sweetness'; 19 October, 'in good time went to my closet where my devotions were full of comfort'; 28 October, 'I am dry, cold and full of distracted thoughts'. The diarist noted Christian celebrations and public anniversaries. For example, on 5 November, Gunpowder treason, she went to church and then returned home to read and meditate on divine mercies. She spent Christmas Day in fervent prayers.[53] The spiritual diaries of many women convey the sense that their lives were spent in dialogue, or even wrestling, with God. Sarah Savage, who longed for a child, wrote in her diary in October 1687 that if God should see good 'to delay or totally deny ye mercy of children to me still by his grace I will wait on him, and love him not one jot the less, tho' I sometimes can scarce quiet my spirit as I would'.[54] Some Nonconformist piety of the late seventeenth and early eighteenth centuries does not read like intense spirituality, but it does convey the impression of a God who was very near, and who was to be argued with in familiar terms.

Religious writing enhanced women's self-awareness. Encouraged to keep records of their spiritual lives, some wrote religious meditations, a few of which were published posthumously in the seventeenth century. Anne Venn's book of meditations, for example, was found after her death and then published.[55] Susanna Bell's reflections were published after her death, in 1673, as she had requested.[56] Jane Turner, however, published her own religious writings in 1653, recognising herself as a pioneer: 'I thought I might seem to walk in an untrodden path, having never seen anything written before in this manner and method.'[57]

In their devotional writings women could confess their sins and find some comfort in the promises of forgiveness. Lady Pakington's papers, found after her death, included a confession: 'the imaginations of the thoughts of my heart are only evill & that continually I weave the spiders web in vaine impertinent Childish thoughts such as are below the dignity of a reasonable Creature'.[58] Some women found in God a friend to whom they could turn with their difficulties and sorrows. Whenever Mary Cary foresaw any suffering, temptation or death, 'my flesh hath crept for feare, my spirit hath fainted . . . but God is the strength'.[59] Women sought a meaning in God's 'providences', events which revealed his intentions. Diaries show women wrestling to find a meaning for their terrible griefs, especially the deaths of children. In 1622, Susanna Bell refused to go to New England. Her child then died. She prayed, and in reply 'it was given in to me, that it was because I would not go to New England'. Later in the 1650s, she was afraid of further judgements because she saw that the Lord's day was not being observed properly.[60] Mary Cary's experience of maternal grief was differently resolved. In a poignant entry for 14 May 1652 she wrote 'I have now buried foure Sons, and a Daughter. God hath my all of Children, I have his all [beloved Christ] a sweet Change; in greatest Sorrowes, content, & happy.' She signed her name at the conclusion of her statement.[61]

The practice of piety, as Mendelson has shown, could provide 'a coherent and satisfying explanation of world-historical events'.[62] It could also impose an order upon the fortuitous incidents which made up female lives. A concept of 'Providence' helped women to make sense of the accidents in their personal lives. They thanked God when they or their families escaped illnesses or death, as can be seen from their diaries, autobiographies and letters. For example, Alice Thornton's account of herself from childhood was influenced by her sense that God was ever-present. She was infected with smallpox as a child, but 'by the blessing of God I recovered very soon. . . . I will praise the Lord our God for my preservation and deliverance'.[63] Many women found comfort in their religious devotions and supernatural help for crises. Most significantly of all, some found a joy in their faith like no other. Reconciled to God through Christ, Mary Cary wrote 'And now I did daily see so much Happiness by an Interest in Jesus Christ, that ye Tongue of Man, & Angell cannot expresse it.'[64]

Although the reformers negated the value of the monastic life, a few Catholic women continued to join religious orders abroad after 1598. While a hostile Protestant literature referred to families deciding to imprison their daughters in convents to save the expense of marrying them, the nuns themselves wrote of their choosing a monastic life as a means of finding spiritual satisfaction. Many nuns confessed that they initially resisted a religious vocation. Alexia Grey was 'in the hight of transitory Glory for youth and bravery', enjoying balls and masques, when she had a 'dream or vision' which prompted more serious thoughts. God called her 'whilst she was actually dancing' and she professed as a nun in 1631.[65] Lucy Knatchbull struggled in her vocation, suffering all her life from 'undertaking such a Course soo Contrary to her naturall Inclination to freedom'. During her novitiate, 'she saw with the eyes of her soul a most Glorious and Supernatural Star', which vision of the greatness of God so comforted her soul that she found that she 'could pray, read, sing, sweep, wash dishes, or whatsoever else with pleasure'.[66] A few nuns were converts. Catherine Holland, in a marvellous spiritual autobiography, narrates how she was born and brought up a Protestant, but became an Augustinian canoness. As a young woman, although she was attracted to Catholicism by her stepmother, she still had a prejudice against monasticism as 'a miserable Life always to be locked up as in a Prison'. After years of spiritual quest, and struggles with her father, she travelled to Flanders, entering the convent without a penny: 'even, as I may say, blindfold; for I was as ignorant as a Child, what a Religious Life was'.[67]

The rule of each monastic order differed, although all shared a pattern of daily prayers and duties.[68] Like her godly Protestant sister, each nun had duties according to her social station, and each lived a daily and weekly routine – idleness as 'an enemy to the Soule'.[69] Yet even in religious houses of the same order, there was no single pattern of piety. The rule of the nuns of Immaculate Conception, known as the Blue Nuns, allowed that not all nuns were suited to silent contemplation: 'if any Religious after a long experience, finds she profitts little in Meditation, she may then be allow'd to employ her time in vocal prayer, or some spiritual Lecture'.[70] Dame Gertrude More wrote a book of spiritual exercises for those who could not meditate.[71] Within the confines of her chosen monastery, each nun developed her own individual devotion and spirituality. Among the Benedectine nuns at Ghent, Dame Alexia Maurice was most remarkable for her 'obedience, fortitude, Zeal of Quire service'. She would kneel at prayer 'whole howers without motion', and went through the spiritual exercises three or four times in less than a year.[72] 'O you souls who are capable of prayer', wrote Gertrude More, 'be grateful to our Lord, for it is the greatest happiness that can be possessed in this life'.[73] Others fulfilled their spiritual vocation by faithful discharge of a humble office, such as that of cellarer. Personal austerity attracted many nuns: 'her Delight was to debar herself of all Delights'.[74] Some found their chief comfort in the sacraments, others were remarkable for charity.[75] Obituary notices for nuns of the English Poor Clares praised exemplary piety: 'a perfect Pattern of Humility, Patience and the fear of God', 'of Singular Humility, Devotion & Piety', and 'a Mirour to all'. Nuns were praised also for their zeal 'in the Divine honour and service', including insatiable zeal for the conversion of England.[76]

The politics of many of the convents focused on disputes over the nature of spiritual direction, whether Benedictine or Jesuit. Historical accounts stress the importance of the role of individual confessors, but it should be remembered that nuns were exercising choices about their preferred modes of spirituality. Gertrude More, who died of smallpox in 1633, had used her spiritual director to emancipate herself from the need for any priest at her deathbed. She had attained such spirituality 'that she could confidently go out of this life without speaking to any man'.[77]

A more active form of monastic devotion was that of Mary Ward who founded a new religious order. She first joined the Poor Clares, but she had a religious experience. Ward's experience was beyond words – 'I know not, and never did know, how to explain' – but to her it 'appeared wholly divine'. It was shown to her that she was not to be of the Poor Clares, but to do some other thing, as God willed.[78] In 1611 she received in a vision the command to model a new order, her Institute of the Blessed Virgin Mary, on the spiritual discipline and active life of the Jesuits: 'I heard distinctly, not by sound of voice, but intellectually understood, these words: TAKE THE SAME OF THE SOCIETY.' Prayers, fast days and penances were all part of the Institute's discipline.[79] Around 1616 Ward set down thirty-five resolutions for her own spiritual life, praying 'Lord, let that be made possible to me by grace which seemeth impossible to me by nature'. She concluded by embracing a suffering life: 'It is necessary that we arm ourselves with a great desire to suffer much and many crosses.'[80] Like many other nuns, she sought an ascetic life.

Although we know most about the piety of those who were literate, this does not mean that piety was confined to the middling and upper levels of society. At the poorer levels of society, women's performance of household tasks in the love of the Lord could satisfy some devotional needs. Protestant theology emphasised the concept of serving God through daily life. George Herbert, an Anglican minister, wrote in one of his poems of the religious satisfaction in household drudgery:

> Teach me, my God and King, In all things thee to see,
> And what I do in any thing, To do it as for thee:
> A servant with this clause Makes drudgerie divine:
> Who sweeps a room, as for thy laws, Makes that and th' action
> fine.[81]

Piety could manifest itself as cleanliness and order. Elizabeth Walker remembered that a minister had taught that 'the Maid-Servant may sweep the House to God, . . . by considering it a Duty, in the condition to which he calls her'. [82]

The poorest women might express piety in daily prayers. However, such women usually elude observation. The Countess of Warwick found that when she tried to instruct 'poor weeding women' in the Christian faith, there was no mutual comprehension.[83] Nevertheless, the sources do provide glimpses. John Bunyan, before he experienced conversion, was working in Bedford when he overheard 'three or four poor women sitting at a door in the sun, and talking about the things of God'. His account of the scene is one of the most vivid descriptions of the faith of ordinary women. Their talk, Bunyan wrote, was about a new birth, the work of God on their hearts, and also how they were convinced of their miserable state by nature:

> they talked how God had visited their souls with his love in the Lord Jesus, and with what words and promises they had been refreshed, comforted and supported against the temptations of the devil. . . . And methought they spake as if joy did make them speak; they spake with such pleasantness of Scripture language, and with such appearance of grace in all they said, that they were to me as if they had found a new world.[84]

Religious devotion may also have been sustained in poorer households by visual means. Tessa Watts has shown how, before the Reformation, painted cloths adorned many walls, and after the Reformation, an increasing number of broadsides illustrating Scriptural stories were printed for the walls of houses. By the mid-eighteenth century there was still a large demand for godly broadsides for household walls.[85] While she does not discuss who was responsible for the furnishings and decoration of houses, it seems likely that women had a larger part in the interior of a household than men. Irrespective of responsibility for these devotional images, they served the function of daily reinforcing religious truths.

THE GODLY WIFE AND MOTHER: PIETY IN THE FAMILY, HOUSEHOLD AND NEIGHBOURHOOD

Protestant preachers emphasised the role of the household in producing godliness. Parents were to rear their children in Christian precepts and practices, and to instruct and discipline their servants so that they too lived a Christian life. None of this was especially novel in the sixteenth century, as several historians have pointed out.[86] What is interesting is to see how an essentially female pattern of piety, one based on the sexual division of labour between men and women, influenced the environment in which children were reared.

Protestantism made the household an extension of the church. As we have seen, male heads of household became spiritual leaders, responsible for family worship. A godly wife also had a role in promoting domestic piety. She deputised in her husband's absence by leading the family prayers. Dorothy Shaw, for example, over twenty-five years of their marriage, never failed to pray twice daily, to sing a psalm and read the Scriptures with her family when her husband was away.[87] Katherine Clark not only prayed with her household morning and evening in her husband's absence, but even in his presence, if he was sick.[88] In the daily life of the pious household, the role of the wife and mother in ordering the activities in a godly fashion was essential. Godly wives of clergymen in particular took responsibility for the smooth running of the household. Elizabeth Walker tried to keep her household small, 'free from disturbing Noise & distracting Diversions'.[89] In some of the households of Puritan and later Nonconformist clergymen we can see the beginnings of the disciplined family which was to be so important in nineteenth-century English middle-class life. Through the publication of lives of the pious family, clergymen established models of godliness in the seventeenth century which were to be significant at later dates.[90]

Women served the Lord by instructing their children in Christianity. If Scripture presented the paradigm for the godly life, it still required interpretation.[91] Literate godly women concentrated on catechising their children and teaching them to read. Elizabeth Joceline, who died in 1622, left instructions for the godly education of her daughter: 'I desire her bringing up may be learning the Bible, as my sisters [children] doe, good housewifery, writing and good workes.'[92] Elizabeth Walker taught her children to read the Bible.[93] Testimony to the effect of maternal instruction and example survived in spiritual autobiographies and other accounts from both sons and daughters.[94] A mother's teaching was, of course, deemed especially appropriate for girls. Preachers commended it in funeral sermons: Lady Frances Digby's mother taught her daughter 'plain Rules, and shew'd it to the life in an admirable & brave Example'.[95] Female patterns of piety could be seen as an accepted part of female culture at various social levels, transmitted from mother to daughter. Some mothers respected their daughters' religious choices more than did fathers. In the 1670s Mrs Churchman's mother tried to protect her daughter Mary from paternal anger when Mary began to attend Nonconformist meetings.[96]

Wealthier godly women who had servants would instruct them also. Lady Falkland, who died in 1649, usually spent an hour each morning in prayer and catechising her maids.[97] Lady Anne Waller catechised her children and servants weekly, while Lady Anne Clifford pinned up texts and sayings all around her room for general edification.[98] A female servant who consulted Lady Elizabeth Brooke about spiritual matters was encouraged by her mistress, and 'required her for that time, to forget that she was a Servant'.[99] At the end of the seventeenth century, Elizabeth Burnet, a bishop's wife, included prayers for servants in her publication, *A Method of Devotion*.[100] However, the practice of instructing servants was not confined to the wealthiest; godly women of middling social status also tried to find time to catechise their maids.[101]

Practical charity was an acceptable public manifestation of the private virtue of piety, as numerous sermons attest. Godly women prepared cordials for the sick, dressed sores of neighbours, and attended at the childbirths of 'meane and poor women'.[102] Women of all theological persuasions engaged in charitable works. In 1669 Mary Rich assisted a poor man falsely accused of a crime. She tried to persuade him to a strict course of religious life.[103] A Quaker gentlewoman, Mary Penington's widowed mother-in-law, provided employment for several poor women in gathering the ingredients she needed to prepare physic for others.[104] Unlike these wealthier women who helped their neighbours in sickness, poorer women who practised healing by charms or prayers were in danger of prosecution for witchcraft, as we shall see.

The wills of wealthier widows reflected their concern for their poorer neighbours. In Norfolk, female testators made bequests for the relief of the poor in similar proportion to male testators, but women gave more money for educational purposes. However, in London women bequeathed 41 per cent of their gifts for the relief of the poor, compared with 35 per cent bequeathed by city testators at large.[105]

The observation of sacred times for church festivals, fasts and thanksgivings also allowed an opportunity to witness to piety. Some of this was under female control, as women determined whether a household feasted or fasted. Dorothy Hazzard refused to acknowledge Christmas as a special day. She sat sewing in the door of her grocer's shop in the High Street on Christmas Day in the late 1630s, keeping her shop open 'as a witnesse for God'.[106] Lady Elizabeth Brooke refused to keep the fasts or thanksgivings of 'the usurpers' in the 1650s.[107]

Prayers. 54

with one drop of the water of thy mercy, for thine only Sonne our Lord and Sauiour Jesus Christes sake, Amen.

✶ A Prayer to be sayd for our
Euilwillers.

MOst mercifull Redéemer, thou hast commaunded vs to pray for them, both which wish vs euill, and (as much as in them lyeth) doe worke vs euill: and that hast thou done, not onely in words, but also in deds, of purpose that we should follow thine example. We pray thee therfore, to them in to vs the spirit of thy mildenesse, that we may patiently suffer both the euill will, and the euill speach, and the euill doings of our enemies, as we hear say thou diddest, and as we dayly perceiue that thou doest still.

Let vs nether requite wrong indede, nor take vpon vs to reuenge our selues

Charitie visiteth the sick.

I was sick & ye visited me, Math. 25.

Let it not greue thee to visit the sick. Eccle. 7

P.ij.

Figure 5. Practical charity was part of a godly woman's life. Border to Richard Day, *A Book of Christian Prayer, 1578*, p. 54 (British Library, London).

89

Personal dress and cleanliness were linked with piety. Elizabeth Walker strove for personal sobriety and decency in her own attire and admonished her son that, since bodies were the temple of the Holy Ghost, he ought to keep his clothes clean: 'All cleanly people are not good, but there are few good people but are cleanly.'[108]

Some pious women found that their household duties actually interfered with their desire to practise godliness. When Katherine Gell consulted the minister Richard Baxter about her spiritual melancholy, he told her to keep busy. She replied that she did continually occupy herself with her household, 'though it would suit better wth my nature to sit & read all day'.[109] Unlike Baxter, who had been able to spend much of his life doing just that, Katherine Gell's life afforded no such opportunity. Had she neglected her housekeeping for her prayers she would no doubt have drawn upon herself the same rebuke as a praying woman received from the Presbyterian minister, Philip Henry. He was disgusted to find a house in disorder in the middle of the day because the woman of the house was at prayer in her closet: 'Is there no fear of God in this House?' he asked.[110] The godly woman's life was in a state of continual tension between the claims of family and her own spirituality. Censured for neglect of her household on the one hand, she would find that should she be too busy in her wordly concerns, she would likewise earn a rebuke. The diaries of Sarah Savage, Philip Henry's daughter, show her in constant anxiety between the cares of the world and the cares for heaven.[111]

The Reformation altered the sacred significance of certain forms of pious behaviour. While Protestant women turned their attention to their Bibles, Catholic women continued to express devotion in traditional ways. Aveling analysed the devotional practices of eight Elizabethan Catholic households for which records have survived. Prayer was of central importance, and included the constant repetition of the Pater, Ave Maria and perhaps the credo. There were rituals such as crossing, kneeling, and prostrations, and kissing holy pictures and bone or wooden crucifixes.[112] Repetition of phrases could comfort many in times of emergency. Catholic women also went on pilgrimages.

Nevertheless, expressions of religious devotion crossed religious boundaries. A comparison of the daily rituals of two women, one a Catholic martyr in the 1580s, the other the wife of a Protestant minister in the 1640s, demonstrates the similarities. Margaret Clitheroe was of middling status in the city of York, where her stepfather was the mayor, and her husband a butcher.[113] According to her confessor and biographer, John Mush, every morning she spent one and a half to two hours on her knees in her chamber at prayer, instructed her children for an hour, and closed the day with an hour of prayer and examination of her conscience.[114] The devotional works she 'most delighted' to read were the New Testament, Thomas à Kempis and Perin's *Exercises*. Her public devotion, secretly performed because of her Catholicism, was confession and the Eucharist twice a week, and a weekly sermon. She also sought to make some of her activity truly secret and personal, performing her household and worldly tasks with her 'mind fixed on God'. At the Sacrament she always chose the worst seat. At her own table, she mortified herself by denial of food, and she devised ways of avoiding social outings, by lying, saying that she was helping her neighbours in childbirth.

Elizabeth Walker's regime of godliness was likewise recorded by a man, in this case, by her husband, a Protestant minister. Like Clitheroe half a century or so earlier, Walker rose early before the rest of her household to spend time in private prayer. She too read godly books, instructed her household, and tried to live a life of personal asceticism.[115] Despite their different social status and religious affiliations, both women shared a desire to express their spirituality in their family and household routines.

Nevertheless, godliness gave women public esteem. They were perceived to be a blessing to households, especially before the Restoration. Good women, said Geere, 'are wonderfull helpefull to their husbands by their prayers . . . indeed, the whole family fares the better for them'. Richard Baxter recognised that his stepmother, by her prayers, was 'a special blessing to our family'.[116] Funeral sermons were occasions when the virtues of the pious woman were publicly acknowledged. Many of these were published for their exemplary value: it was 'useful to propose some women as patterns to others'.[117] Nothing, said Kettlewell in his funeral sermon for Lady Frances Digby in 1684, 'is more instructive to the world . . . than to draw it out in the Lives and Acts of Pious Persons'.[118] Some of these funeral sermons were expanded into godly lives, and some husbands also lauded their wives' virtues in published lives. Thus, even though much of the exercise of piety was through private actions in the household, the virtue was publicly acknowledged and so redounded to the praise of the woman herself and of her family. Piety was one way in which women could bring honour to their kin.

ASCETICISM, SPIRITUALITY AND ACTION

Through the regime of piety many women developed a personal asceticism which enhanced their spiritual awareness. Self-denial was always an option readily open to women, since they controlled the preparation and distribution of food and the household routine. For wealthier women, piety could include a simple diet. Since a rich diet was believed to promote lascivious thoughts, it is not surprising that godliness was linked with abstinence, wantonness with 'the excess of dainties'.[119] Katherine Stubbs ate sparingly, refusing 'to pamper her bodie with delicate meats, wines, or strong drinke, but refrained from them altogether'.[120] Elizabeth Walker had fasted in her youth, and as an adult was abstemious at dinner eating only a small piece of white bread with a draught of household beer.[121] Jane Ratcliffe, a wealthy brewer's wife, was able to fast without appearing to do so.[122] More famous for her asceticism was Dorothy Traske, imprisoned in the Gatehouse with her husband in 1618 for her Sabbatarian views. She ate only vegetables and drank only water.[123] The Catholic church required fasting as part of a devotional ritual. Margaret Clitheroe fasted on Monday, Wednesday, Friday and Saturday. Even her normal diet was spare: rye bread, milk or pottage, and butter. Although the wife of a reasonably prosperous citizen of York, she tried to avoid accompanying her husband to banquets. When she was the carver, she took the worst piece for herself.[124] Elizabeth Cary, at a later date, was noticeably less conscientious, and even her Protestant husband was on occasions forced to remind her that she was supposed to be fasting.[125]

Limited sleep was also part of the regime of devotion. Among urban women of middling social status, the exercise of piety might involve early rising for private prayer before the rest of the household. Elizabeth Walker was up at 4 or 5 a.m. even in winter while her husband, a minister, was still in bed.[126] In some cases, fatigue undoubtedly played a part in creating the physical states conducive to visions and trancing.[127]

Self-denial and self-sacrifice could extend beyond questions of food and might include household chores. Margaret Clitheroe allowed her maids to 'do sweeter business' while she undertook the drudgery of sweeping the house, making the fire and washing the dishes.[128] Lady Magdalen, Viscountess Montague performed personal services for the old Countess of Bedford which were deemed beneath one of her social status: she 'did not disdain . . . to perform that base kind of service which curious ears refuse to heare related'.[129]

If Catholic and Protestant piety for women had common features which came from the similarity of life styles of the middling and upper ranks in society, there were differences in the forms of spirituality. The attitudes of Catholics and Protestants to the body differed. Catholic medieval devotion encouraged people to focus upon bodily experiences. Devotional manuals glorified and celebrated the physical sufferings of Christ and the saints, and encouraged individuals to think of ways of mortifying the flesh. Early modern Catholic devotion included the personal ownership of relics, pieces of the body. Protestants were uncertain about pain, suffering and sacrifice, uncomfortable with rituals of humiliation.[130]

From the diaries which some women kept of their spiritual condition we can see the ways in which they assessed their own experiences and the value which they placed upon them. Sarah Henry had thought for a long time about keeping 'something in ye Nature of a Diary' and was encouraged by the knowledge that others had received great benefit thereby, '& by ye hopes yt I may therby bee furthered [in] a godly life'.[131] Katherine Gell described her diary as a book of the state of her heart, which reads as a book of accounts: 'I count ys booke to be like a booke of expenses wr euery peny laid ot is set down & yr to be found & sumed up at ye yeares end.'[132] Frequently this writing was secret, but it was socially sanctioned. The Protestant faith stressed the value of individual struggle, so that the habit of daily introspection was more characteristic of godly Protestants than of godly Catholics.

Piety, an apparently conservative activity, could be used by women for their own purposes. Some women's piety even led them deliberately to write for publication. A good woman was supposed to be silent, but her duty to God, or to her children, could compel her to speak. Prayers and devotions published for the benefit of others, women authors said, could arouse no criticism. During the Civil War and Interregnum, when the amount of publication by women increased, religion was an important motivating force. Nearly half of the total of publications by women for the period 1600–1700 were works of piety, prayers, meditations, godly advice, prophecies, Quaker warnings, admonitions and lamentations.[133] Religious publications probably constituted a slightly higher proportion of women's publications than they were of total publications. Up to 1640, around 44 per cent of all publications were religious in theme.[134] After that date, publications were probably more diverse. A religious justification for publication was more important for women than for men. Educated men, having no inhibitions on speaking because of their sex, as did educated women, needed no special justification for writing for the press. Men published in a wider range of genres than women. They did not need the special justification which religion provided in order to overcome the obstacles to writing.

'Practical Godliness', which might include works of charity, required some knowledge of God. Thus, although it was generally agreed that women's need for education was limited, no one could deny that education could improve the knowledge and the true worship of Christ. Some parents, in educating their daughters, went beyond the norm and taught them of the 'controversial and critical' parts of Scripture.[135] In the 1660s Susanna Perwich cautiously approached the Book of Revelation, saying that she thought it 'not unproper for her (though of the female sex)' to read 'with humble reverence and prayer'.[136] Education could lead to social comment. Elizabeth Bury was a conventionally pious woman, yet she censured as 'uncharitable' the learned divines who refused to translate more devotional books for women's use.[137] As a good woman, she asserted the right to criticise.

Bible study could increase self-confidence. The parable of the talents encouraged women to develop what abilities they had. Everyone, wrote Rachel Speght in 1621, was expected to give an account, even if only of one talent.[138] Each must contribute her mite, the parable of the poor widow taught, and no one was allowed to hide her light under a bushel.[139] Furthermore, Scriptural study could develop skill in religious argument and provide precedents for action. It could even encourage women to suggest an alternative exegesis of the Christian stories. In 1611 Aemilia Lanyer put forward a different version of the Fall from the traditional one which blamed Eve. It was Adam's fault, because God had told him to watch over his wife: 'We know right well he did discretion lacke.'[140] Women turned to the Bible for a range of female role models: Deborah, a nursing mother in Israel; Jael, a heroine who slew Sisera; and Judith who beheaded Holofernes. They knew about the woman of Samaria who brought the news to the city of Christ's coming as the Messiah. They could cite examples of women whose words had been heeded: Mary Pope begged the members of Parliament to consider her arguments in 1647, just as David had listened to the woman of Tekoah (2 Samuel 14.12).[141] Furthermore, a few women glossed over the Biblical texts about women's duty of silence in church in the light of texts which spoke of sons and daughters prophesying.[142] They claimed the right to reinterpret Scripture.

Religious belief could assist a woman in worldly negotiations. With dignity and courage, an abbess negotiated with a niggardly father for the dowry of a postulant in 1676. When Sir Thomas Clifton was unwilling to pay £500 and argued that £300 or £350 was sufficient, the abbess told him that such behaviour was contrary to what she would have expected from her own parents, 'for I should have much resented had they not taken the same care of me in Religion as if I had betaken my self to the world'.[143] Anne Clifton, too, protested at her father's behaviour. 'I cannot but know', Anne wrote, 'had I bine in the world my fortune would haue bine answerable to my quality'.[144] Sir Thomas did agree to £500, and an annuity of £20, although the following year he reduced the annuity to £16.[145]

In the cause of godliness, some women involved themselves in politics.[146] Hannah Brograve tendered political advice to her nephew, the MP Symonds D'Ewes: go the whole way to advance the interest of Christ, she urged him,

> pray take hede of leaving us wors then ye found us[.] study the word to (find?) out the way of Christ. . . . I pray pardon my bould rewdnes and take it out of love and the earnest desir of my sowle.[147]

As we will see, a godly life and a search for salvation was also the basis of much of the female activity described as religious radicalism during the 1640s and 1650s.

Finally, godliness and piety could develop a woman's sense of rectitude which would enable her to defy her husband. From Anne Askew onwards, a few women had left their husbands for the sake of their faith. In minor ways, too, women could use religion to authorise wifely defiance. A Catholic subject of King James II appealed to him from Denmark in 1687 for his support against her husband who denied her the benefit of a confessor. She confessed, 'with blushing, & shame', that she petitioned against her husband, 'whom she acknowledges she has been always ready to obey in all things but those that are against her conscience, or contrary to her salvation'.[148]

A fascinating example of a woman's insistence upon what she called 'her little liberty of conscience' comes from the household of the Anglican minister Samuel Wesley, father of John and Charles.[149] After the Revolution Settlement of 1689, all Anglicans were required to accept the monarchy of William and Mary. The bishops and clergy who found themselves unable to take the required oaths were forced to resign from their places. This party of Non-Jurors, as they were termed, was thus an all-male party, but non-juring views were not confined to the clergy. Some of the Anglican laity shared them. Susannah, Samuel's wife, had been reared a Nonconformist. However, she married Samuel Wesley, an Anglican minister, and became a strict Anglican, accepting theories of divine right, which occasioned a famous quarrel with her husband in 1702.

In 1702 Susannah Wesley was aged 32, had been married for twelve years, and borne several children of whom only six survived. Susannah confided her problem to a sympathetic woman friend, Lady Yarborough. When her husband had recently observed that she refused to say Amen to his family prayer for King William, he summoned her to his study, and asked the reason.

> I was a little surprised at the question and don't well know what I answered, but too well I remember what followed: He immediately kneeled down and imprecated the divine Vengeance upon himself and all his posterity if ever he touched me more or came into a bed with me before I had begged God's pardon and his, for not saying Amen to the prayer for the Kg'.[150]

Susannah regarded herself as 'an Original of misery', and knew of no way either of them could come off from their consciences. She put the conventional arguments to Samuel, that his oath was unlawful and unreasonable, because of his marriage vows: 'that the Man in that case has no more power over his own body than the Woman over hers'. She also argued that since she was willing to let him enjoy his opinions quietly, 'he ought not to deprive me of my little liberty of conscience'. Susannah was convinced that to ask pardon was to 'mock almighty God, by begging pardon for what I think no sin'. Faced with such intransigence, Samuel left Susannah and their six children, and set off determined to become a naval chaplain.[151]

Meanwhile, Susannah's case had been submitted to George Hicks, a non-juror, who condemned Samuel for his oath contrary to his marriage promise. Samuel had threatened to refer the whole matter to the Archbishop of York and the Bishop of Lincoln, from whom Susannah expected no justice. Nor, from her comments, does it seem likely that she would have submitted. 'I very well know before such Judges I'm sure to be condemned without a fair hearing'. Samuel was dissuaded from his journey by a fellow minister, but it is not clear on what terms the couple resumed sexual relations. Susannah did subsequently bear several more children, including the famous John, but she retained her non-juring opinions, observing in 1709 that kings were accountable to God alone: 'I cannot tell how to think that a King of England can ever be accountable to his subjects for any mal-administrations or abuse of power: but as he derives his power from God, so to Him only must he answer for using it.'[152]

By symbolic reversal, some women could use ideas about female weakness to attain spiritual power. As the Magnificat celebrated, the Lord had chosen the lowliest of his handmaidens to work his mighty effects. Female weakness was emphasised by most women who wrote on religious subjects. Sara Wight's titles reflected this: *Strength in weakness* and *The exceeding riches of grace advanced by the spirit of grace in an empty nothing creature*. Other works repeated these ideas about God choosing one of the humblest to have pre-eminence.[153] Women petitioners to Parliament in the 1650s claimed additional authority from their very weakness: 'nothing is more manifest then that God is pleased often times to raise up the weakest means to work the mightiest effects'.[154] Men might abase themselves as the chief of sinners, but women, as members of the weaker sex, were by nature lower. Through self-abasement, women could unite with God in a mystical state where the differences and disadvantages of sex associated with the female condition could be transcended. There was no disadvantage to a woman in the female condition in approaching the Lord. Since everyone was weak and feeble compared with the Lord, women may have found self-abasement easier than men did.

Clearly the apparently natural religiosity of women was a social construct. Women's piety was not so much a success story in social control, as a story of women gaining control over their own lives. Piety was an area of religious life which they were able to make very much their own. Piety could provide a kind of self-imposed career for women,[155] which in some cases led to writing, publication, and political action. But more importantly, piety developed female spirituality. Religious beliefs and practices could meet women's emotional needs. The regime of piety which was so widely publicised through the funeral sermons and lives of certain women depended upon a degree of education and leisure, but it could manifest in other ways. It was a domestic virtue which many women could practise in their proper sphere, at home. Christianity involved discipline and self-control for everyone. For women, piety involved establishing and keeping to daily household routines. Spirituality was their personal goal, and an important part of female culture. Piety helped women to transcend the limitations of their earthly condition, to find spiritual satisfaction and to 'apprehend the divine'.

5

Dangerous beliefs: magic, prophecy and mysticism

HISTORIANS AND POPULAR BELIEFS

Women and men in early modern Europe sought supernatural help for the problems of daily life and for comfort about the life to come. Not all of their beliefs were Christian. For the populace at large, the boundary between orthodox and unorthodox belief was not always clear. Before the mid-seventeenth century, to foretell the future by astrology or to cast a horoscope seemed to many Christians to be legitimate activities. But contemporaries were concerned about the status of those who were involved. Queen Elizabeth could safely consult John Dee about astrology, but when other women turned to cunning men or cunning women for help, they risked the danger that their actions could lead to charges of witchcraft.

Studies of non-Christian beliefs of early modern England were previously the province of the folklorist and local historian, but more recently attitudes have altered. First, religious belief has declined among historians. Historians are less committed to the idea of religious history as one of Christian ancestors fighting over the truth. Second, historians have developed an interest in the methodologies of other disciplines, particularly of the social sciences. Like anthropologists who had long been studying the beliefs of non-Christian societies, historians sought to explore the beliefs of their own societies from a different perspective. Keith Thomas first advocated this new anthropological approach in 1963, and his full-length study of popular beliefs in early modern England has effected a major change in our understanding of the religious history of the sixteenth and seventeenth centuries.[1] In particular, Thomas has shown that although the Reformation deprived people of access to various kinds of supernatural power which the church had previously offered, magical belief continued and even flourished afterwards.

A third factor affecting studies of non-Christian belief has been a democratisation of historians' interests. Social historians have sought to understand the beliefs of the masses as well as the elite, and studies of popular religion have multiplied.[2] They have understood popular beliefs in two different ways. Some see popular beliefs broadly as those of the mass of the population, the other more narrowly, in opposition to elite beliefs, as forms of protest produced by the masses in resistance to the institutionalised beliefs of the dominant groups in the society.[3] Here I will use the term in the wider sense to refer to beliefs spread through the populace. Although historians have been sensitive to regional factors influencing popular beliefs, they have devoted less attention to gender differences, and to questioning the relative importance of these beliefs in the daily lives of the two sexes.

During the medieval period, popular religion modified some of the forms and beliefs of elite Catholicism. Individualism was strong, and women as well as men could negotiate with God. However, the church was never happy about direct communiction with the Lord, and periodically had made attempts to control and authenticate spiritual experiences, as the example of Joan of Arc shows.[4] During the sixteenth century, both the Catholic and Protestant churches intensified their drive to Christianise the masses.

Christianity was, of course, a most significant influence on popular belief, but there is no agreement as to how important it was. While Delumeau has drawn attention to the ignorance and ungodliness which concerned contemporaries in Europe, Collinson has stressed the centrality of Christianity in the lives of the vast majority of the population in England.[5] Certainly Christian beliefs influenced all aspects of social life, but this chapter is concerned with beliefs which were not strictly orthodox and therefore potentially dangerous to women. Some of their non-Christian beliefs have been described as magical or superstitious, but this implies that their beliefs lacked a coherent framework, which is not the case.[6] Ginzburg's study of the beliefs of a sixteenth-century miller in Friuli have revealed the rich, imaginative and complex world view which the miller constructed from the belief systems available.[7] Unfortunately, there have to date been no comparable studies of the beliefs of 'ordinary' women. One way of thinking about women's 'magical' or 'superstitious' beliefs may be to consider them as a form of resistance to 'orthodox' Christianity in their society.

By discussing popular beliefs, magic, prophecy and mysticism together, this chapter focuses on beliefs which, while they may have been satisfying to women, could also be dangerous to them. However, piety and popular beliefs should not be polarised into the good and the bad, for both were part of the same spectrum. Deep spirituality, visions and mysticisim developed out of an intense search for the divine, from a longing for oneness with God. But whereas the institutional church approved of certain forms of piety, it distrusted less orthodox or more intense forms of spirituality. Society was suspicious of mystics and prophets.

WOMEN'S DAILY LIVES AND POPULAR BELIEFS

A range of popular beliefs affected the daily lives of women and men. Some beliefs were specific to female work. Dairying, making butter and cheese were processes subject to irrational forces. Thomas has argued that where the technology was uncertain, popular belief flourished. Churning butter and making cheese were sometimes unpredictable: beliefs about the role of fairies and gnomes encouraged cleanliness in the dairy.[8] If a woman performed her tasks with reference to magical beliefs, she helped to protect her household from malign supernatural forces.

Women as well as men sought to know the future. Servant maids used to smooth the ashes of the fire after supper to try to divine their future husbands, Aubrey recollected.[9] Some women hoped that their horoscopes would help them to plan their lives. The case books of the Elizabethan astrologer, Simon Forman, reveal that many women consulted him about a range of concerns. They asked him whether they were pregnant, about suitable days for a journey, or whether their lovers or husbands would return from voyages.[10] The use of astrology in healing the sick could be contentious. In the early seventeenth century, Richard Napier, clergyman and astrological physician, offered magical amulets to cure people. Some godly people believed that it was sinful to use such magic.[11] They were even more suspicious of cunning folk. Florence Smyth sought to exculpate herself when her cousin 'went to the divell' about a lost dish. She said that her cousin had sent to a woman in Bristol 'before I knew it, which hath mutch troubelled me for of all things I hated witchcraft, but I have prayed God not to lay the sin to my charg'.[12] Yet not all the godly shared her scruples. Later in the seventeenth century, some young women who were members of Nonconformist sects had recourse to cunning men and women to find out about marriage partners or lost goods.[13]

Women believed that rituals and beliefs helped to preserve them from harm when their natural functions – menstruation, childbirth and lactation – placed them in danger. Many women used prayers, the conventional form of divine aid. Women's medical commonplace books reveal a different range of remedies for female problems and disorders, some of which were magical. For example, one remedy for menstrual disorders instructed a woman to take a branch of a mulberry tree, cut when the moon was full, bind it to her wrist, and let her blood run into a hole in the ground with a three-cornered stake buried in it.[14] A pregnant woman who sought to prevent a child being born with a hare lip was advised to slit her smock.[15]

There was a female lore about child-rearing which drew upon folklore, natural remedies, and magic. For teething, some believed that a necklace of henbane seed was good, but others recommended anointing the child's gums with the brains of a hare, or the comb from a cock. If a child were weak with rickets, 'let it blood in the hollow hole with the eares three days before the change of the moon, and let the Child bee tossed in ones armes the heeles highest'. Recipes advised women to anoint a child's scaled head three days before the full moon, and to prevent fits by anointing the soles of a child's feet with the hair of the hind legs of she-bear boiled in brandy. Mothers could ward off sickness in their children by arranging the letters of the alphabet in a pattern and hanging them around their children's necks. Warts could be cured by cutting off the head of an eel, rubbing the warts with the blood, and burying the head. When the eel's head was rotten, the warts would fall off.[16] Recipes invoked moonlore and sympathetic magic. For example, in 1734 Sarah Savage, daughter of a Nonconformist minister, advised her daughter to wean her son in the waning of the moon. An old woman had recommended it to her, she said, and although Sarah expressed some scepticism, she did pass the idea on.[17] Popular astrology could be practised in conjunction with Christian beliefs.

Many people suffered sickness without much hope of relief or cure in early modern England. The medical profession had little to offer, and indeed some contemporary practices, such as blood letting, may have been harmful to health. However, there was a wide range of medical practitioners and women had an important role in nursing and curing the sick. Some of their practices for healing relied upon beliefs which were outside orthodox Christianity, but beliefs in magical healing were widespread through the society. In the regular process of healing, there ı little distinction between natural and supernatural objects. ınds of supernatural healing were generally accepted. After the ʀeformation, when exorcism was abandoned, many Protestant clergy used prayer to try to heal those who were troubled in mind.[18] Theories of sympathy explained how an individual could be cured of a wound by anointing the weapon which inflicted it with a salve.[19] The clergy agreed that eaglestones possessed power to help in childbirth. In the later seventeenth centry, the Anglican Dr Bargrave, Dean of Christchurch, Canterbury, said that an eaglestone was so popular his wife 'can seldom keep it at home'. Bargrave suggested that a clergyman's wife should continue to keep it in her custody 'for the public good' and be careful into whose hands it was committed, 'so that it shall be the Cathedral's stone'.[20] The monarchs all possessed the power to heal by touch, and an elaborate ritual was developed so that kings and queens might cure those suffering from scrofula, known as the King's Evil.[21] Seventh sons of seventh sons were also recognised to possess a power to heal by touching.[22] There was no parallel belief in the powers of daughters: the only female who could legitimately exercise a healing touch in early modern England was an anointed female monarch. Consequently, many of the supernatural healing practices exercised by women, which were extensions of their traditional role in helping the sick, could bring them into danger. For example, Margaret Neale of Aldeborough was presented to Bishop Redman in 1597 because 'she taketh upon her to cure diseases by prayer, & therefore hath recorse of people to her farre & nighe'. She confessed 'that she useth a prayer to God, and then a paternoster, the creed, and an other prayer devised'. She was ordered to do penance in the church porch with a paper on her breast in capital letters, for witchcraft and inchantment.[23] Healing practices could easily lead to witchcraft accusations.

WITCHCRAFT

Witchcraft beliefs were widespread through early modern Europe, declining only towards the end of the seventeenth century. Even then, belief in witches may have continued among the populace at large, while they lessened among the educated. In England, there were far fewer prosecutions than in Scotland and on the Continent. Macfarlane has estimated that in England in the years 1560–1706, roughly 2,000 people were tried, of whom about 300 were executed.[24] Despite extensive discussion of witchcraft beliefs and the witchcraft craze of both Europe and England, only recently have historians focused attention on the significance of gender.[25] Christina Larner's work on witchcraft in Scotland has been valuable especially in raising questions about the high proportion of the prosecutions which were directed against women.[26] In England, the percentage was around 93 per cent, in Scotland nearer 80 per cent.[27] Macfarlane's analysis of the social status of those prosecuted in Essex reveals that they were at the lowest levels of the society, and that labourers' wives and widows predominated.[28] Contemporaries thought that just as women's nature, 'being the weaker sexe', inclined them to heresy, so their natures, 'being displeased more malicious, and so more apt to revenge according to their power', inclined them to the devil and witchcraft.[29] Nevertheless, contemporary misogyny seems an inadequate reason to explain why large numbers of *women* were killed for witchcraft in early modern England. Women's own lives and beliefs also played a part.

Witchcraft beliefs arose partly from various practices which called upon supernatural aid. Such appeals to maleficent powers were closely related in the minds of many to orthodox Christian beliefs; that is, belief in God logically implied a belief in the devil. The witch was the opposite of the saint: instead of using her power for good, she used it for harm, for malificarum. In England witchcraft was less involved with the demonic pact, the pact with Satan, than was European witchcraft, and in England, the courts did not use torture to obtain confessions.[30] More common in England was what Larner has classified as the simplest form of witchcraft involving both sorcery, the manipulation of objects and or words, and witchcraft, harming through the release of power activated by hatred.[31]

The purpose of this section is not to debate the causes of witchcraft beliefs or crazes, but rather to discuss the question of witchcraft belief from a more narrow focus. Witchcraft beliefs had meaning for women, both as victims of witchcraft and as witches, and were related to other forms of religious activity. Contemporaries believed that women who sought supernatural aid to harm others invoked evil powers in similar ways to those employed by women who implored more orthodox assistance.

Women, like men, believed in witches. Women shared the view that there were supernatural forces which could both help and harm them. In so far as they summoned supernatural aid for their life crises and for sickness, women helped create a milieu which sustained witchcraft beliefs. Larner argued that the stereotype of the witch was the woman who did not conform to the male idea of proper behaviour. She was independent, assertive, not nurturant and had powers which did not derive from the orthodox order. As such she was a threat not just to men but also to conforming women and their children. Hence it is not surprising that women participated in the processes of the witch trials by bringing complaints and acting as witnesses. Evidence from the trials suggests that there was normally a personal relationship between the accused and her victim. Analysis of the patterns indicates that victims were frequently of higher social status, which was hardly surprising given the impoverished state of most of the witches. A woman might believe herself to be menaced by a woman of lower status, and retaliate by accusing her of witchcraft. Larner suggests that some may have practised supernatural arts to give vent to their aggression or to gain power.[32] There is no doubt that some women nourished malevolent feelings towards their neighbours. Macfarlane argues that it was the disputes between neighbours over gifts and loans which precipitated the majority of attacks in Essex.[33]

More recently, historians have begun to explore the tensions between women which could express themselves through the medium of witchcraft accusations. Lyndal Roper, in an analysis of German witchcraft material, has argued that female jealousy and anxiety focused on maternity. A common category of those accused were lying-in maids – post-menopausal women who assisted mothers who had just given birth. If a child failed to thrive, the mother and other women would accuse the nurse of feeding the child not to nourish but to harm it.[34]

Women's belief in witchcraft had several effects: it provided them with help when more orthodox assistance, such as that from priests, ministers or medical practitioners, had failed. It reinforced women's need to be careful about their own behaviour and to remain on good terms with other women in their community. Jealousy and hatred between women could lead to witchcraft practices or, alternatively, to witchcraft accusations.

The question of why women became witches is more complex and interesting. In the light of Larner's suggestion that women had recourse to witchcraft as a means of gaining power in a society, to what extent can we see women in early modern England choosing to gain their objectives by means of witchcraft?[35] Of course most women did not choose to become witches. The process of making a witch was in part a labelling process which exposed a woman to trial and, if she were found guilty, death. But some women certainly did try to harm others, and their invocation of evil power needs to be explained. Thomas suggests that in a society in which people believed in the devil, it may have been tempting for the economically deprived to turn to Satan for help.

Typically, the devil did not promise great riches but only that those who served him should not want. Women said that he offered food or small sums of money.[36] However, as we have noted, the demonic pact features less in English witchcraft trials than in the European. More usual was the woman who called upon power to harm. In 1632 Mariam Cutford 'did most wickedlie wishe herselfe to be a witche for a tyme that she might be revenged of her adversarie', another woman.[37]

The social situations of many of the women who were accused – widows, older women in poverty – were of relative powerlessness. These impoverished women may have begun with trying to help other people, casting spells to find lost objects, to cure sick animals or children.[38] Thomas has shown how traditional female practices in healing could be a danger. The use of herbs, for example, could be construed as conjuring. Thomas cites a case in 1592 of a woman who claimed that she did not use charms, 'but that she doth use ointments and herbs to cure many diseases'.[39] To help to cure their neighbours was part of the charity of godly women of higher social status, yet in the hands of poorer women, the attempt to cure could be dangerous. Poorer women, with fewer resources, had fewer material cures to offer, but they could deploy supernatural power. In some cases, witchcraft may have offered an alternative access to divine aid. Here again, the power to label belief is vital. Those who ruled in the society promulgated one set of beliefs as orthodox and desirable, while they labelled another set dangerous and punishable with death. Yet the processes of supplication were remarkably similar. A priest could pray for deliverance from plague and be commended; a woman who offered an amulet for protection from plague could be accused of conjuring.

Orthodox religious practices could be perverted for evil ends. For example, fasting was approved by the Christian church, but in some cases, especially before the Reformation, the practice of 'black fasting' was undertaken to secure the death of some specified person.[40] A widow, Mabel Brigge, was executed for fasting in 1537 to cause the death of Henry VIII and the Duke of Norfolk. She had successfully fasted an earlier victim to death.[41]

In a society in which women who were poor were socially deprived and relatively powerless, some may even have turned to witchcraft for excitement. Given the dangers of prosecution, few may have consciously embarked on witchcraft, but many may have nevertheless tried to achieve their ends by means outside the Christian framework.

VISIONS, DREAMS, TRANCE AND PROPHECY

Many women of middling social status could practice a private regime of personal asceticism in their daily lives. Taken to extremes, this could lead to an altered physical state in which a few women experienced ecstasy, saw visions and uttered prophecies. Just as the Christian duty of helping the sick could lead to charges of sorcery, so women who prophesied were frequently suspected of whoredom, insanity or witchcraft.

Women who heard voices, saw visions or spoke in trance are the archetype of religious enthusiasm. The role of handmaiden, vessel of the Lord, has a long history. Weber argued that women were attracted to non-political prophecy, and Norman Cohn has associated the phenomenon with a context of widespread religious disorder.[42] Mary Douglas has suggested that widespread social and religious disorder were necessary for a religion of ecstasy.[43] Such conditions existed in the 1640s and 1650s.

Prophecy was important for a small group of women in seventeenth-century England. It was a marginal activity within the Catholic Church and the Church of England, but the sects brought it more to the fore, and during the period 1640–60 prophecy increased dramatically. Phyllis Mack has identified around 300 women prophets during the 1640s and 1650s.[44] Most of the prophetic writings by women were published at that time: around seventy-two of a total of ninety-two titles published between 1600 and 1700 appeared between 1640 and 1660.[45] Not all those whom others have identified as prophets spoke in trance or in visions. Quaker women, for example, usually spoke, as did Quaker men, in the power of the Lord. Unless there is some evidence of a visionary or ecstatic experience underlying the woman's utterance, I have discussed it elsewhere as preaching.[46]

While social and economic conditions played a great part in creating the situation in which men and women prophesied, I want to discuss the role of women's own religious practices which in some cases predisposed them to trance, vision and prophetic utterances. Female prophecy was far more common than male. While several women prophesied while in trance in early modern England, men rarely did so. Indeed, trance prophecy was a form of communication particularly attractive to women. As Phyllis Mack has shown, prophecy was especially suited to women because they were less proud, and exemplified the traditional Christian paradox that the last should be first.[47] Women prophets spoke of themselves in lowly terms in relation to the Lord – 'a poor, dark, forlorn nothing-creature'[48] – but most of them were not, in social terms, the dispossessed. Some, such as Eleanor Channel, were poor, and Elizabeth Poole earned her living 'by her hands', but on the whole, as Mack has shown, these women were not desperately poor.[49] One in the 1530s was a gentleman's daughter, in the seventeenth century Lady Eleanor Davies was a peer's daughter, and others were of more middling origins with education enough to teach them to read and to write.[50] Nor were they all loners. Many of the Quaker women, whose prophetic activity was of a slightly different kind, combined their prophesying with their normal family duties as wives and mothers.[51]

Female prophetic utterance had a long history, and prophecy should be linked with women's religious practices and spirituality as well as with social upheaval. Virginity, adolescence or youth may have predisposed women to prophecy: the gentleman's daughter mentioned by Thomas More was only 12 years of age.[52] The ability to have visions or to prophesy was doubtless enhanced by regimes of fasting and wakefulness. Eating and refusing food were important to the religiosity of medieval women, and as we have seen, the pious regime in early modern times could involve asceticism.[53] Deprivation of food and sleep have been shown to cause alterations in people's sensory states,[54] and Mary Douglas has pointed out that women's marginality to the social system made them favour forms of inarticulateness and bodily dissociation.[55] A number of female prophets' statements suggest that they had experienced a physical alteration. Ann Venn, in 1658, wrote of how a persuasion 'darted into me' and 'my arched heart, which was like a wild thing ready to break out'.[56] Fasting could precipitate trance in susceptible individuals. Anna Trapnel first heard voices as an adolescent after she had fasted, prayed, and reduced herself to a 'sad condition'.[57] Sara Wight also fasted. In addition to fasting, a trauma such as the death of a husband or child could precipitate physical symptoms.

In trance, senses were altered. Women answered questions although they seemed not to see the people around them. Trapnel said that after fasting, 'Many times God appeared in visions of glory to me.' She attained the state for which all Christians longed: 'The soul wrapt up in the glorious discovery of the brightness of God, would fain be always in that condition.'[58] Trapnel reported feeling 'smoke in her mouth, hot in the belly, the smell of brimstone & she heard a voice saying Thou art damn'd, damn'd'. However, her own later judgement was that this was 'but a fancy'. Subsequently, she was in trance for twelve days in 1654, and for ten months from October 1657 to August 1658 when she was sustained only by drinking small beer and eating toast. In June 1646 she was so ill that those standing by thought that she 'was going out of the body' but in this state she had 'Visions of the Eternal God', and amazed the watchers with her continued speaking.[59] Earlier, Elizabeth Barton's trances were preceded by sickness.[60]

All the women prophets shared a common experience of ecstasy, which took the subject outside of herself and gave her authority. Many prophets said that they heard voices from outside themselves. As the Flanders prophet Antonia Bourignon explained, 'the Spirit which is in me, is not my own'.[61] The voice came in different ways. Eleanor Channel felt 'a Blow given her upon her heart'.[62] Other women, after fasting and prayer, experienced an altered physical state, as did Sara Wight in the 1640s: 'I was in a trance [this was 6 April at night] I lay in visions. And in that time the Spirit of God was powr'rd in upon mee.' She also said that she had dreams.[63] Bystanders reported that women in trance spoke as if they heard a voice. Prophets might speak in different voices: in the 1520s Elizabeth Barton uttered with two voices.[64] A Catholic mystic in Europe, Mary Magdalen Pazzi, was in trance for two hours daily for forty days, in which state she spoke with many different voices.[65] Trapnel spoke swiftly and loudly, and Sara Wight spoke 'as with a new tongue'.[66] Another feature of some female prophecy was the ability to speak in rough rhymes. Elizabeth Barton was said to utter 'sundry metricall and ryming speeches, tending to the worship of our Lady of Court of Strete'.[67] In 1629 Jane Hawkins, who was in trance for three days, spoke in verse to an audience of around 200 people.[68] Anna Trapnel spoke in rhyming couplets for hours.[69]

Contemporaries were deeply interested in the source of women's prophecies. Writing in 1530, Sir Thomas More listed a number of criteria for authenticating the prophecies of Sir Roger Wentworth's daughter: she had no pretext of begging; no possibility of counterfeiting; her parents were of honourable social esteem; there were many witnesses of great repute; the girl was too young for fraud; and finally, the outcome was virtuous, since the maid forsook the world 'and professed religion'.[70] Yet to speak prophetically could be dangerous to women, in proportion to the political content of her message. For Elizabeth Barton the outcome was disgrace and death. Her prophecy touched matters of great political importance, namely the King's marriage and issue. There were at least two books of Barton's prophecies published, but apparently they were successfully suppressed, and survive only in an abstracted form in Lambarde.[71] Another woman, Mrs Amadas, prophesied the death of the King in 1533.[72] Eleanor Davies prophesied the death of the Duke of Buckingham in 1628. When the Duke's death followed, Charles I had her imprisoned.[73]

Magistrates questioned women prophets, because they feared that the prophecies would be heeded by the populace at large and would lead to disorder. Thus they sought to discredit the female prophet's message by arguing that she was demonically possessed. In the fifteenth century in France, Joan of Arc had claimed to hear divine voices, but those who condemned her believed that her voices were from the devil.[74] Allegations of witchcraft or sexual impropriety were standard. In 1654 when Anna Trapnel, a Fifth Monarchist prophet, was in trance in Cornwall, some people wanted to send for a witch tryer to test her with a pin. Trapnel said that she was described as a witch, a whore, a vagabond, 'a Monster, or some ill-shaped Creature'. Her self-esteem was such that she declared that she would have proceeded against her detractors at law if she thought she had any chance of justice, 'if there were any Law up save the Wits of men'.[75] In 1651 Elizabeth Poole was attacked as a witch, one set up by Oliver Cromwell and Ireton as 'a precious saint'. Earlier, in 1629, ecclesiastical authorities accused Jane Hawkins of St Ives of faking her prophecies.[76]

Men entrusted with authority knew that if a prophet was the voice of God, they should obey. Elizabeth Poole, who was examined by the Army Council in 1649 about her vision, said that 'when I was with the Councell, it was in a Vision, or Revelation'.[77] Examined closely as to the source of her vision, on 5 January 1649 she expatiated further: 'I saw noe Vision, nor noe Angell, nor heard noe voice, butt my spirit being drawne out about those thinges, I was in itt. Soe farre as it is from God I think itt is a revelation.'[78] The Army Council's problem was to decide whether or not she was a messenger from God. For her, the experience was of oneness with divine power: 'I was in itt'. She also referred to herself as pregnant with the divine, of her message as 'the Babe Jesus in me'.[79] Anna Trapnel who also had dreams as well as visions, was asked 'was it only a spirit of faith that was upon you, or was it a Vision wrapping up your outward senses in trances, so that you had not your senses to see, nor hear, nor take notice of the People present?' Her questioners were concerned with the origin of her prophecy – personal or divine? She replied with the classic statement of the Christian mystic: that she heard nothing of the people, only the voice of God.

> It was as if the Clouds did open and receive me into them: and I was as swallowed up by the Glory of the Lord, and could speak no more.[80]

From this ecstatic state, she was able to recall what had taken place on waking.

Figure 6. A woman prophet: Anne Bathurst, 1707 (Bodleian Library, Oxford).

Weber's characterisation of women's prophecies as a-political thus seems misleading, for some women prophets were taken seriously by a range of men of different political persuasions. In early modern England, Henry VIII, Charles I, the Army Council and Oliver Cromwell were all at different times concerned with the political significance of the revelations. In 1654 Anna Trapnel was examined by the Council of State about her prophecies which included explicit statements about the failings of Cromwell's rule.[81] She had spoken of her dream of Cromwell as 'a kind of cattle' who came at her, but the Lord promised to protect her. Cromwell had 'backslidden'. Once over several nights, she spoke a long poem in which she praised the Lord's handmaidens, and prophesied wrath upon the rulers.

> Wo to the Rabbies and Wise men
> That the people do deceive.[82]

Prophecy, revelations and visions may be different phenomena. There were obviously several different types of prophecy. Mary (Rande) Cary's prophecies were political, but not associated with fasting or trance, and Jane Lead's, at the end of the century, were more poetic and mystical with no apparent references to contemporary political events. Other women expressed religious ecstasy which had no obvious political overtones. Anne Bathurst compiled a number of books of writings around the 1680s about 'the depth of the love of God'. She sought God early in life, at about 10 years of age, but sickness, fear of death, sorrows and difficulties oppressed her until she was about 40 years of age. Then, on 23 December 1678, her life was transformed. She was 'taken out of the Bewildered place, and put into such a Calm as is not to be expressed'.[83] Her language was ecstatic. 'There be divers operashans' of the spirit, she wrote,

> for as I haue said somtims it works as one Drunk wth loue, sometimes by Aire, as the body is full of devin joyfulnes, & a body wth in a body carying it very swift in moshan to goe or walking as wthout sences or feling ye ground, or sence of wery-nes . . .
> I speak now also of a sperit quick & powerfull deviding betwixt ye marrow & the bone, & works in my heart . . . that I am licke one drunck . . .[84]

Some visions had sexual overtones. Sara Wight had a terrifying 'Dream or Vision' in which she was rescued by

> one like the appearance of a man (but the Glory of him was so great, I cannot express it;) he came, and took me in his armes.[85]

111

Anne Bathurst's nightly dreams were of sensual union with Christ:

> Then I was caught up higher, where I saw Jesus in the appearance
> of a Man, all surrounded by a most glorious Light, wch greatly
> transpoorted me; for now I knew I was come to the place wch I
> had so long desired to behold. Whilst I was there I appeared to my
> self (I mean my Angel apper'd to Me, but I understood it not) at
> wch being surpriz'd, and the flesh shrinking at the greatness of the
> Glory, I perfectly felt a touch on the top of my head, wch drew my
> spirit out of me, as you draw a knife or sword out of a Sheath, & it
> cut as it was drawn forth. Thereafter I appeared as a spark of
> Light, and according to my desire i sometimes mounted up to see
> Jesus; and then descended again to Paradise; all wch motions were
> very swift.[86]

These visions remained private, recorded in Bathurst's notebooks, and
led to no public stir.

Mack's analysis, which focuses on audience, suggests that ultimately
women's prophetic activity reinforced existing negative female stereotypes. By claiming to speak with voices, and with visions of a spiritual
millennium outside historical time, women left intact the view that
women were weak and despised.[87] However, I would argue that
although the women prophets stressed a negative attitude to their sex,
this was a way of magnifying both the Lord, and themselves in relation to
other people. Women's authority as prophets was enormous. 'The
things which are written above', declared Elizabeth Poole, 'I have
shewed you my authority for.'[88] Women believed that their visions were
given to help others, especially those who were troubled: 'The Saints
should declare the goodness of God to each other.'[89] In uttering
prophecy, some women transcended weakness and experienced great
power.

MYSTICS, FEMALE SPIRITUALITY AND SYMBOLISM

Beyond visions, prophecies and trances lay the religious experience
known as mysticism. Although comparatively rare in early modern
England, it was an orthodox part of Christian faith. Women may have
been more likely to become mystics than men, for the pattern of pious
women's lives may have developed a more inward-looking spiritual life.
The Catholic church may have been more sympathetic to mysticism
than the Protestant. Gertrude More sought total dedication to God
through the Benedictine order. She found satisfaction in resigning

herself to the divine will and pleasure, and prayed that she might 'dy to al created things that I may live alone to thee'.[90] It would be interesting to know of the reactions of the clergy to the experiences of nuns. Mary Ward's mystical experiences were questioned not only by her clerical critics but also by one of the sisters in her convent.[91]

A few women attained a mystical state in solitude and occasioned little or no contemporary comment. Anne Bathurst in the 1690s wrote several volumes of mystical visions, expressing her closeness to the divine through her fully human and female nature.

> The word *divine* multiplies in me & fills me, taking away my herts life into it. . . . O Sea of redeeming love, what wilt not thou do! & fountains of blood what canst thou do! O, a fountain seal'd, breasts full of consolation. I am as pent milk in the breast, ready to be poured forth & dilated into Thee, from whom my fullness flows with such fulness and plenitude & pleas'd when eas'd.[92]

In this extraordinary passage, she wrote of nurturing God in a symbiotic relationship; she was the milk flowing into God. Her body rejoiced in her nurturant role, satisfying her completely. Hers was one of the many ways in which early modern women apprehended God and tried to live in harmony and closeness with him. What interests me here is the interplay between mysticism and gender.

A woman's sexual identity, which was always a sign of comparative inferiority in social terms, could become a means by which she could triumph with God. Antonia Bourignon, a Flanders mystic whose works were translated into English in the later seventeenth century, was initially unwilling to obey the Lord's command. When the Lord told her to serve him by declaring his plans, she objected that she would be unsuitable because she was female:

> she being a simple Girl, void of all Force and Authority, every way weak. He said to her, *I will be thy All; My power is not limited; Give thy Consent.* She said, wherefore hast thou not made me a Man? I would have had more Advantage and capacity that thou mightest serve thy self of me. He answered, *I will serve my self of vilest Matter to confound the pride of Men. I will give thee all that thou shalt need; be faithful to me.*[93]

Such abasement and abnegation of self, even denial of sexual identity – 'wherefore hast thou not made me a Man' – served the purpose of allowing her to become a vessel for the Lord. Bourignon attracted a wide following, and her influence spread after her death in 1680. By the

1690s her followers, according to critics, were 'some of the better sort, who have been reputed, Men of Sense, Learning and Probity'.[94]

Jane Lead (1624–1703) also published mystical prophetic visions. When her husband died after twenty-five years of marriage, her spiritual development flourished, and she began to experience ecstatic visions: 'There came upon me an overshadowing bright Cloud, and in the midst of it the Figure of a Woman.' This woman she identified as Sophia, the Goddess of Wisdom.[95] She founded a religious movement known as the Philadelphian Society which attracted male disciples who took part in publishing her works.[96] Many of Lead's writings were visionary or prophetic. *A fountain of gardens*, for example, which was published in three volumes in 1696, was to enlighten, lead and refresh others with 'these Love-Visitations from the Spirit of my Lord'.[97] Lead urged all pastors and teachers to heed her prophecies from 'the Day-spring on high' and to reject their previous teachings as 'a dead draught of literal Knowledge'.[98] Lead was influenced by the work of Jacob Boehme, a German mystic, whose writings were influential in the seventeenth century.[99] Like Boehme, and Joachim of Fiore before him, Lead expounded a doctrine of the age of the Holy Spirit 'which will Excell all before it, to Unseal and Reveal what yet never was known or understood'.[100] If Scripture was silent on a subject, Lead reported what was 'visionally and Communicatively made known by the direct inspiration of the Spirit'.[101] She believed in universal salvation.

Lead's revelations have not received a sympathetic reading from some historians. Walker criticised her style as unnatural, ungrammatical and often obscure.[102] However, for those with an unconventional message, language is often difficult. There are some fascinating insights in Lead's writing to the way in which she used the existing social situation of herself as a woman to express her oneness with God. Lead adopted a classic female role – 'I my self was wholly Passive, and the Spirit altogether active'[103] – which allowed God to use her. Passivity became a source of spiritual strength and advantage. In her writings, she speculated on sexuality and gender, arguing that God was both male and female, and Adam, created in his image, was likewise androgynous.

Both Bourignon and Lead applied to themselves the Scriptural types of the female, especially that of the woman clothed with the sun, in Revelation 12. Later, in the eighteenth century, Joanna Southcott founded a large religious movement, and was influenced by Lead. Southcott also pictured herself as the same woman clothed with the sun.[104]

The language in which men and women spoke of God was sexed, and mystics had no difficulty in responding to the idea of God in physical terms. When Lady Packington thought of death, she prayed to God to 'receive her into thine own Embraces, into the blessed armes of they unspeakable mercyes, into the sacred rest of thine everlasting joy'.[105] Sometimes, when female mystics dreamed of heaven, they saw Christ in physical beauty. One night in January 1680, Anne Bathurst saw Jesus in a dream or vision 'in a figure like a Man, in clearness & colour like a Jasper Stone, wth his legs of white beryl-stone: which did greatly ravish me, yt one day I should be like Him'.[106] Although Protestantism discouraged contemplation and favoured the active life, some women were able to develop their spiritual gifts to achieve an ecstatic union with the divine.

CONCLUSION

By the later seventeenth century, educated male public opinion was hostile to religious enthusiasm and prophecy. Even the Quakers tried to tone down the wilder prophetic utterances of their adherents, and women's prophetic publications declined accordingly.[107] The reactions of other women to prophecy are rare. One comment survives from the early eighteenth century, in Elizabeth Burnet's private observations on the work of Antonia Bourignon. Elizabeth, the wife of Bishop Gilbert Burnet, believed that harsh accusations of imposture only made enthusiasts more extreme, encouraging in them the belief that they were the people spoken of in Scripture who suffered for truth and holiness, so her own attitude was mild. She thought that Bourignon's book had 'many true & noble thoughts of religion & virtue', but that Bourignon was deluded by her disordered imagination and 'followed her own reasonings without restraint'.[108] In this censure the voice of educated rationality can be detected. Even so, prophetic and millenarian movements continued to command widespread popular support in eighteenth century Europe.[109]

Faced with uncertainty and sorrow in life, early modern women sought supernatural help of various kinds. When women prayed to God, and sought his blessing through a regime of piety, they won praise from their contemporaries. But if women sought a more intense relationship with God, or turned to alternative sources of divine aid, they found themselves in dangerous areas where they could be suspected as enthusiasts, prophets or witches.

Part III

Women and radical religion in the English Revolution 1640–60

6

Radical religion: separatists and sectaries 1558–1660

These *English Crocodiles* leave no politick ways untried to work
upon *Weak Proselites*, they prevaile most upon the femall *Sex*, as
knowing the *Woman was first seduced*, and then seduced the man.
The Quacking Mountebanck, 1655[1]

The history of enthusiasm is largely a history of female emancipation, and it is not a reassuring one.
R. A. Knox, *Enthusiasm*, 1950[2]

WOMEN IN SEPARATIST CHURCHES AND VOLUNTARY RELIGIOUS MEETINGS, 1558–1640

In the century before the outbreak of the Civil Wars, women were
prominent in what the ecclesiastical authorities called 'conventicles'. So
far as the established church was concerned, these conventicles were all
separatist, and dangerous, and therefore to be suppressed. But these
groups did not all share the same principles. A few were separatist only
for reasons of expediency. They considered that the Anglican church
was so unreformed and corrupt that believers should separate from it
lest they be contaminated.[3] Others had a theology of separation. They
believed that the true church consisted of believers only, separate from
the Anglican establishment. However, Patrick Collinson has pointed
out that most of those who were involved in extra religious activites
before the Civil Wars were neither conventiclers nor separatists but
were engaged in forms of 'voluntary religion'.[4] Godly women as well as
godly men sought to supplement the spiritual activities of the established church.

Hostile witnesses commented on one common feature of these
separatist groups and of 'enthusiastic religion' generally: the presence

119

and participation of women.[5] In this the heresiographers followed a long tradition which declared that women were especially prone to error and heresy. As Miles Hogarde declared, 'in all ages at any tyme when one had devised some foolishe errour or other, straight way woemen were readye to apply to their fancies'.[6] In the Elizabethan period, the Catholic writer Nicholas Sander set out a typology of female heretics. These included Athalia, who made herself a queen; Manacha, a priestess of impious and filthy rites; Jezabel, who persecuted and slew the prophet Elia; Selene, a woman of evil life; Constantia, a cruel and ruthless woman; and the empress Eudoxia, the persecutor of St John Chrysostom. Sander reminded his audience of the view of St Jerome that nearly every heresy was spread by women.[7] The point of Sander's misogyny was to discredit the Protestant church and its leaders. In reply, the Anglicans attacked not so much the women 'whose judgment', Richard Hooker said, 'is commonly weakest [sic] by reason of their sex', but rather the men who deliberately misled women,

> for that they are deemed apter to serve as instruments and helps in the cause. Apter they are through the eagerness of their affection, that maketh them . . . diligent in drawing their husbands, children, servants, friends and allies the same waie.[8]

Hooker thought that the natural compassion of women made them generous to preachers. Besides, women knew a great deal about the attitudes of people around them to the cause, and so had opportunities to procure support. Whatever the reason, Hooker believed that both women and men were difficult to convince, once they had chosen differently.[9]

The printed word spread a heresiography about the presence of women among the sects. They were stubborn in heresy: Elborow thought that five men could be convinced of their errors sooner than one woman.[10] Most heresiographers believed that women were seeking power and authority over men in religious matters. Some writers equated heresy with sexual licentiousness.[11] When a group met together, contemporaries questioned their sexual morals. Thomas White described the men and women whom he called Brownists as 'cages of euery uncleane bird'.[12] Some groups met by night. Not only was the night and dark associated with private sexuality, it was also the antithesis of the public and open worship of God which Anglicans believed bore witness to true Christianity. Some of the lines of the Civil War debates can be seen in these earlier discussions. This was the context in which any female attempt to separate from the Anglican church was understood.

While historians of early separatism in England have been preoccupied with dating origins and tracing formative influences on its history,[13] this chapter is concerned with the female presence in religious radicalism. Before 1640 the evidence does not allow us to ascertain women's motives for joining the early separatist churches nor to discuss their experiences. After 1640 the much fuller sources permit a more detailed consideration of women's views and of the effects of issues of gender on separatist congregations and sects. Feminist scholarship has recently focused new attention on the women in radical religious movements in early modern England. New questions and a re-reading of the sources enable us to attempt a fresh look at questions of gender and radicalism in the revolutionary period.

Terminology is difficult. 'Sect' is a value-laden term which many of the groups themselves would have rejected and implies a more formal constitution than many of these radical religious groups possessed, especially those of the 1640s and 1650s.[14] Over the centuries of Christian history, there had always been groups who separated from the main body of the church, claiming that they were restoring the true faith which had become polluted. In the words of Geoffrey Nuttall, separatists had a 'passionate desire to recover the inner life of New Testament Christianity'.[15] Although they were usually distinguished by high moral standards, they were frequently persecuted as heretics. Surviving information often originated with their enemies rather than with the separatists themselves.

From the mid-sixteenth century, records survive of separatist congregations meeting in out-of-the-way places. Some were at taverns and upper rooms of buildings in London. John Stow mockingly referred to the congregation at Holy Trinity Minories as 'Puritans or Unspottyd Lambs of the Lord'.[16] However, the congregation at the Minories were not separatists on principle, but rather a group meeting for extra religious worship.[17] A few details about meetings emerged from some prosecutions in Essex in the 1580s. Helen Colman and Dorothy Fenning testified that they went into the woods one midsummer afternoon, where they joined a mixed group of about a dozen who shared a meal and then listened to William Collett read words out of a book. From the descriptions of mossy seats and the ladder which Collett used, it sounds like a regular meeting place, but one witness denied that Collett actually preached, while the other was carefully evasive.[18]

In Elizabeth's reign several sects worried contemporaries, including Brownists, Barrowists, and the Family of Love. Hostile commentators believed that the Family of Love was socially exclusive. John Rogers thought that Familists believed that anyone outside the Family was a beast without a soul, that marriage should be made among themselves, that alms should be distributed only to those of their sect, and that when wives were in labour 'they must use the help of none other but their own sect'.[19] Yet the recent work of Christopher Marsh has overturned such views, showing that men who were Familists were also integrated into parish life to the extent of serving as churchwardens.[20] The Familists were followers of the Dutch mystic Hendrich Niclaes. His works were translated into English and his ideas were spread by itinerant preachers.[21] The Familists annoyed contemporaries by their claim to greater moral rectitude: 'they bragge very much of their owne sincere lives', 'Marke, how purely we live'.[22] Among those charged with Familism, in 1580 Margaret Colevill of the Wisbech group 'confessed also that perfection might be attained unto in this life'.[23] Predictably, the Familists were charged with libertinism, the customary allegation made to discredit a separatist group. Perhaps the charge related to views about the incarnation: Rogers reported what to him was blasphemy, that the women of the Family believed that they were all Marys, 'and say, that Christ is come forth in their fleshe', and that the Angels Gabriel and Raphael were born of woman.[24]

In the early Baptist churches the model for the true church was Scriptural. English Baptists were influenced by practical experience of separation in English congregations in Amsterdam. A troubling question to the Amsterdam Baptists was the place of women in the true church. In 1610 Henry Robinson, a Baptist pastor, argued that women were debarred from exercising authority over men 'by their sex'. All they could do was profess their faith, confess their sins, say Amen to prayers and sing Psalms. They could share also in church discipline by accusing or defending a brother who was accused of sin. Finally, Robinson conceded that 'in a case extraordinary, namely when no man will, I see not but a woman may reprove the Church'. Robinson also believed that Scriptural example authorised women speaking in public in the role of prophets.[25] In practice, the Amsterdam congregation found it difficult to discipline female members of the church.[26] A hostile pamphlet alleged sexual sins in the congregation, including adultery and incest.[27] Because the congregation excommunicated a wife who obeyed her husband and refused to bring their child for baptism, the pamphlet's author believed that the church was encouraging wifely insubordination.[28] In defence of his church, the pastor Johnson argued that there was a distinction to be drawn between private sins, which could be forgiven if confessed and repented of, and those which were public, and therefore a matter for the church. Failure to baptise a child was a public sin, and therefore the church was right to censure a mother who refused to bring her child for baptism. In matters of adultery, on the other hand, it was permissible for the innocent party to take back the sinful one privately; it was no defilement, no 'coupling themselves with an harlot'.[29]

Many early separatist congregations were persecuted. The Court of High Commission's records of the examination of John Lathrop's congregation in 1632 show that sexuality, female insubordination and separatism were associated in the bishops' minds. Humphrey Barnet, at whose house in Blackfriars the group had met, admitted that while he still attended his parish church, 'his wife will not'. The Archbishop of York was incredulous: 'will you suffer that in your wife?'[30] Bishop Laud implied that there was sexual promiscuity, asking Lathrop 'how manie women sate crosse legged upon ye bedd, whilest you sat on one side & preached & prayed most devoutlie?' Lathrop denied keeping 'such evill companie, they were not such women'.[31] When the women came before the court they refused to take the *ex officio* oath. Some pleaded that they did not understand it, others, their consciences: 'I am afraid to take Gods name in vaine', said Sara Jones.[32] 'I see you are an obstinate woman', the Archbishop of Canterbury replied. The Archbishop accused the entire group of ingratitude: a godly church was provided for them, but 'the Church is nothing wth you, & his Ministers not be regarded, but you runne into woods, as if you lived in persecution'.[33] They were all imprisoned for two years. But not all separatists were persecuted. In Bristol in the 1630s, Dorothy Hazzard led a group of Baptist sympathisers who worshipped together and escaped persecution.[34]

In some parishes, a decision was made before 1640 to gather believers together as a true church. John Goodwin was minister of St Stephen's, Coleman Street, in London. By 1639 his congregation had constituted itself as a gathered church, by which was meant that worshippers covenanted together with God to be a true church.[35] Goodwin's congregation, known as Independents or Congregationalists, believed that each congregation was autonomous in matters of worship.

The most prominent example of Independency came from New England. The ecclesiastical experiment there was watched with interest from England and Scotland. In the 1630s, New England was deeply divided by disputes about two issues: the place of women in the church, and the Antinomian question – whether Christians were free by grace from the moral law. Anne Hutchinson publicly discussed religious matters before a mixed audience, and when put on trial for her temerity, proved unrepentant. Her story is an intriguing one which has been widely studied.[36] Hutchinson's activities both in expounding Scriptures to people who gathered at her house and in defying the magistrates became a horror story which discredited religious separatism. She was excommunicated and expelled from the colony.

Gender was a central issue to Anne Hutchinson's case. Contemporaries believed that a woman should not exercise authority and that she should be subordinate and submissive. When Hutchinson gave birth to a misshapen or monstrous child, and was finally massacred by Indians 'contrary to their wont', her opponents interpreted her fate as a punishment from God vindicating her expulsion. Her unhappy history featured in the anti-separatist propaganda of the 1640s in England. She was cited as an awful warning of the consequences of license in matters of religious belief. Anti-separatist writers pointed out that her 'unnatural' fate was a fitting judgement for her unnatural behaviour. As Robert Baillie, the Scottish minister, observed with satisfaction, 'God let loose his hand and destroyed her'.[37]

Later historians have not been favourable to Anne Hutchinson. Rather than portraying her as a martyr for liberty of conscience – which she was – they have characterised her as a woman who did not know her place. James Anderson, the nineteenth-century Reformation historian, summed up her story as revealing 'the defects of her character' which betrayed her into error and delusion.[38] In the 1960s Hutchinson's history was reinterpreted in terms of the female life-cycle. Her behaviour was explained as a function of menopausal disorders.[39] More recently, accounts sympathetic to Hutchinson have shown her as a woman struggling to exercise her spiritual gifts.[40]

Many voluntary religious groups and separatists were persecuted before 1640 in England. After ecclesiastical control broke down in 1641, sects multiplied and attracted many more followers.

GENDER AND HERESIOGRAPHY

Thus by 1640 a well-developed heresiography existed in England. Certain known features were thought to characterise the sects. Fissiparous by nature, they attracted the socially disadvantaged, including poorer men and women. Indeed, a major weapon in the contemporary attacks on the separatists was to depict them as a collection of impoverished men and unruly women. Some of the historiography of the sects in the early modern period has been hostile, which has made other historians conscious of the need to 'be fair' to the radicals.[41] Among the defenders of the sects have been religious believers whose current institutional allegiance is to denominations with their roots in the seventeenth century. Practitioners of 'believer history' recognise that such commitment has its difficulties, but argue that it gives insight and sympathy which other historians lack.[42] Yet even this empathy can be distorting, for it is with the survivors rather than the losers. Furthermore, a denominational interest in origins has imposed more order on the religious scene than appeared at the time, when groups were frequently fluid and disorganised. The search for 'founding fathers' has obscured collective effort and the contributions of women. Just as women's presence presented problems to early modern pastors and leaders of congregations, so they have continued to present problems to denominational historians, many of whom have been ministers themselves.

Images of the female were central to people's religious understandings in the 1640s and 1650s. Little work has been done on female symbolism in the early modern period to date, although the forthcoming study by Phyllis Mack of gender and religious prophecy raises exciting and important issues. Mack argues that women were understood at two levels: in a social context, as humble, meek, and subordinate, and at a spiritual level, as immensely powerful.[43]

Religion was a gendered subject: that is, religious belief and practice were understood in terms of human relationships. As social roles altered, so religious changes occurred. But it was no simple, one-way process. Any alterations in religious ideas, in the boundaries between the sacred and the profane, had profound implications for relationships between men and women. We need to understand how a female preacher threatened masculine control in English society. But the social context which allowed a woman to claim the right to preach affected the way God was perceived: the divine could be more accessible to a wider range of people. The power to define belief was no longer the property of an elite, and God was less remote.

When the members of the Long Parliament assembled in 1640, religious reformation was one of their first priorities. All the MPs knew, as fathers of families, that just as they were accountable to God for what happened in their families, so as magistrates they were answerable to

God for England's religious state. Religious policy always had implications for gender. The public reformation of religion was claimed by men as their own. At their fast in December 1641 the Commons heard their chosen preacher, Edmund Calamy, tell them what kind of a reformation they were to effect:

> Now this is the great work that the lord requireth at your hands, Oh ye Worthies of Israel! To stub up all these unprofitable Trees, and to repair the breaches of Gods House, to build it up in its beauty, according to the pattern in the Mount, and to bring us back not onely to our *first Reformation* in King *Edwards* dayes, but to *reform the Reformation it self*.[44]

Reformation was a clearing and building project: this was men's work, for according to the sexual division of labour, building was labour in the male domain, even if it was work more familiar to lower-class men than to the gentry and wealthier citizens who sat in the Commons.

Although men were convinced that the public work of reformation was their responsibility, they knew that what women did could render their labour in vain. Just as a wife's sexual disorderliness impugned the honour of her husband, so her religious disorderliness would be charged by God to the account of her husband. As the chief heresiographer of the 1640s, Thomas Edwards grimly reminded the members of Parliament in 1646:

> A man . . . is accounted by God to be guilty of all the Idolatry committed by his wives and their followers . . . And yet I do not say Your Honours have done these things. . . . Now I humbly submit to your deep judgement, whether God account not men guilty of that which is committed by others under them, they having power to hinder it.[45]

Whatever happened in private families was thus of significance in the eyes of God. Women's behaviour in a sphere which might be thought and even labelled 'private' was, in fact, a matter of public concern. Women too were aware that their actions in their families and houses were publicly significant.

Thus, although historians usually write of the religious policies of the 1640s and 1650s as though they were part of the public male domain – the world of ministers in their pulpits and in the Assembly of the Divines, and of men who were members of Parliament – they overlook the importance of gender relations, something which no contemporaries would have forgotten. Religious policy was influenced by the interaction between men and women in 'private' houses seeking the worship of God. Neither ministers nor members of Parliament could, or would have wished to, separate religion from its family and household meaning. They wanted women to obey, not to initiate reform.

In order to understand why the presence of women so discredited the separatist cause, we need to examine the underlying assumptions more closely. Scripture was the basis for the arguments. The Bible showed that woman was designed to be man's companion. Even before the Fall, she was under man's authority, as most people agreed. After the Fall, she was to be ruled by man as part of her punishment. The power of the keys, namely the power to discipline, was therefore crucial. If the power to excommunicate was in the whole church, then 'men, women, young, old, the meanest and weakest part of the people [would be able] to decide by the number, not the weight of their voices'.[46] Ministers were as fathers to their congregations, and as such to be obeyed. As Brinsley explained,

> *Ministers* in their places endeavouring as *spiritual fathers* to beget sons and daughters unto God, by the incorruptible seed of the word, that so we may every one of us be able to say at that great day, . . . *Behold, Lord, here am I, and the children whom thou hast given me.*[47]

Any woman who tried to challenge male power was therefore acting contrary to God's order in a deeply sinful way, endangering the whole society because she might infect others with her disobedience and might also provoke God's wrath against those who permitted such license.

Historical examples were adduced as evidence that heresy and sexual licentiousness went together. Stories of the Anabaptist attempt to establish God's kingdom in 1534 in Munster were reprinted in the 1640s.[48] Robert Baillie, the influential Scottish minister, blamed the sexual promiscuity at Munster on the revival of Old Testament polygamy.[49] Baillie tainted sectarianism with sexual freedom, citing the New England case of Anne Hutchinson.[50] Yet it was not just Hutchinson and other women whom the opponents of the sectaries were attacking: it was the men who countenanced them, such as Cotton, Wheelwright and Vane. These men were powerful in the Boston community, and Vane was especially feared in England after his return there in 1639.

The Ranters Declaration, 2

WITH

Their new Oath and Proteſtation; their ſtrange Votes, and a new way to get money; their Proclamation and Summons; their new way of Ranting, *never before heard of*; their dancing of the *Hay* naked, at the white *Lyon* in Peticoat-lane; their mad Dream, and Dr. *Pockridge* his Speech, with their Trial, Examination, and Anſwers: the coming in of 3000. their Prayer and Recantation, *to be in all Cities and Market-towns read and publiſhed*; the mad-Ranters further Reſolution; their Chriſtmas Carol, and blaſpheming Song; their two pretended-abominable Keyes to enter Heaven, and the worſhiping of his little-majeſty, the late Biſhop of *Canterbury*: A new and further Diſcovery of their black Art, with the Names of thoſe that are poſ-ſeſt by the Devil, having ſtrange and hideous cries heard within them, *to the great admiration of all thoſe that ſhall read and peruſe this enſuing ſubject.*

Licenſed according to order, and publiſhed by M. *Stubs*, a late fellow-Ranter

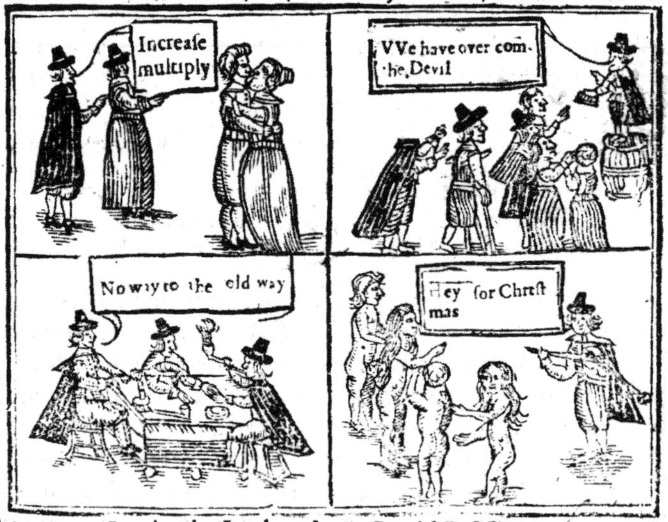

Dec: 17 Imprinted at London, by J. C. MDCL. 1650

Figure 7. Women's presence discredited the radical religious sects. Thomason Tract (British Library, London).

The heresiography of the 1640s and 1650s followed the lines already established in earlier periods. Women were said to join the sects because they were weak and foolish and therefore easily seduced. Indeed, Baillie believed that the sects deliberately enticed women to join by offering them the chance to preach, prophesy and speak. Since a woman was allowed to join a sect without her husband's knowledge or consent, the wife could virtually divorce her husband and free herself 'from the bond of obedience to him'.[51] It was a scenario just like the Fall. While Brinsley recognised that all Christians should exercise independent judgement, he thought that women should not question fundamental truths without good reason. Brinsley assumed that all women were wives, and censured 'the unwarrantable rashness and presumption of some women' who espoused errors without their husbands' consent.[52]

In the 1640s the heresiographers published reports from all over England of the outrageous behaviour. The picture was one of disorder and confusion. Women's religious actions were sexualised by male commentators who found it impossible to believe that women could act from religious motives alone. A clever rhyme mocked Katherine Chidley's sexual morality and slyly cast doubts upon her authorship of her work:

> Oh Kate, O Kate, thou art unclean I heare,
> A man doth lye betweene thy sheetes, I feare.[53]

Heresiographers attacked the men who misled their female disciples. They claimed that male cult leaders preached doctrines of sinlessness, and seduced the minds and bodies of their female disciples.[54] Naked men went into the water with naked women, 'holding them in their arms'.[55] It was a titillating vision, which sold well.

Some of the hostile opponents of the sects gave vent to their anger in satires, and the foolishness of women was one of their prime targets. Such material is difficult to use for an understanding of women's motives, for neither Thomas Edwards nor Robert Baillie is to be trusted on this subject. However, their writing has exciting possibilities if analysed as a source describing male fears about women. Why male satirists found actions performed by women inherently ridiculous gives insight into men's anxieties. Satire is a rhetorical device which works off normative values. Like jokes and laughter, it comes from a sense of the ridiculous in life, but in this case, behaviour does not provoke mirth, but anger. For a woman to act in areas which men considered to be their own territory aroused men's fury. Consequently, men held women up to ridicule. Satire worked from known and accepted values which an author assumed that his readers shared. It was not a genre so open to women writers, who lacked the confidence that their assumptions were widespread through the literate public.

Popular wisdom announced that 'It is a sad house where the hen crows louder than the cock.'[56] More sophisticated satirists mocked the preaching woman. At both levels, however, it was assumed that the actions were ridiculous because they reversed the natural order. No argument was felt to be necessary in this context. Furthermore, contemporaries believed that women joined the sects because they sought freedom, which meant sexual freedom or licentiousness. Subsequent writers have also assumed that women sought greater liberty in the sects. How much freedom women found in the sects is to be considered.[57]

WOMEN'S RADICAL ACTIVITIES 1640–60

One of the most remarkable features of the 1640s and 1650s was the public religious activity of women. People saw or heard of women teaching, preaching, leading worship and missionising. The breakdown of ecclesiastical control led to female participation in public religious and political life on an unprecedented scale. By the 1650s some women had moved away from the Anglican, Presbyterian, Congregationalist and Baptist churches and sought a religion based on the immediacy of the spirit. They became Quakers, Fifth Monarchists, Familists, Muggletonians, Adamites and Ranters, to name some of the sects. The total numbers involved were only a minority of the female population, for the majority of women remained loyal Anglicans or secret Catholics, unsympathetic or hostile to the religious radicals. John Morrill has estimated that the radicals were only 5 per cent of the population between 1643 and 1654.[58] Barry Reay, the most recent historian of the Quakers, agrees that they may have amounted to only 1 per cent of the total population, but he points to their impressive penetration of every county. Bristol and London were important, but the Quakers also flourished in many villages.[59] But the significance of the sects extends beyond their numbers. Contemporaries themselves thought that the sectaries were important, and the actions of female religious radicals aroused widespread contemporary comment. Furthermore, women outnumbered men in congregations for which lists have survived.[60]

The terms 'radical', 'sect' and 'heresy' are value-laden terms with reference to a specific historical context. Contemporaries were very conscious of the significance of language, and in the 1640s the Independents successfully insisted in the Assembly of Divines that the term 'church' should not be used of the building, but only of the collection of believers. This still left open the question of who was a believer, and who was outside in error. Individual groups defined themselves as a church, and others as sectaries. In the 1650s, for example, it was common to denigrate the Society of Friends by referring to 'the sect called Quakers'.[61] After the Civil Wars, in the 1680s, Locke was able to view the situation with a detachment not possible in the 1640s: 'every church is orthodox to itself', he coolly observed, 'to others heretical'.[62] Many religious beliefs were labelled heresies during the English revolution by their opponents, and the triumph of one label represents a victory for one group over another.

Thus, although I will use the term 'sect' in these chapters, it is as a convenient shorthand. Beyond this, it can be useful, if not too rigidly applied, as it draws upon the typology of Ernst Troeltsch who distinguished between 'church-type' and 'sect-type' theology. His ideal types draw attention to certain distinct features of church organisation. 'Church-type' refers to religious groups whose theology included everyone: the church had powers to discipline unbelievers. During the early modern period, Anglicans, Catholics, Independents, Presbyterians and some Baptists shared a 'church-type' theology. 'Sect-type' religious groups, on the other hand, were for believers only. Admission was by application of the individual and was subject to the approval of the group.[63] The Quakers, some Baptists and a range of other groups shared a 'sect-type' theology. Characteristics shared by sects, according to the sociologist Bryan Wilson, include claims to exclusivity and to a monopoly of religious truth, a tendency to be lay rather than clerical, a demand for total allegiance, a willingness to expel people, and a general character of protest.[64] Sometimes, the term 'sect' seems too formal for what were fluid religious groups in the 1640s and 1650s, and the term 'movement' is often more appropriate for some of the newer churches, especially for the Quakers, Seekers and Ranters.[65] After the 1660s the term 'denomination' can be used of the more settled religious groupings.

Because a disproportionate number of women were active participants in the sects, a discussion of religious radicalism during the 1640s and 1650s thus provides an opportunity to examine a wide range of evidence about women's activities. In addition, by analysis of separatist thought and practices, we have an opportunity to explore the limits of radicalism so far as the gender order was concerned. What did the different groups of Independents, Baptists and Quakers, to name the main churches, decide about women and their place in the household, the congregation, and the community? What did the sectarian experience mean for women as individuals and as a sex? These issues raise questions about the long-term significance of religious radicalism for the position of women in English society.

In the richer source material of the religious history of the 1640s and 1650s, more evidence about women can be found than at some other periods. Women themselves wrote a greater proportion of the published work than ever before. The breakdown of censorship allowed a wider variety of publications, and women wrote in increasing numbers after 1640. Particularly in the Society of Friends, women had recourse to the public press.[66] There are also the conventional sources of religious history – tracts, sermons, debates and letters – which can be interrogated afresh for their evidence about questions of gender. In addition, there is one valuable source which has been relatively underutilised: early church books. These were corporate records, kept by men, marking a new stage in the group's evolution into a church. Some date to the 1640s, others to the 1650s.[67] Church books provide evidence both about women's role in the congregations and men's reactions to them. They can be used in conjunction with other records about early congregations, including histories of the sufferings of the faithful.

Many women published writings in the 1640s and 1650s. Some works were controversial, discussing the important issues of the time, such as religious separation and the execution of the king. Prophecies were also widely printed and reported, especially in the 1640s.[68] Authors came from a range of social backgrounds. They included daughters of ministers, wives of printers, comb-makers, poor tradesmen and soldiers, and servants. Many of the churches required evidence of spiritual development before they would admit new members in the 1640s. This rule led to further publications, and encouraged others to nurture their spirituality.[69] After being almost totally ignored, women's writings have attracted more recent attention than any other aspect of female activity during these years.[70]

Katherine Chidley is probably the best known of the female controversialists for her arguments with the Presbyterian minister Thomas Edwards. We know comparatively little about her background. Chidley attended conventicles in Shrewsbury in the 1620s and moved to London around 1630 with her husband, who was a tailor, and their seven children.[71] She had so developed her views of separation that she was able to contribute an important tract to the debate about Independency in 1641. In *The justification of the independent churches of Christ*, Chidley argued that separation from the Church of England was not only lawful but also a duty since that church was subject to the discipline of Antichrist.[72] A congregation made itself a church, and had the right to choose its pastor. Subsequently Chidley debated with the Presbyterian champion, Thomas Edwards. Edwards claimed that the separatists had stolen his parishioners, whom he called his children. 'This', said Chidley, 'is an unjust comparison and crosseth the whole tenour of the Scripture.'[73] Like her contemporaries, she grounded her arguments and rhetoric in the Bible. For example, she mocked Edwards as 'a mighty champion', echoing 1 Samuel 17.45 where Goliath is referred to as such.[74] Her writing was remarkable for the force and confidence of her arguments. She deployed the standard rhetorical ploys about lack of scholarly training, but in such a way that this became a strength: her answers were 'not laid downe in a Schollerik way, but by the plaine truth of Holy Scripture'. Mocking the hireling ministry of the Anglican church, she protested against their inordinate desire for fees.[75] Chidley was to write again during the 1640s for the separatist cause. She did not believe in toleration of all religions, 'for there is but one true Religion, and that is it which hath Gods Word for their rule'.[76] Her son Samuel was prominent in the Leveller movement, and she was active in women's protests. Chidley was last heard of in 1653 reportedly leading 6,000 women to petition the Rump to halt the trial of the Leveller leader, John Lilburne.[77]

The dreams and visions of women and men recorded in print were gendered. Even the most radical men shared the conventional assumptions about the different natures of the two sexes. Gerrard Winstanley, powerful advocate of a more just society, still believed that the sun of righteousness represented the masculine light of reason, while the moon and the earth were the dark, fleshly, feminine part.[78] Even in his ideal society there was a sexual division of labour: sewing, knitting and spinning were women's work.[79] The ideal world envisaged by the Fifth Monarchist, Mary Cary, started from a different premise. Her first object was an improved mortality rate. The saints should be grieved by the deaths of their kin: 'No infant of days shall die; none shall die while they are young: . . . They shall not be afflicted for the loss of their children.'[80]

After 1640, widespread millenarian expectations encouraged women to think that the existing social constraints were irrelevant. Scriptural texts justified active female participation: 'your sons and your daughters shall prophesy' (Joel 2.28–9) seemed more suited to the times than the Pauline texts that women should keep silent in church. There was a greater variety of ideas in print than before 1640, and more choice of religious groups. As individuals, women expressed themselves in speech and in writing. Collectively, women extended the traditional freedom of all subjects to petition to present petitions on a range of public issues.[81] Female petitions called for the restoration of trade and for peace in 1641 and 1642. By 1643 women's petitions for peace were less welcome to the MPs, since the petitioners' views no longer accorded with the views of the Parliamentary majority. Undeterred, women continued to present petitions. In the years of Leveller agitation after 1646, women supported the Leveller cause. In April 1649 when women petitioned and demonstrated for the release of the imprisoned Leveller leaders, they were told to go home to their housewifery. Instead, they returned a week later with an even more strongly worded petition in which they claimed political rights as Christians. It was a high point for female political activity, and women justified their claims in religious terms. In 1659 a large number of Quaker women – 7,000 handmaids of the Lord – petitioned Parliament against tithes.

After 1640, informal religious meetings were widespread, although only a minority of the population was involved. Usually the church courts summoned those who attended 'conventicles', but in 1641 ecclesiastical discipline broke down, which opened the way for greater religious choices. Parents such as the Venns had gone secretly to meetings for prayers around 1639, 'not daring' to tell even their daughter, 'the times being so dangerous'. In the 1640s they allowed her to go with them.[82] Testimonies from women tell of a search from one religious group to another until they found spiritual satisfaction. It would be a mistake to formalise the labels for religious adherence too firmly. Among the lists of 'Grand Blasphemies' published were a range of individual views: a woman 'playing the fool, said, that that was Preaching the Gospel'; another claimed that she could serve God just as well in her bed or at work in her garden as by attending the ordinances on the Lord's day; a butcher's wife affirmed 'that she hath her tribe as well as Christ'.[83]

It is difficult to separate fact from fantasy in accounts of early religious gatherings. Women and men called Adamists were said to have met naked, 'thinking thereby to imitate our first Parents in their innocency'.[84] There were popular stories of people having revelations which justified their rejection of conventional morality. Anne Wells married Mathew Hall without any ceremony, there being 'nothing in Scripture concerning marriage'. One Nicholas Ware then had a revelation that Anne 'was a type of the Church of the Jews', and that since Judah and Israel should be one, he should have sexual relations with her.

Somewhat reluctantly, with her husband's approval, she agreed, but was later abandoned, pregnant, by both.[85]

Within months of the meeting of the Long Parliament, women were reported to be preaching. The numbers and details may have been exaggerated by hostile observers. One claimed that she had a dream of the prophet Anna, who authorised her preaching. Another preached that husbands who crossed wives might lawfully be forsaken. From Kent, there was a report of a woman preaching that the devil was the father of all who did not love Puritans.[86] Those women who preached in London were probably the best known. Mrs Attaway, a lace-maker, was a member of a London General Baptist congregation which met in Bell Alley, Coleman Street. She held meetings for religious exercises, with the approval of the congregation. By 1645 women preached there regularly on Tuesday afternoons, attracting an audience of over a thousand people, or so the heresiographer Thomas Edwards reported. Attaway preached against current Calvinist orthodoxy, saying that 'Christ died for all'.[87] Among other women preachers was one in the Queen's chapel in 1653 described as 'an audacious virago' who was mocked for thumping the pulpit cushion, although this may have been a popular male style of preaching in the early seventeenth century.[88] The most prominent female preachers in the 1650s were Quakers, and they will be discussed in chapter 8. Nor did all those with a message confine themselves to formal preaching. Women engaged in various kinds of dramatic performances. In 1652 one stripped off all her clothes in the back of a crowded Whitehall church for motives unrecorded.[89]

Many men tried to limit women's public participation in religious debate. During the 1640s and 1650s, formal public disputations on religious issues were relatively common, but Ann Hughes has found no examples of ministers permitting women to take part. Certainly women lacked the formal training, but more significantly, few male clergy would consent to debate with women.[90] This did not deter some women from challenging ministers. Katherine Chidley, for example, argued with the Independent William Greenhill, until he grew angry and left.[91] Public female defiance enraged male contemporaries. Christopher Fowler was infuriated when a woman questioned for causing a disturbance on the Lord's day refused to give her name, replying three times in the words of the Lord, 'I am that I am'.[92] Such blasphemy would have aroused ire if a man had uttered it, but it was worse in a woman because she was expected to be submissive and obedient in general, and silent in church.[93]

Some women followed messianic leaders, including Lodowick Muggleton and John Reeve who claimed to be the two last Witnesses of the Spirit.[94] Mary Gadbury, a 30-year-old deserted wife, believed the claim of William Franklin, a married man and father of three, to be the messiah. Her visions, in which she 'saw such a brightness, which she was not able to behold', convinced her of his divinity, and she sold everything in order to follow him. When the magistrates prosecuted them, to Mary's astonishment, Franklin recanted and admitted that his claims were fraudulent. In prison, Gadbury was confused about the status of her visions, sometimes saying she was deceived, but at other times holding to their divine origin. The magistrates deemed 'her offence was the greater, because she so committed it under the cloak of religion'. They punished her more severely than Franklin.[95]

A few women in the sects claimed divine power. It was reported around 1650 that Joan Robins, the wife of the millenarian John Robins who said he was God, claimed that she 'shall bring forth a man child that shall be the Saviour'.[96] Among the Anabaptists, said Baillie, women 'professe themselves to be the church of Christ and Messias to all their own sexe'.[97] Ralph Farmer, antagonist of the Quakers in the 1650s, reported that a woman had claimed she was God, saying that she could make a book like the Greek Bible. Asked where the book was, she replied 'In my fancy'.[98]

Some women offered spiritual leadership themselves. Martha Simmonds in the mid-1650s sought to lead the Quakers.[99] Several women prophets had a following. The breakdown of ecclesiastical control and strong millenarian expectations encouraged female prophecy. Phyllis Mack has estimated that there were over 300 women prophets during the Civil Wars and Interregnum.[100] Prophecy was discussed earlier in chapter 5 as a source of spiritual satisfaction for women close to mysticism and ecstasy. However, during the revolutionary decades, a few women uttered political prophecies which were widely heeded. Women prophets acted as individuals. Although their utterances were gendered, they did not see themselves as spokespersons for their sex.[101] Their message was what mattered. Frequently a woman prophet had a male amanuensis who recorded her words while she was in trance and later published them. There was usually a crowd of visitors of both sexes, including people of high social or political status.

Some examples may indicate the political importance of female prophecy. At the end of the second Civil War, the Army was divided on what to do about the King, whether to put him on trial, and whether to execute him. Some members of the Army were convinced by the testimony of their victory in the war that Charles Stuart was a 'man of blood' against whom the Lord had witnessed. Many of the officers disagreed.[102] On 29 December 1648 and 4 January 1649, Elizabeth Poole appeared before the Army Council and told them of her visions. Her appearance there was probably authorised by Cromwell and Ireton, to reinforce resistance to Leveller demands.[103] Certainly Poole would not have appeared without the support of some powerful officers. But her message of clemency towards the King – to bring him to trial, but spare his life – was not one that the majority of the Council wished to hear. Subsequently Poole was disowned by the Baptist congregation of which she was a member, and the pastor, Kiffin, testified against her to the Council. A letter from a friend, probably another woman, alleged that by casting her out the congregation had deprived her of her livelihood, for she had nothing 'but what she earns by her hands'.[104]

Poole's source of authority was 'the divine will' which, she told the Council, 'cals me to believe, and you to act'. Her view of events was couched in gendered terms. When she read the Army's Remonstrance, which asked for punishment of the King as a capital offender, she felt that 'the pangs of a travelling woman was upon me'. Her message received in a vision was 'the Babe Jesus in mee'.[105] While men might speak of 'Christ within', they did not claim to be pregnant with the divine. Poole used the analogy of husband and wife to explain to the Army why they should put the King on trial but not execute him: 'You never heard that a wife might put away her husband, as he is the head of her body.' There were limits to the subject's obedience, just as to the wife's. Since Charles had treated his people as 'a wife for his own lusts, thereby is the yoake taken from your necks'.[106] A wife might hold the hands of her husband 'that he pierce not your bowels with a knife or sword to take your life', but resist no further.[107] It was a chilling view of the lawful limits of wifely resistance. Men in the Council believed that they could take stronger action.

Anna Trapnel (fl. 1642–60) was a Fifth Monarchist, and her prophecies also had political import. On 7 January 1654 she prophesied while in a trance for twelve days, but it was not until she attracted a large following on her mission to Cornwall that the government took notice of her. After she spoke on behalf of the poor and against the pomp of Cromwell and the rulers of England, the Council of State summoned her to London for questioning and imprisoned her in Bridewell for a time. From October 1657 to August 1658 she was in trance for ten months, sustained only by small beer and toast, and continued to criticise the Protectorate.[108]

Prophecy was not confined to sectarian women. Katherine Johnson, a woman 'of a good Family', warned Charles I not to sign Strafford's death warrant. She prophesied Charles's own destruction, 'but he took none of my counsel, though I was sent from God'. Later in 1653 Johnson told his son, Prince Charles, that his right to the crown of England 'must be in peace, not by the Sword'. She was confident of her authority: 'what I say is by Faith, and I shall justifie it with my life'. The Speaker of the House of Commons, John Lenthall, heeded her warning and stayed away from the House at one point.[109]

Female participation in public religious activitiy during the 1640s and 1650s distinguished these two decades in the early modern period. While the majority of women engaged in private spirituality in their own relationships with the divine, others were active and imaginative in the public religious issues of these revolutionary decades. Their actions were not unprecedented. Indeed, Dorothy Ludlow, in her valuable study of English preaching women, has concluded that the 1640s and 1650s were no new awakening, but rather brought to fruition a long tradition of independent action by women.[110] However, it is my view that women's participation not just in preaching but in the whole spectrum of religious life of the period was on such a massive scale that it did amount to a qualitative change.

FEMALE EMANCIPATION?

Why did women join the sects? Even from hostile accounts by the sectaries' enemies, there is evidence that women exercised judgement in leaving established congregations. In 1645, John Brinsley, a Presbyterian minister in Great Yarmouth, said that women were 'distasted with the publik Ordinances'. They wanted 'pure Ordinances', and hoped for sweetness, spiritual edification and 'soul nourishment' in separation.[111] Broadly, the 'ordinances' with which women were dissatisfied were the administration of the two sacraments, the Lord's supper and baptism, and the preaching of the Word. These women wanted a reformed church which satisfied their spiritual needs.

Women's opportunities to witness to their faith in the 1640s and 1650s were different from those of the Protestant and Catholic women martyrs of the sixteenth century. Seventeenth-century women's conflicts were with local authorities, ministers and justices of the peace, and with assize judges. They took a public role, but they were not martyrs, although many of them suffered imprisonment, physical punishment and violence for the sake of their faith. Because women were assumed to be accessories rather than instigators of action, they were treated more leniently in their conflicts with the established authorities in the 1650s, as the Nayler case illustrates.[112] There are other instances where difference of sex worked in women's favour. For example, Quaker principles about worldly respect and giving 'hat honour' meant that men who refused to remove their hats at the Assizes as a sign of respect for the courts were in trouble for an additional offence. As the early Quaker historian Besse recorded, against women 'the Occasion of the Hat could not be taken'.[113] Yet even if women were viewed as a favoured sex, their participation – and its differentness from that of men – should be examined seriously.

It would be anachronistic to suggest that women found 'emancipation' in the sects. It should not surprise us that the conventional views of woman's nature and place in the world remained essentially the same during the revolutionary period of the 1640s and 1650s. Women's economic opportunities were still restricted and their rates of pay less. There was no alteration in the basic connection between sexuality and reproduction; no change in the concept of woman as the weaker vessel. Language reveals the same fundamental concepts about sexuality that had been current earlier. Men explained their religious behaviour in sexual metaphors which relied for their effect upon clearly understood ideas about good and bad women. For example, when Dennis Hollister left the Baptists for the Quakers in Bristol, he was charged with leaving 'the church'. His denial was phrased in the familiar sexual metaphor: 'to witness the Church I have left the harlot'.[114] So the sects did not offer a fundamentally different view of woman from that of the Anglican church or of society at large.

Yet the sects did provide different opportunities for women to worship. Assumptions about the two sexes continued to influence men's and women's behaviour and spirituality, so there was a gender dimension in all the religious upheavals of the revolutionary decades. How much freedom women found to express their spirituality in the separatist churches and sects of the 1640s and 1650s remains to be considered in later chapters.

7

Separatist churches and sexual politics

GENDER AND THE FORMATION OF SEPARATIST CHURCHES

In contemporary literature and woodcuts, the picture of life in the separatist churches and the sects was of sexual licentiousness. It is the argument here, however, that while there was sexual politics, this was not so much of the kind imagined, but rather of men struggling with women for authority and control. Two paradoxes affected the sects: they promised no distinction between the clergy and the laity, and they asserted the equality of all believers, male and female. In practice, ministers and lay members, men and women were all viewed differently.[1]

There is a range of evidence for discussing the role of gender in the churches of the Civil Wars and Interregnum. Especially valuable are church books and minutes which provide evidence of the churches' views on issues of morality. Unlike the heresiographies, church books deal with named people in specific geographical locations. In addition to primary sources, there is also an extensive secondary literature about the separatists, or radicals.[2]

In the 1640s, after the church courts ceased to function, individuals who wished to meet together to discuss religious matters had less fear of prosecution. As we saw earlier, from Elizabethan times onwards the separatists had disregarded the conventional ideas about sacred places, and there were records of separatists meeting in rooms upstairs in taverns in the City of London or out in fields. Frequently, there were meetings in private houses. 'They account their own houses as holy as the Church' observed John Taylor in disgust in 1641.[3] This use of private dwellings and meetings at night made it harder for the separatists to be detected, and Baillie was convinced that such meetings were 'a very pregnant meanes to steale way men and women from their own Pastors'.[4] Among the Baptists, the essential rite of baptism was not performed at the font of the parish church but rather in rivers and streams. Nevertheless, although many sectaries were not restricted in their attitudes to places of worship, not all of those even among the radicals shared these views. Some places still seemed inappropriate for worship. For example, in 1640 in Bristol one radical, Mr Cann, preached on a green. He wanted to hire a barn, but the congregation could not accept this because 'the tincture of consecrated places was not off the people'.[5] However, some of the less radical separatist congregations took over regular places of worship, such as cathedrals or parish churches.[6] In Exeter, for example, the cathedral was divided in two by a wall, with a Presbyterian congregation meeting in the chancel, while an Independent congregation worshipped in the nave.[7] More radical groups refused to occupy such churches because of their beliefs about the objectionable nature of tithes and of a settled ministry.

Not surprisingly, the men and women who later formed separate congregations found it difficult to date 'the first gathering of the church'.[8] In the early, less formalised stages, women often played a significant role which has been obscured by historians' concentration on the role of ministers in the 'foundation' of a particular church. In Bristol, the process of separation for the Baptists began with meetings to read over notes of the sermons, pray together and fast. The Broadmead records indicate that this had been the pattern for over twenty years until 1645. At this time, the congregation was divided, and some people separated and covenanted together to be a church. They usually met every Sunday afternoon at a brewer's house, 'namely, at one Mrs Nethway's, a woman who in her day was very eminent for godlinesse'. When the church became dissatisfied with their minister, Nathaniel Ingello, for 'his Flaunting apparell' and his enthusiasm for music, it was Mrs Nethway who rode into Wales to hear another minister, Thomas Ewins, and who 'was ye Instrument, when she came home, to perswade ye Leading brethren of ye Congregation that they were to endeavour to gett ye said Mr. Ewins'.[9] Both as a householder and a woman of initiative, this widow was instrumental in the formation of the church.

Among those of Independent theology, the decision to gather together as a church was followed by the formal process of signing a covenant. If a covenant was to be made by all the church members, each church had to decide if women were to sign. What happened is not always clear. Surviving church books for Independent congregations of the 1640s and 1650s suggest that women did swear the covenant, but they were usually listed in separate columns, which suggests that their position as members was ambiguous.[10]

Admission to an Independent congregation was usually by testimony of the believer. The profession in words of a personal Christian experience may, Nuttall comments, 'seem to be asking too much of the common man'.[11] It asked even more of the ordinary woman who was required to speak for herself. Some congregations did make allowance for female modesty and women's alleged inability to speak before an audience. In the Keysoe congregation in the 1670s, once Independent, later Baptist, women 'being bashfull and fearefull to speake publicly' were permitted to give their testimonies privately to two or three friends.[12]

In their public admission statements, women spoke of their spiritual struggles and offered their own views about significant religious experiences.[13] They engaged in a new form of self-expression. Elizabeth Avery stated that public worship gave her 'no comfort, nor ease, nor could I eat or drink' in the 1640s. But after nine months of despair, she found full assurance, as she testified to John Rogers' Independent Dublin congregation three years later.[14]

There were some common elements in the testimonies. Very often the experiences dated to impressionable adolescent years as girls came to terms with their adult responsibilities. There was no expectation that salvation would be won easily, for did not the Bible tell of Jacob 'wrestling with the Lord'? Traditional Christian theology encouraged women to accept their suffering: 'no cross no crown' was a commonly heard saying. Personal experiences, such as bereavements, often precipitated crises. One woman explained that after she had buried a child, with great grief, 'then was I more fully convinced of sin'. Her response was the conventionally pious one. She studied the Scriptures, listened to sermons, and 'thought I might make use of those full promises which was made to those that came to him'.[15] Another woman had several misfortunes, including a husband wounded in the Wars, but it was not until her son died suddenly that she recognised the hand of the Lord. In despair for her sins, which she feared had caused the deaths of her children, she learned to find comfort from the sermons of one minister and from discussions with another.[16] A widow, cast down by the death of her husband, also found comfort in sermons and several Scriptural texts.[17] Here it is important to recognise that women did not set out to defy fathers, husbands or ministers: rather, the intensity of their search for individual salvation, and their strong assurance of the authenticity of their own experiences, meant that their defiance of the world was apt to be a logical development from initial premises. There is no evidence in women's own testimonies that they joined the sects for the sake of freedom or licence, and we should be careful of attributing motives to them on the basis of the comments of their critics.

It is often difficult to decide in what sense women were members of the congregation. No doubt this reflected contemporary uncertainty. As we shall see, many of the divisions in the churches related to debates about women's role, and ultimately practices varied. Evidence from Goodwin's gathered Independent church from 1639 to 1660 indicates that while women could join in discussions, none ever signed a public declaration of the church. Ellen More concluded in her study that women seemed disqualified from office-holding, from voting, and from publicly representing the church. Nevertheless, More has listed four women out of fifty named persons as representing the active core of the congregation, although she did not state the basis for this classification.[18] The Hubbard–How–More covenant was signed in May 1648 by men only, 'In the behalfe of the Rest'.[19] The Baptists did not make a formal church covenant, but members' names were usually listed near the beginning of the church book. In one London Baptist congregation, known as the Chamberlen congregation,[20] the issue of female membership is puzzling. Women's names were listed separately from those of men, as though they were a different type of church member. However, there are no signs of women's marital status or occupations, which suggests that women were accepted in congregations as individuals. Yet the metaphor in which members discussed their congregation was of an organic whole, the body. If an individual left the church, they spoke of amputation: 'our small body cannot be but much defiled, weakened & disenabled by the amputation of so many members'.[21]

Although questions about female membership are difficult, one point remains clear: in most of the separatist congregations, women outnumbered men. Surviving membership lists in church books indicate that women might outnumber men by as many as two to one. For example, the Great Yarmouth Congregational church began with thirteen men and seventeen women in November 1642, but in the Bunyan congregation in 1655, there were seventeen women and eight men.[22]

MINISTERS AND LAITY: POWER IN THE SECTS

The crucial question was who had power or authority in the sect. Voting about church membership, discipline and the appointment of officers all raised the issue in an acute form. Did women and the people generally, John Bastwick questioned in 1645, 'have the power of the Keyes'?[23] If women participated, then they were exercising authority over men. In the Independent congregation of John Rogers in Dublin, women had full voting rights, but Rogers admitted that there had been bitter contention, as 'most men doe arrogate a Soveraignty to themselves'. He concluded that 'Votes concern all, ergo all must vote.'[24] The issue of voting marks the limits of radicalism in the sects. Either voting was on the basis of church membership, and all were to share in calling church officers and in discipline, or women's rights to vote were denied, and they were not full church members.

If churches accepted the idea of a ministry as one of their 'ordinances', then women's participation in the choice of a minister involved authority. By the mid-seventeenth century, the Protestant ministers were a professional group distinct from the laity. They expected to lead and to advise the laity on matters of church government, worship and social relations. The Congregationalists and Baptists accepted a ministry, paid either by existing tithes or voluntary contributions; the Quakers did not. In the Independent churches, a pastor was usually chosen by the congregation. It was said by the Independents' enemies that women participated in the choice. Practices appear to have varied from church to church, and over time. In 1675 the Norwich Congregational church recorded explicitly that only the men chose the ministers.[25] Baptist pastors were usually selected by the congregation, but as each congregation was autonomous, practices varied. Some church books from the end of the seventeenth century indicate that women voted, by raising their hands.

The duties of the minister, pastor or leader varied. In most sects, whatever the sacraments were deemed to be – and this was contentious – they were administered by men. Although in earlier heresies, some women had been priests and may even have administered the sacrament of the Lord's Supper, I have found only one example of a woman, that of Martha Simmonds, who offered bread and wine to the congregation. No church ever gave to women this sacred power. No women in the Independent or Baptist churches could be church officers, that is, pastors or elders. No women were ever sent as messengers when the church wanted to resolve vital policy, as in 1656, when nine men went to find what to do about 'the personall appearing of Christ' and what policy they should adopt towards the present government, even though women were concerned.[26] However, there was one specifically female office in the Independent and Baptist churches, that of deaconess. The

Independent church at Great Yarmouth instituted the office in 1650 on the basis of the New Testament precedent.[27]

The minister's position in relation to his congregation was a matter of dispute. On the whole, ministers believed that they were parents, fathers, or even husbands of their people.[28] This role conferred great authority upon them, including that derived from the fifth commandment. At the same time, ministers were vulnerable, as was any father of a family, to the disobedience and disorder of wife or children. Katherine Chidley denied the ministers this patriarchal relationship in one of her printed works. She argued that Christ gave the keys to his spouse, the true church, the congregation. Just as in a husband's absence, a wife was not subject to servants, so the congregation, the bride of Christ, was not subject to the minister, her servant. This was an extraordinary reversal of customary authority as it gave women a share in the power of the keys.[29]

During the 1640s and 1650s many women as well as men challenged the rights of the ministry. Mrs Attaway, a preacher around 1640, apparently denied 'that any in the world this day living had any commision to preach'.[30] Such a challenge to the minister's pre-eminence, to the boundary between him and the laity, threatened the whole doctrine, or ordinance, of the ministry. What logical exception could there be to their administering the sacraments? And if women could be priests, why could they not aspire higher, to bring forth the divine, or even, to be God?

If women could speak in church, they could exercise authority over men, and also have sacred power. Two Pauline texts were regularly cited about women keeping silence in church:

> Let the woman learn in silence with all subjection.
> But I suffer not a woman to teach, nor to usurp authority over the man, but to be in silence.
>
> (1 Timothy 2. 11–12)

But what did silence and speaking mean? Even in the Anglican church women's voices were to be heard as part of the congregation's liturgical response and in the set words of a service, such as that of marriage. Certainly in private, women had a role in talking of Scripture, teaching their families and, with due deference, admonishing their husbands.[31]

The 'speaking' which caused most difficulty was the public preaching by women, in which they exercised authority over the congregation, including men. The Bible authorised female as well as male prophecy: 'I will pour out my spirit upon all flesh; and your sons and your daughters shall prophesy' (Joel 2.28). All the churches directly inspired by the

Holy Spirit – Baptists and Quakers particularly – recognised that women could receive the Lord's messages. Even if female prophecy seemed an extraordinary rather than an everyday occurrence, the times appeared to justify it. Millenarian aspirations were widespread in the 1640s and 1650s, encouraging many people in the belief that the last days of the world had arrived. Women speaking as prophets could therefore be accepted as a sign that the 'latter days' were upon the church.

Problems about female speech arose when any church functioned in public, that is, was at worship according to the ordinances established by Christ. In public, before the world, women had no authority or right to participate. However, in some of the sects, there was certain business which the church conducted in private from the world, as a group of believers. For example, the records of the Particular Baptist churches in the Midlands in the 1650s show that distinctions were made between the church business which was to be performed before the world, and what was private, purely for the church. Baptism, preaching, prophesying, prayer, 'breaking of bread', and excommunication were all public, while admonitions, the trial of preaching gifts and the fitness of officers were private church business.[32] In one congregation, when a woman's speaking was complained of, the minister said that she should speak, 'but it must be by a Brother'.[33] Whether women were to be involved in the church's private business, and on what terms, was an issue for most separatist congregations.

Speaking could involve formal argument and debate, skills in which women were not trained. Anne Pharepoint, of the Fenstanton church, was forced to debate her choice of spouse when she was visited by two elders who charged her with 'taking a husband contrary to the mind of the congregation'. One elder swept aside her answer that she thought it was no sin: if she had not sinned, 'then the church has sinned in charging of you'.[34] Yet while these women lacked debating skills, nevertheless they still asserted their point of view, and their right to differ.

Among the Quakers, women had the greatest freedom of speech. Ann Audland was an active speaker in the 1650s, although a later testimony to her as Ann Camm showed how women's position had changed. By the end of the century, she was praised as

> not forward to appear in preaching or prayer in public meetings, . . . for without extraordinary impulse and concern, it was rare for her to preach in large meetings, where she knew there were brethren qualified for such meetings.

146

Camm was said to have advised her own sex not to be 'too hasty, forward or unseasonable in their appearing at such meetings'.[35] In the Particular Baptist congregations of the Abingdon Association, the meetings considered 'how far a woman may speak in the church and how far not'. In 1658 they reiterated the earlier resolution of 1656: 'A woman may not publikely teach in the church. . . . She may not speake in prayer as the mouth of the church.'[36] In the Chamberlen congregation, the question of which women might properly speak was raised. Ultimately, after great debate, they decided that a woman's marital status was irrelevant: any maid, wife or widow could speak. However, if it was a question of uttering a prophecy, men were the ones to decide if this was appropriate.[37] Similarly, in Rogers' Independent congregation in Dublin, if speaking meant preaching, then women had no permission to speak. Because of the danger of disorders in the church, 'your silence may sometimes be the best advocate of your orderly liberty'. [38] Biblical models could encourage a woman to break her silence. Just as the woman of Samaria had rushed to tell the people of the coming of the Messiah, so some women in the 1640s and 1650s experienced the call to preach Christ's message.

THEORIES AND PRACTICES OF FAMILY RELATIONSHIPS IN BAPTIST AND INDEPENDENT CHURCHES

The sects' attitudes towards family relationships were varied and sometimes contradictory. At one extreme is the statement of the Quaker, Thomas Parnell, in 1655: 'Christ is come to set at variance father against son, and son against father, and the wife against the man, and the man against the wife.'[39] At the other is the separatist churches' record of discipline. They consistently supported conventional family values against disobedient wives, children and servants. Yet their contemporaries were unaware of this conservatism. Instead, they focused upon the danger which the sects represented because the sects encouraged female participation. Not surprisingly, many people likened the sects' apparent disregard of family bonds to the tactics employed by the Papists, and particularly the Jesuits. Earlier in 1624 John Gee had published a story of a young gentlewoman whose mistress had tried to persuade her to become a nun. To her protest that her widowed mother would object, the Jesuits replied 'you must not respect your mother in these matters. Shee is an Hereticke'.[40] Just as the Papists had allegedly urged individuals to defy family duty, so the sects were accused of encouraging family disunity. During the 1650s many people feared that the Papist cause was being advanced under the guise of the sects.[41]

During the period of the Civil Wars and after, the question of suitable marriage partners for believers was discussed in various congregations. Behind the practical question of whether a believer might marry an unbeliever was a theology of marriage: what kind of partnership or union it was to be. The Particular Baptists of Abingdon resolved that while it was not unlawful to marry an unbeliever, church members should be careful. They upheld one of the conventional restrictions on marriage within the prohibited degrees. It was neither 'expedient nor of good report', they noted, for a saint to marry with his dead brother's wife.[42]

Many of the sects took a conventional view of marital conduct. Wives were to be obedient and faithful, respecting their husbands' authority. Relatively few domestic issues came before the churches in the years before the Restoration. Possibly because the churches were more fluid, there were fewer records kept. In the early stages, too, the level of commitment required may have meant that believers were more careful about their conduct. As time passed, strains developed. The church itself may have concluded that the definition of social relationships and the exercise of discipline were all marks or signs of the true church, and therefore have been more concerned to censure sinners. Nevertheless, there are a few examples of discipline from some of the sects as early as the 1650s. In 1654 Sister Smith, a member of Peter Chamberlen's Baptist congregation, was questioned for abusing her husband, calling him 'Dog &c'. There were differing responses from the male leaders of the church. One man told Brother Smith that he should put up with her abuse, but Chamberlen disagreed, translating her offence from a private to a public one: a husband 'might bear with offences to him: but not to God'. The record, probably kept by Chamberlen himself at this point, noted that Sister Smith was humbled and reconciled.[43] Husbands, too, were expected to conform to conventional ideals of behaviour. In 1657 Tiverton Baptist meeting resolved that there was no Scriptural precedent for a man to strike his wife. Twenty years later, in Bunyan's Baptist church, a man was expelled 'for beating hir [his wife] often for very light matters'.[44]

By contrast, household duties were less emphasised in the more radical sects than they were in the Anglican church. Possibly this was in part explicable in terms of the millenarian excitement of the 1640s and 1650s. As the New Jerusalem was imminent, long-term planning was less significant. Furthermore, wives and mothers might themselves receive the call of the spirit to bear witness, and this was more important than any child-care or household responsibility. A poor woman, Elinor Channel, was struck dumb until her husband gave her permission to leave him and their small children to deliver the Lord's message to Oliver Cromwell.[45]

Parents were less directly responsible for their children's salvation in a separatist church, where membership was by the individual's decision. This raised some awkward questions about baptism. Was baptism to be something done for the child, to bring it into the church, or was it for an adult believer only? Differences on this issue were fundamental to the existence of the Baptists as a separate church. Even in the established church, some mothers expressed doubts about the ceremony of infant baptism, or the 'sprinkling' of their babies. Mary Penington listened to all the ministers she 'formerly delighted to hear' on the subject of her duty to have her child baptised, 'but I could not consent and be clear'.[46] Lucy Hutchinson also examined the arguments for infant baptism, but could not be persuaded.[47] In both these cases the women were of gentry status, which no doubt assisted them in holding to their own opinions. Baillie said that the Independents would not baptise all: 'who can say that an particular Infant is holy?'[48] Parents were nevertheless concerned with the godly upbringing of children, hoping that this might pre-dispose them to salvation, even if it could not guarantee the immediate call of the spirit. It is not clear from the records, however, at what age the sects would admit children who were acting in defiance of their parents. There are many instances of adolescents being accepted, but I know of no very young children. Nor is it clear what the separatist churches decided about the fate of unbaptised children, nor stillbirths and miscarriages.

Masters had a duty to instruct their servants in true religion and to restrain sin. But just as the limits of obedience needed definition for the believing wife of an unbelieving husband, so too the servant could raise the question of how far obedience should extend. In 1656 the Baptist congregation at Tiverton resolved that while servants should obey their masters' just commands, they should obey God rather than men.[49]

After a woman was admitted to a church, the men who led the congregation expected her to behave submissively. There is evidence that some women continued to think independently. The records of the General Baptist congregation of Fenstanton show several cases of women ceasing to attend. In 1652, two elders from the congregation visited Sister Smith to admonish her. She told them that she had withdrawn for a 'private walking', in which she found comfort. Nor was she persuaded to return by their argument that 'she had no Scriptural warrant'.[50] Another said that she absented herself from the ordinances because 'I find no comfort in them. . . . I have received greater manifestations; for God dwelleth in me, and I in him'.[51] Widow Sanders claimed 'her own experience' as her justification for what she said, although one of the two visiting elders, Henry Denne, deprecated her personal authority, arguing that 'we have a more sure word of prophecy'.[52] When some of the sisterhood were dissatisfied, they did not mince their words in saying so. Elizabeth More told Chamberlen's London congregation that she had not found Christ with them, only confusion and disorder 'when I haued stayed all night big with child to watch and pray exspecting the comfortabell presence of god amoungst you wch he hath promised to his, Matt. 18.20'.[53]

Male leaders of the sect wanted women to obey them – or the church – rather than husbands. Rebecca Eliazer was the wife of a Jew who had converted and joined Chamberlen's congregation in order to marry her. After she allowed her husband to take their child to be 'sprinkled' by the Presbyterians, the church summoned her for questioning. In a written plea she attempted to distinguish between her duty as a church member and her duty as a wife:

> as i ow subiection for my self to you as a chuch soe i also ow subiection to him as a husband in such things as he ought to haue the command . . .[54]

The church ruled that she was responsible for her own actions, and could not shelter under the protection of wifely obedience. Ministers and husbands could thus come into conflict with each other over female behaviour.

Women were not, of course, the only absentees who were questioned. But in their case they were visited by members of the opposite sex, to whom they were expected to be subordinate. They were probably more accustomed to submit than men, and did comply in some instances. In Chamberlen's London congregation in 1654, Sister Anne Harriman stayed away because a man in the congregation objected to her speaking in public. He would 'not walk with such as gave libertie to women to speak in ye church. . . . And therefore rather than Brother Nandon should withdraw, she would withdraw'.[55]

According to the church books, the elders usually had the last word. Yet even from these records, something of the women's attitudes can be deduced. Sometimes their actions were expressive. In the instance cited, Ann Harrison manifested her displeasure by leaving. At Fenstanton, in

1652, John Denne went with another man to admonish widow Sanders four months after the first confrontation. This time they reported that she was angry. She said that she could prove her position out of Scripture, but she would not, because she knew that would not satisfy them. She declined a debate in which she would be outnumbered two to one, and from which there could be no witness to her victory. Furthermore, although the men reported that she 'multiplied many words to no purpose (which are too tedious here to relate)', they did record the encounter. Sanders spoke of

> how God had carried her out of the one dispensation unto another, and now He had brought her out of those fleshly ordinances which we walk in, and truly she would not be brought back again to them.

Her challenge touched the very basis of the sect's existence. Elders could conclude that they 'were confident she was deceived', the church could excommunicate her, but they could not compel her to agree.[56] Whether a woman's departure from a congregation is understood as excommunication or withdrawal frequently depends upon the stance of the reader.

During the 1650s, men leading the separatist congregations found themselves challenged by women, as ministers of the established church had earlier. Around 1657, for example, Thomas Ewins, a Baptist minister, was interrupted in his sermon by Sarah Latchet, a former Baptist who had joined the Quakers. Ewins was addressing the congregation who had assembled to break bread, when Sarah began speaking 'with a loud shrill voice'. The terms in which Latchet was both attacked and defended were conventional. Ewins declared that 'It were fitter such an idle huswife were whipt, and sent to Bridwell to work, then to go about rayling at people as she did.'[57] The defence was that she was 'diligent in honest employment'.[58] Any woman who participated in violent or radical public activity risked her sexual identity. Her behaviour could outrage other women: the wife of a justice labelled the Quaker, Ann Blaykling, 'no woman but a man'.[59] Gradually the conflicts between men and women in the sects in the 1650s fell into a predictable pattern and were resolved in favour of men.

Contradiction and ambiguity marked the attitudes of both sexes to female roles in the church. Women who wanted to speak of the Lord, to tell of his messages, were uncertain about the propriety of their public witness. Responsible members of the congregation soon found that if they did not follow the male leaders, they were branded as contumacious and in some cases excommunicated. Their personal lives might be more restricted than before. Although men too were subject to the discipline of the churches, they could participate in making the rules; no women had the power to attend the Baptist assemblies to determine the rules. Women of an independent spirit, who continued to think and who expressed criticisms, found that they were in trouble. Patriarchal authority was to be respected in the sects, just as in the world at large. Women were expected to subdue the independent thinking which had taken them into a sect as soon as the authority of a minister and elders had been established over the congregation. Basically, the sects were conservative in their views of family relationships. Although individual men might come into conflict with the patriarchal authority of the church, on gender issues they usually closed ranks. Ultimately, collective male authority in the sect was substituted for the authority of an individual husband or master. A non-believing husband was not to be obeyed, but wives of believers were to be conventionally good. Similarly, the children or servants of non-believers were to obey the church rather than the parent or master. While contemporaries sought to discredit the sects for countenancing the disobedience of wives, children and servants, and certainly they did in the matter of joining, once the believer was a member of the church, conventional social norms were enforced. To outside observers, the sects apppeared to condone disruptive family behaviour; from inside, their discipline was usually stricter than that of the Anglican church before or after 1660.

But conventional norms were not upheld in the sect without a struggle. While the men who ruled in the sects had one eye to the censures of the outside world, the other was to their own interests within the sect in controlling the female element. Since women within some sects challenged their authority, this led to conflicts. Not surprisingly, few records of disputes survive, but one conflict in Stucley's Independent congregation in Exeter in the 1650s aroused such contention that various people published their versions of the controversy.

A CONGREGATION IN CONFLICT: SEXUAL POLITICS IN EXETER 1650–7

In 1657, Susanna Parr and Mary Allein were excommunicated from the Independent congregation meeting in Exeter cathedral. The incident caused something of a stir. Six pamphlets which discussed the events were subsequently published.[60] The conventional story, first told by Edmund Calamy, and later recounted by Geoffrey Nuttall, was that the minister, Lewis Stucley, accused the two women of being disorderly because they had gone to hear other ministers preach. Admonished and told to return, they refused, so the ministers excommunicated them. Nuttall, described as the doyen of historians of later Nonconformity,[61] apologised for his lengthy discussion of the incident. It may 'seem too trivial to merit the space allotted to it', he wrote, but he believed that it illustrated the gap between the Congregationalists' ideals and their practices. To be visible saints was sometimes too difficult. Nevertheless, he concluded, 'the troubles of the church at Exeter should not irritate us but deepen our sympathy. Heroic or pathetic, they were men of like weaknesses with our own.'[62]

There is another way of looking at this incident, and that is from the women's point of view. While the sources are more limited, the pamphlets, especially those by Susanna Parr, the anonymous E. T., and Mary Allein's husband do provide an alternative interpretation. The women's version heightens various conflicts: the purpose of the church, they claimed, was 'to have the Gospel more discovered in greater light and beauty', not separation.[63] There are hints of the minister claiming excessive power over the lives of his parishioners and even of sexual harassment.

Susanna Parr wanted a church which would meet her needs. Not much is known about her, except that she was a married woman in 1654, well-enough educated to be able to write, with friends in the City government and the Parliament. In the 1640s she looked for the realisation of public promises of 'a thorough Reformation'. She was impressed with the New England congregational model, so in 1650 she joined Stucley's secret weekly meetings.[64] Gradually the word spread of its 'purity of Ordinances and excellent Administrations'. Others sought admission in the customary sectarian way, by testifying their experiences. Among those who joined were Tobie Allein, a prosperous Exeter serge maker who had friends among the town's oligarchy, and his wife, Mary. She was probably in her late twenties or thirties, had young children and was pregnant again in 1657.[65]

Around 1654, differences arose. Susanna Parr left the congregation a little later and returned to the Presbyterian church. In 1657, Mary Allein left also, and her husband subsequently followed her.[66] Lewis Stucley and his co-minister, Thomas Mall, alleged that both women were disorderly because they went to hear other ministers. Since they refused to listen to the church's admonition, the ministers excommunicated them.[67]

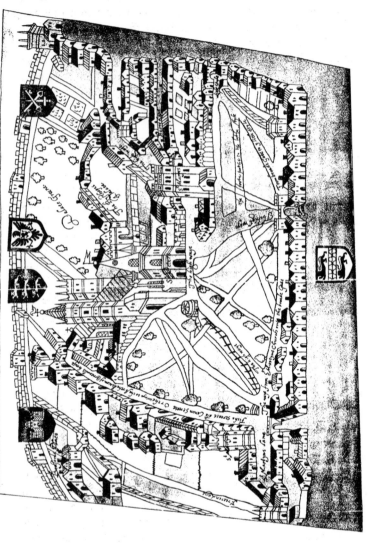

Figure 8. Susanna Parr and Mary Allein worshipped with an Independent congregation meeting in Exeter Cathedral. The illustration shows the Cathedral in the late sixteenth century. From John Vowell, alias Hooker, *The Discription of the Cittie of Excester, c. 1587* (Bodleian Library, Oxford).

Excommunication presented problems to small separatist congregations. It was vital to a true church that it could discipline its members and, as a last resort, cast sinners out.[68] Earlier, in the medieval church, the excommunicant was denied civil rights and Christian burial and barred from the company of Christians. While the effectiveness of the censure had waned before the Reformation, and continued to do so afterwards, studies of the church courts show that the exclusion from burial in consecrated ground and the denial to women of any assistance from a midwife still caused anxiety. The social effects often depended upon popular opinion.[69] In the 1640s, after the Long Parliament abolished the ecclesiastical courts, the situation changed. The multiplication of religious sects meant that denial of communal rights was no longer possible. Those excluded from one congregation could join another. Hence the sentence actually delivered by Stucley and Mall was more than the conventional delivery to Satan and call to repentance, because the ministers needed to intimidate the two women. Just how far they went was a matter for dispute. One version claimed that there was 'a hideous howling cry', followed by a lengthy prayer from Thomas Mall that the Lord would fetch them back: 'O let Satan torment them home . . . there is that upon them, will cost them eternal flames, unlesse they return.'[70] The social effects did worry the two women, for they found themselves vilified everywhere, 'at their doores; and stops, and tables'.[71]

The history of this congregation thus becomes one about the power of ministers over laity, men over women. We can analyse the excommunication in terms of conflicts over women's roles, and who should define these, men or the women themselves. The disputes focused on three main issues relating to women's position in the congregation.

First, there was the question of women's speaking. Clearly, the Biblical prohibition was not intended to be absolute. Susanna Parr said that initially, speaking 'was usually practised amongst us by the rest of my Sex'. The power to speak was said 'to be in the body of the people, in the multitude, so that everyone had the liberty . . . whether men or women'.[72] Some of the men found Susanna Parr's speaking burdensome. Perhaps it was because she had a different view of worship and disliked debate: she objected to psalm singing and to arguments about forms of church government. In her view, 'the work of this generation is not the constituting, but the Reforming of Churches, which I conceived separation did hinder'.[73] Nevertheless, since she knew that speaking out was not usual for women, when Stucley told her that someone in the congregation objected, she readily agreed to keep silent in future. Later, it was argued against her both that she had not made public her disquiet, and also that she was contentious.[74] As Tobie Allein pointed out in defence of his wife's silence, it was an impossible situation, for Mrs Allein was blamed for speaking and blamed for silence.[75]

The author of one of the pamphlets offered a more generalised analysis of the situation. From the citation of Scriptural examples of women advising and admonishing men – David heeded the advice of Abigail, so 'you may mine' – and the passion of the argument for the rights of women as church members, I suspect that the author was a woman.[76] The author argued that to cite the Pauline texts about women keeping silence in church was ridiculous. It was only when women of the congregation criticised Stucley's irregular proceedings that he reproved them for speaking. There were at least four occasions when women should speak as members of the congregation. First, just as Priscilla delivered a rebuke, Acts 18.26, so should all women. Second, women could teach their own sex. 'Yea', E. T. claimed, 'you were formerly very free, and also practised it, to have Women pray in your company, and your selfe Joyning with them in spirit only, whilest they were the Mouth in the Duty.' Furthermore, E. T. said that women had to give their views of those applying for admission, and that when women sang, they could be asked questions. (This latter point seems to refer to a special kind of solo singing for which Baptists later claimed that special gifts and training were necessary.) The final occasion for female speech was the extraordinary occasion, for which again there was Biblical warrant cited. Just as Anna, a prophetess, spoke (Luke 2.37, 38) and the four daughters of Philip, virgins who prohesied (Acts 21.9), so women might be called to speak in a church.[77]

Second, was a good woman permitted to interpret events which revealed God's intentions? When one of Mary Allein's children died, she decided that this was a sign that the Lord had withdrawn from their congregation so she left too, in defiance of her husband, who remained a member for some time.[78] Susanna too, had a dear child die, and then began to think about church policy. Separation, she concluded, was a sin. Both women interpreted their personal griefs as providences sent from the Lord to guide them.[79]

Most significant of all, there was the question of women's involvement in the politics of the nation and of the church. In 1657, when Mary Allein learned that the men in the congregation were engaged in petitioning the Lord Protector not to take the crown, she begged her husband to have no part in it. She argued that the signatories to the petition were in danger of treason. Mary Allein had a political position which influenced that of her husband. Subsequently, she defended her action on the grounds that she was a good wife who acted to save her husband.[80] Susanna Parr claimed that she too had political connections. She said that her attendance at Presbyterian sermons was winked at 'so long as I had a friend that might pleasure them in the City and in the Parliament'.[81] On the issue of the excommunication of the two women, it was alleged that the female members of the church were wrongfully disenfranchised. Biblical precedents were cited by E. T. for the exercise of church discipline:

> Did the Apostle meane only the officers and major part of the Brethren of that Church? and that the Rest, together with the Women, might stay at home, and needed not come together to inflict this Censure? how came you to take away these Keyes from the Minor part of the Brethren and from the Sisters? Are they not all Believers? Have Women no Soules? or no Faith?

Finally, E. T. asked Brother Stucley whom he meant by speaking for the church: 'Doe you meane your selfe, and the Major-Part of the Men?'[82] The implication was that the congregation was divided on sex lines and that the women in the congregation were not consulted; Stucley and the major part of the men were only a minority usurping control of the congregation.

Not surprisingly, the ministers concentrated on attacking the women's characters. Mary was a bad wife who could not be trusted, acted without her husband's authority, and brought scandal on him by her disorder. She did not accept her wifely role, finding her house a prison and her husband a 'Nabal'.[83] By quoting Proverbs verses 8 and 9 against Mary Allein, the ministers insinuated that she was 'a very strumpet'.[84] In attacking the character of a woman as wife, the ministers brought dishonour to her husband: 'he sucks the blood of my reputation', said Toby Allein. Allein attempted to counter the ministers' attacks by showing what a good and obedient wife Mary was. He also claimed that his domestic affairs were his own business. He alleged that the ministers usurped power which properly belonged to a husband, because they asserted that he, Allein, had no power to forgive his wife for actions which had offended him. Among the incidents in contention were that Mary had made a journey to consult a minister without her husband's knowledge, that her companion on the journey was an infamous woman, that Mary had quarrelled with her husband's sister three years earlier, and that she had dismissed a servant. The ministers claimed that since all these sins were public, no husband could forgive them. Toby's pardoning of his wife's journey they paralleled with pardoning incest.[85] Here they intruded into what a man considered was the private sphere between husband and wife. Allein complained that the minister had no business overseeing his household: 'this looks but like a sneaking trick, to pry and peep into other folkes cupboards and kitchens to discover their household-affaires'.[86]

Clearly, the women were challenging the minister's power and control in the congregation. Paradoxically, the stereotypes of women as weak and feeble jostled in the dispute with images of them as powerful and dangerous. In her published defence, Parr herself appealed to the classic stereotype of the weak woman:

> Weakness is entailed upon my sex in generall, and for my selfe in particular, I am a despised worme, a woman full of naturall and sinfull infirmities.[87]

'Weake women', she claimed, were not so well able to defend themselves 'so well as men, especially Schollers'.[88] Yet in composing and publishing her own version of events, she challenged the ministers' version. Neither she nor Mary Allein was poor or friendless. Parr was well-enough educated to be able to write, and Mary Allein often took charge of her husband's serge-making business, which employed over 500 workers, when he was away for a month or so.[89]

Most interesting of all is that Susanna Parr claimed the right to define the quarrel as one about sexual power. The very title of her pamphlet gives this clue: *Susanna's apology against the elders.* Her Biblically well-read audience knew that Susanna's case was one of sexual harassment. Parr said that Stucley allowed people to speak of sins not fit to be mentioned. She implied that as a modest woman she was able to state that his reputation was tarnished. Mary Allein was also troubled that when some people applied for admission to the church, they spoke publicly of sins not fit to be named. For herself, she declined to speak with Stucley 'single or alone', thereby implying that he was not to be trusted.[90] But worst of all, Parr alleged that men in the congregation attributed inappropriate husbandly power to the minister. One elder said that when she went to hear other ministers preach, expecting some benefit thereby, 'I might as well take delight in another man that was not my husband'. On another occasion, Stucley and an elder told her that to seek other ministers' preaching was the same as 'to goe after another man because of fruitfulnesse'. Parr was troubled at 'this gross discourse' and told him that the relations between husband and wife and minister and congregation 'were of a different nature'.[91] The implications of the minister's remarks seem extraordinarily revealing: did he really see himself as a husband to all his female parishioners? If so, he was vulnerable, for his masculinity was undermined when women went to other sermons.

Perhaps when historians write of 'redoubtable women' and 'formidable ladies' they should ponder why they find women who defy male authority so threatening. In reviewing this story from the women's perspective, we can see how ideas about the respective roles of men and women were central to the dispute. While this is not the only possible reading of the incident, for there is undoubtedly a history about Exeter politics and the relationship of the town to the central government, nevertheless to ignore this gender issue distorts our understanding of the personal interactions in a religious sect. The politics of the congregation were not all about theological issues. Sexual politics, which involved women's desires to play a part in the decision-making of the congregation, and men's desires to keep them under control, were central to the life of the separatist congregations. Women's determination to claim their rights and responsibilities as good Christian women posed a challenge to the male leaders. In this case, although the women subscribed to conventional notions of female inferiority, such arguments could be turned around: as Parr said, Christ gave the weak power to confound the mighty. Both Mary Allein and Susanna Parr were strong women who challenged the power of the ministers and elders in their congregation.

8

Sex and power in the early Quaker movement: the case of Martha Simmonds

WOMEN IN THE QUAKER MOVEMENT

Named derisively for the trembling, or quaking, which shook many of the believers, the Quakers, or Society of Friends, were one of the most prominent of the religious movements of the revolutionary period.[1] Although their numbers were probably not great, their public profile was high, and contemporaries increasingly feared that they were growing in converts and power during the 1650s. Their theology was one based on experience: they believed that God was present in all human beings, and that an established church and ministry were unnecessary. Women were highly visible in the early stages of the movement, from roughly 1650 to 1670. The Quakers were affected by the Restoration rather less than other religious sects. Some of the changes that came to the movement in the 1660s were more a response to the growing need for strategies for survival. With organisation, female participation lessened. But the process of containment of women had begun earlier. The history of the early Quaker movement shows the defeat of some female challenges to patriarchal power within the sect.

The story of the beginnings of Quakerism in the 1650s is often told in terms of the biography of George Fox. Certainly his role as a charismatic preacher was important, but in the early 1650s he was not so clearly the leader as he later became. He was a prolific writer, but many of the ideas which he preached and published were familiar ones from the radical religious ferment of the 1640s.[2] The origins of the Quaker movement, as its most recent historian, Barry Reay, has argued, lay less with Fox as a prophet and more in 'a linking of advanced Protestant separatists into a loose kind of church fellowship with a coherent ideology and a developing code of ethics'.[3] Subsequently, the Quaker movement's survival owed much to organisation, and here the role of Margaret Fell – later

160

Fox's wife – as well as Fox himself was significant. Contemporaries witnessed that Fox was a preacher of great power; surviving records witness that Fell was an organiser of great skill.[4]

Women's activities were well recorded. The Quakers themselves were highly conscious of record-keeping, and later Quaker historians have chronicled the sufferings of women and men. Some of the Quaker historians have claimed for their faith the credit for enlightened attitudes towards women. Indeed, W. C. Braithwaite celebrated the 'equality of men and women in spiritual privilege and responsibility' as one of the glories of Quakerism.[5] This offer of equality seemed to provide an answer to the reasons for women's participation: they became Quakers because they sought spiritual freedom from restriction. However, the Quakers did not offer women secular equality – it would be anachronistic to expect them to have done so – but they did give more independence than that offered by society.[6] Furthermore, as Phyllis Mack has argued in an important essay, the early Quaker movement should not be seen as meeting women's non-religious needs, but rather as satisfying their quest for spirituality.[7]

The question of recruitment to a radical religious movement is sometimes discussed in terms of social dispossession, but analysis of the social origins of the women and men who were active Quakers appears not to support this conclusion. Adherents were drawn from the middling and lower ranks of the society, not from the very poorest. Agricultural work occupied many of the men; occupations among the unmarried women included domestic service.[8] It is also curious that the women who were prominent appear to have come from a range of age and marital groups. Although Richard Baxter believed that the Quakers were 'a Company of young raw Professors', there were many wives, mothers and widows as well as a range of ages among the earliest converts.[9] Elizabeth Hooton, one of the earliest women preachers, was 51.[10] Regional explanations are not altogether satisfactory. While Quakerism had many adherents in the North and West, it also enjoyed strong support in London and Bristol.[11]

Perhaps the appeal of Quakerism to women was similar to that of other religious movements: it offered access to the divine in a direct and immediate way. For those seeking the Lord, Quakerism could be deeply satisfying. Temperance Hignell, when asked how she knew she was moved of the Lord, 'answered, it was like a fire in her bones'.[12] Like other experiential religious movements, it was especially attractive to women with limited educational opportunities, as Susanna Bateman's poem of 1657 showed:

161

Cease then a while you humane learned men,
And know your wisdome cannot find him out.
. . . It's not the prudent, learned, wise, that shall
Him comprehend, who is the light of all.[13]

A Baptist 'Sister Cornish' said 'that she had long wandered as a lost sheep hither and thither' but from the Quakers she had received such declarations 'so suitable to her owne experiences that she had found rest and had found Christ within'. Like many other women, she was attracted by the Quakers' 'Zeale, holiness, & activity for God', and disliked 'the formality, want of love, pride, earthly-mindedness among the churches'.[14] Similarly, Martha Simmonds, a married woman of middling social status, came to Quakerism after years of searching 'from one Idolls temple to another'.[15] Believing that the Lord inspired their actions, these women sought to tell the truth to the rest of the world.

Women who joined the Quaker movement, or perhaps more accurately we should say, women who became the Quaker movement, did so as individuals. In the earliest years, before a hierarchy of male leaders was established, women's role was more prominent than later. While many of the leaders did believe that men and women both had responsibilities in the movement, there were limits to male acceptance of female participation.

Certainly women played a conspicuous and important role in preaching the Quaker message. They spoke whenever the Lord moved them. Sometimes they denounced the ministers in church – priests in the steeple-houses, as they termed them – for taking money for talking of God. Examples abound. Elizabeth Marshall denounced the minister Ralph Farmer in Bristol in 1654. She was abused and dragged into the street where boys followed her with dirt and stones.[16] Temperance Hignell entered Temple Church in 1655; when the minister finished, she began saying 'Wo from the Lord God to thou, Jacob Brent'. She was knocked down, beaten and imprisoned. Charged with making a disturbance, and questioned about the reason for her words, 'She replyed, she spake not her own words, but his that sent her.' Since she was thrown down before she finished denouncing Brent, she sent him a one-page letter 'that thou mayst not be ignorant of the minde of the living God concerning thee . . . Wo from the Lord God unto thee Jacob Brent, thou Idol, and dumb Shepherd, that seekest for the fleece, and cloathest thy self with the wool, and devourest the souls of the people for dishonest gain.' She died three days after her ill-treatment.[17] In 1656 Ann Blaykling entered a church and 'Affronted the Minister in the

Pulpit, calling him Priest hirelinge & deceiver, greadie dume dogge wth manie more words of the same nature'.[18]

Preaching among the Quakers was a less formal activity than in many other churches, because individuals spoke when inspired by the Lord – women and children as well as men. Some women became famous preachers, such as Elizabeth Hooton and Ann Camm. Missionary work during the 1650s was considerable.[19] Frequently two women journeyed together, as did Elizabeth Williams and Mary Fisher who were reported to the Mayor of Cambridge for preaching and reprehending the scholars. They infuriated the mayor, who demanded of them their husbands' names, by telling him that 'they had no Husband but Jesus Christ'.[20] Elizabeth Leavens and Elizabeth Fletcher went to Oxford together in 1654, first preaching in the streets, then in the churches.[21] In the same year the pair went to Shrewsbury, 'where ye people were rude and brutish but . . . severall convinced of ye Truth'.[22] The sufferings of many of these early women preachers at the hands of the congregations and of magistrates were well documented by the Friends from the earliest period.[23]

Not only did Quaker women preach the truth in England, they also embarked on missionary journeys to the Turks, to Barbados and Massachusetts. Again, two women often travelled together: Sarah Cheevers and Katharine Evans were journeying to Jerusalem when they were imprisoned in 1659 in Malta, where they remained for over three years.[24] Among the missionaries to the New World, in Massachussetts Mary Dyer refused to be silenced. She was hanged in 1660. The 60-year-old Elizabeth Hooton journeyed there with Joan Brocksopp in 1661.[25]

The subjects on which women preached were the major spiritual and political issues of the day. They lamented the public sins of the kingdom, warned citizens to repent of their sins, and admonished the rulers about the state of the nation. Furthermore, many were sharply critical of various social ills. They attacked governments for their cruelty to the poor and the oppressed, and were particularly critical of the inadequacies of the ministry.[26]

Another form of witness was to publish. More Quaker women wrote for publication than might be expected from their numbers in English society. They were among the few women who published during the seventeenth century without any reference to their sex, impelled directly by the power of the Lord. They wrote warnings, admonitions and lamentations. Some wrote of their spiritual experiences. Altogether, in the decade 1651–60, their writings amounted to nearly half the total publications by women, despite their relatively small numbers in the community generally.[27] Phyllis Mack has estimated that in the years 1650–65, there were over 240 women preachers and writers among the Quakers.[28]

Some Quaker women sought to bear witness to the Lord by re-enacting 'signs' in public places. Given the conventional view of the good, religious woman as private and secret in her religious duties, their actions were a bold challenge to the gender norms. A few individuals showed a distinct flair for the dramatic. Early in 1660, Elizabeth Adams from Kent went to London, and bought 'a great painted Earthen Vessel' which she carried to Parliament house. She

> stood there two Days with the Vessel, at first on her Head, and afterwards sat upon it. At another Time she stood below, and plac'd her Vessel with the bottom upward. The People gather'd about, and ask'd her many Questions, to all of which she gave read and pertinent Answers: Amongst others, one asked her, What was in the Pot? she answered, It is bottom upward, and many things are turned and turning.[29]

On other occasions, she caused a tumult merely by silently carrying two lighted torches through the streets of Gravesend and Canterbury.[30] Sara Goldsmith, in 1655, was 'moved to put on a Coat of Sackcloth of hair next her, to uncover her head, and to put earth thereon, with her hair hanging down about her, and without any other clothes upon her, except shoes on her feet'. Her intended witness against pride of dress resulted in her committal, and that of two women who supported her, to Bridewell.[31] The re-enactment of signs was a complex business, and in this case, as in others, the intention was not realised. Some women were moved to go naked 'for a sign', such as Elizabeth Fletcher, who 'Contrary to her owne will or inclination, in obedience to the Lord, went naked through the Streets' of Oxford in 1654.[32] While witness by sign was not a specifically female act, the meaning of nakedness in men and women was different. Female nakedness was so shocking to contemporary ideas of modesty that, as Bauman has argued, its effect usually misfired.[33] Later Quakers were sensitive to their enemies' association of such an immodest act with sexual promiscuity, and in 1695 Penn indignantly denied that any woman ever went naked.[34]

Although many of the women's public activities such as preaching, heckling, and publishing were similar to those of men, their behaviour was viewed differently. Like men, women declined to support any established ministry, believing that the word of God should be taught freely.[35] Men as property owners were more likely to suffer for refusing to pay tithes than women, although women also were active in refusing tithes and in organising a huge petition against them.[36] Brought to court, Quaker women also refused to swear oaths.[37] Since women, unlike men, were not expected to remove their hats in courts, they did not offend the courts in this particular as did men. In other ways, women's support of the Quaker cause fitted more conventional stereotypes. For example, some women worked at relief of those in prison for their faith, at helping families in difficulties, and for the poor.[38] Furthermore, many women bore witness by a personally austere lifestyle. After hearing one of the Quaker leaders preach, a captain's wife tore off her silver lace crying 'This is the power of the Lord'.[39] By the end of the century, adherents of the Society of Friends were distinctive in their wearing of plain dress as a witness against pride and luxury. Again, since women were generally thought to be more sensitive to following fashions than men, Quaker dress separated Quaker women from the neighbourhood more than it separated men. Quaker women's meetings urged mothers to forbid their daughters to wear 'high dressed heads with Ruffles and double Gause; . . . Stript Gownes, of divers Colours wrapt into a narrow Compass hanging behind them'.[40]

In the campaigns to win converts in England, the Quakers developed a loose form of organisation based on meetings. Separate women's meetings for charitable purposes began in London in the late 1650s. Two meetings concerned with relief of the poor were founded, and similar women's meetings sprang up around the country, although they were not established formally until the late 1660s.[41] Margaret Fell, a widowed gentlewoman, played a vital role in the organisation of the scattered groups out of which Quakerism became a powerful movement in the 1650s. Kunze argues that Fell's influence on early Quakerism and on Fox was greater than traditional Quaker historiography has recognised.[42]

Much of this activity by Quaker women is well known. Undoubtedly, women played a prominent part in spreading the Quaker message. Compared with other women in England in the 1650s they took certain public freedoms. But the argument here is a different one, designed to show how the men and women in the Quaker movement, radical as it was, nevertheless were affected by conventional ideas about the two sexes. In the Quaker movement, despite its radical theology and the high public profile of women, men did not want women to be leaders any more than they did in any other religious movement. That we know so little of the most radical women, or know them only as disorderly, deranged, or enigmatic, speaks not only to their failure but also to the conventions of their time and of historical explanation.

A few women among the early Quakers aspired even more highly than has been imagined. This can be demonstrated by a re-reading of a well-known incident, that of James Nayler's entry into Bristol in 1656. By re-examining it from the perspective of Martha Simmonds, the woman who organised it, we may understand better the sexual dynamics of the early Quaker movement and the role of gender in a religious movement.

JAMES NAYLER AND THE QUAKER LEADERSHIP

James Nayler, one of the Quaker leaders, rode into Bristol on 24 October 1656 in an attempt to re-enact Christ's entry into Jerusalem. Martha Simmonds and another woman led his horse. He was accompanied by a small group of men and women crying 'Holy, holy, holy, Lord God of Sabaoth' and strewing garments before him.[43] The Bristol magistrates arrested the group. Rather than dealing with the incident themselves, they sent Nayler and his friends to the Protectorate Parliament in London. Members of the Second Protectorate Parliament felt the need to demonstrate abhorrence of what they believed was blasphemy, thereby showing their own religious soundness: 'All the eyes of the nation are upon you for it, to see what you will do for God in this business', said one MP.[44] Many members wanted to put Nayler to death. In the end, he was not executed, but a savage punishment was carried out. On 18 December 1656 Nayler stood in the pillory for two hours and was then whipped 310 times. On 27 December he was bored through the tongue with a red hot iron and branded with a B for blasphemer on the forehead.[45] In Bristol, he was whipped again on 17 January.

Nayler's case is notorious because of the savage punishment inflicted upon him, but his re-enactment of Christ's entry into Jerusalem was an awesome and extraordinary event. It is one of those moments when, to use Robert Darnton's term, the past seems most opaque to us.[46] Either we follow contemporaries, and take it seriously as a terrible blasphemy, or we dismiss it as a bizarre manifestation, in which case the puzzle becomes the ferocity of the contemporary reaction. Yet where the evidence seems most puzzling, we may find a valid point of entry into an alien mentality.

The Nayler incident has been widely discussed from many perspectives. There is a substantial body of literature about Nayler

JAMES NAYLOR

Of all the Sects that Night, and Errors own
And with false Lights possesse the world, ther's none
More strongly blind, or who more madly place
The light of Nature for the light of Grace.

Figure 9. James Nayler, branded B for Blasphemer. From *Ephraim Pagitt's Heresiography, 1661* (Library of the Religious Society of Friends).

himself.[47] His entry into Bristol sent a shudder of horror through contemporaries as it seemed to realise the blasphemous potential of religious liberty. It exacerbated growing fears of the Quakers. As one MP said, 'The sect is dangerous'.[48] Nayler's case, as Christopher Hill has pointed out, placed the whole religious policy of the Protectorate in the dock.[49] The incident has been seen as an important milestone in the history of liberty of conscience.[50]

In the contemporary debate and subsequent discussion, one theme emerges very clearly: women were held to be in some way responsible.[51] It was said at the time, and has been repeated through the historiography, that Nayler's troubles were largely caused by his women admirers, in particular, by one Martha Simmonds.[52] The basis for the charge of blasphemy was that Nayler believed that he was Christ. Women certainly provided contemporaries with evidence that suggested they worshipped Nayler as the Messiah. Sarah Blackbury addressed him in language usually employed for Christ: 'Rise up my love, my dove, my fair one, and come away.'[53] Dorcas Erbury told the Bristol magistrates that she believed that Nayler was the only begotten son of God. She had taken off his stockings and put her clothes under his feet 'Because he is the Lord of Israel and worthy of it.' Most significantly of all, she claimed that she had been dead for two days when James Nayler raised her: 'I was dead two dayes and he laid his hands upon my head, and said Dorcas arise, and from that day to this, I am alive.'[54] Women participated in Nayler's entry into Bristol: Martha Simmonds and Hannah Stranger were said to have led his horse, and others sang and strewed garments before him.[55] Much was made of letters from various people who saluted Nayler in terms which suggested they thought he was Christ. When he was in prison, Martha Simmonds was with him. Moreover, there were reports of three women – Simmonds, Stranger and Erbury – being grouped around him, in imitation of the three at the foot of the cross, at the time of his public punishment on 27 December.[56] Rebecca Travers testified that she had washed his wounds after he was whipped.[57] As one MP said, when urging that women as well as men be kept away from Nayler in prison, 'it is a woman that has done all the mischief'.[58]

In the debate in Parliament some members professed to be more shocked by the women's behaviour than by Nayler's. Nayler, they argued, had been foolish rather than blasphemous. According to Bulstrode Whitelocke, Nayler sinned 'in suffering adoration to be done to him'.[59] It was women who gave him the honour, Disborowe said, and Strickland added that Nayler did not believe he was Christ, 'though I

Figure 10. Contemporary accounts said that two women led Nayler's horse into Bristol, but twenty years on, women have taken the rear position. From *The Quakers' Ballad, 1674* (Library of the Religious Society of Friends).

believe the women do believe him to be Christ'.[60] The issue of what Nayler actually believed provided a loophole at the time for those who wanted to exonerate him. Theologically, he seemed close to believing what Colonel Sydenham told the Parliament was 'a glorious truth, that the spirit is personally in us'. Or, as Whitelocke put it, Nayler believed, like the Lutherans, 'in the ubiquity of Christ'.[61] Sydenham argued that the women were greater offenders than Nayler 'inasmuch as they actually committed idolatry'. While this may have been a debating ploy, designed to reduce the hysterical hostility of the MPs to Nayler, it raised the question in Parliament of women's part in the incident, and touched deeper fears about their involvement in sectarian religion generally.

Disorderly women were generally disturbing to MPs in December 1656. On 22 December the MPs leaving the House had to pass a Quaker woman who told the Speaker and everyone who passed her 'that justice was turned into wormwood, and equity into gall'.[62] One MP reported on 26 December what a merchant's wife had told him of Nayler's whipping, that there was no skin left between his hips and shoulders after his punishment. MPs indignantly repudiated this tale of barbarity, adducing the apparently more credible information from a gaoler who said that Naylor's skin was broken only in three places. After this, Colonel Markham went so far as to say that the merchant's wife who was the source of the accusation should be sent for 'and whipped'.[63] Such an over-reaction betrays the Parliamentarians' anxieties. Quaker women were not the only ones causing the MPs anxiety over the December and January period, 1656–7. Interspersed with debates on Nayler, MPs were also debating the case of Scot, a gentleman of good family seeking a divorce from an adulterous wife. The members' hostile language betrays their sensitivity: 'the bold face', they said, had injured her husband, for which 'She deserves no more than a dog.'[64]

Two traditional stereotypes of the disorderly woman were the witch and the whore. Both were brought into play against the women involved with Nayler, particularly against Martha Simmonds. The examining magistrates in Bristol questioned Martha Simmonds for 'a Witch, a Sorcerer, and a Whore'. The accusation of witch was linked to her London visit to Nayler, after which he fell into a trance for three days.[65] Allegations of sexual misconduct were rife. A minister, Hall, stated that Simmonds was suspected 'to be a Witch and a Whore'.[66] Martha Simmonds 'a very Baggage' and Hannah Stranger 'is a deceitful Trull'.[67] One of Williamson's correspondents in France had heard news of Nayler pretending to be the Messiah with twelve apostles 'and 2 sinful Magdalens'.[68] Contemporaries were quite clear that sexual promiscuity was a characteristic of sectarian life. Nayler was married,[69] but various stories circulated about him too. It was alleged that he was expelled from an Independent church in York for 'wanton carriage' with one Mrs Roper 'as that she should sit on his knee and kiss him before divers other persons'. One amplification of this allegation was that he had begotten a bastard on her in her husband's absence. In Somerset Nayler was said to have been discovered in his chamber with three women, and leaning on the bed with one. Further, a servant had found him on a bed with a woman while the curtains were drawn.[70]

Martha Simmonds was also married when she was observed to be involved in 'some unseemly communication' with James Nayler in prison. 'She stroked his head, and sat breast to breast, and desired him to go with her'.[71] Quaker writers refer to 'filthiness' but do not make clear whether there was anything more at issue than this public behaviour in prison.[72] Simmonds was labelled as a whore. Later historians have not wished to go so far, although their comments suggest that they are uncomfortable about the sexual implications of the relationship. Watts, however, thinks that the witchery went the other way, and explains the female element in the incident in terms of James Nayler's physical attributes and eloquence exercising 'a fatal fascination for the ladies'.[73]

In the event, Simmonds, Stranger and Erbury were lucky to have suffered no more than imprisonment and questioning. Several factors were probably significant. First, they had done less than Nayler. Second, in any criminal activity, the contemporary assumption was that the man was the active instigator, the woman merely the passive agent. Women were usually convicted as accessories to crimes.[74] Third, while contemporaries immediately tried to convict the women of the classic female offences, whoredom or witchcraft, none of these charges was pursued with any vigour. This was probably because the main issue for the members of Parliament was the religious policy of the Protectorate and their concern with the spread of Quakerism. In this case, being female protected the women from punishment, although it did not save them from being vilified.

Just as some of Nayler's contemporaries blamed women for his excesses, so too have later historians. First, historians have accepted the theological argument that Nayler never said he was Christ, only a sign of Christ. They argue that it was Martha Simmonds and others who hailed him as the Messiah. Matthews, in his study of English Messiahs, asserts that Nayler was 'thrust into the assumption of divinity by the unwelcome enthusiasm of a handful of women', 'unbalanced female admirers of a type that still plagues the lives of well-looking ministers of religion'.[75] Nayler's later biographer, Fogelklou, argued that the women's actions had set Nayler up.[76] Yet although the women's excesses of language in addressing Nayler still carry some of the overtones of blasphemy, the historian Geoffrey Nuttall has rightly pointed to the significance of the contemporary context. Messianic language which might seem strange was generally used in certain seventeenth-century contexts.[77]

Finally, contemporary Quakers and later historians have blamed women for Nayler's misguided behaviour, claiming that he was either bewitched or under psychological domination by Martha Simmonds. Surviving Quaker correspondence from 1656 is full of abuse of Simmonds and her 'unclean spirt'.[78] The legend of blame was given further substance by remarks of Nayler himself. George Whitehead later recollected that Nayler told him in 1657 that 'a few forward, conceited, imaginary women, especially Martha Simmonds and some others, under pretence of some Divine Motions, grew somewhat turbulent'.[79] Nayler's dismissal of Simmonds's inspiration as 'pretence' confirmed Fox's earlier judgement of the whole business. Subsequent historians have accepted the contemporary view of Simmonds. Thus Braithwaite writes of Nayler being weakened by a long imprisonment and fasting in Exeter gaol, isolated from the counsel of Fox, coming under the sway of 'this misguided woman'.[80]

It is worth looking closely at the language which historians use for describing Simmonds and the other women. Barbour refers to them all as 'a group of intensely emotional women'.[81] Breward, in the *Biographical Dictionary of British Radicals*, calls them 'the fanatical women', Nayler's 'unbalanced followers', and reiterates the theological point that Nayler distinguished between himself as son of God and Jesus as son of God which the women did not.[82] Mabel Brailsford describes Simmonds as 'the villain of this piece'.[83] Kenneth Carroll, in his article about Simmonds, entitles her 'a Quaker enigma', but it is clear that he considered she was unbalanced from the time she stood up against the Quaker leaders in mid-1656, 'earning a place with the worst of the Ranters'. He believed that it was she who separated Nayler from Fox, gained an 'almost hypnotic influence' on him, and 'was largely responsible for what took place in Bristol'.[84] As Mgr Ronald Knox earlier summed up this tradition of interpretation, the story 'is usually told as that of a muddle-headed Quaker who underwent a brief apotheosis at the hands of a few crazed women'. Knox, too, blamed the women, but he reverted to an earlier theme, namely that the story was one of the 'overshadowing of the founder by one of his own disciples'.[85] It can be argued that this challenge to Fox was not just from Nayler: it came from a group of women too. And the level of abuse of those women by other Quakers indicates to us the seriousness with which contemporaries viewed that challenge.

Similar behaviour has a different meaning in men and women. While Nayler could hold a sophisticated theological position, women were simple literalists. Being female meant that Simmonds, Erbury and Stranger could not be the Messiah, but it saved the women from such savage punishment as Nayler suffered. Gender was central to the incident, but the female perspective has been largely distorted.

MARTHA SIMMONDS AND THE CHALLENGE FOR LEADERSHIP

Given the brutal punishment of Nayler, it is not surprising that contemporaries and historians have focused attention and explanation upon him. Even so, as we have seen, women featured largely in discussions of the incident. Their actions, however, were viewed in the light of the male protagonists and their concerns. In this section the incident will be discussed from the perspective of one of the women, Martha Simmonds. Although the sources are limited, and largely hostile, there is enough evidence to question the account of unbalanced, hysterical or mad women, and even to offer an alternative interpretation. In addition to allowing us to focus on the ways in which women's religious options differed because of contemporary assumptions about gender, discussion also reveals a struggle between women and men in the early stages of Quakerism for leadership, control, and power.

Martha Simmonds was not atypical in her spiritual development and practices as a Quaker. She was born in Somerset in 1624. Her brother, Giles Calvert, was a printer, and her husband, Thomas, was also a printer. In an autobiographical reflection, she spoke of seeking the Lord for seven years until she joined the Quakers. This was probably in the early 1650s. She then began to speak in meetings; in 1654 she set off on missionary journeys to cities, towns, and market streets. She wrote her messages from the Lord and her brother printed them. Her first pamphlet was a warning to sinners, 'longing for your soules good am I made open to you'.[86] The following year she admonished sinners: 'I cannot but mourn over you, to see how you lie wallowing in your filth.'[87] In 1655 she went to Colchester where she walked 'in sackcloth and barefoote with her hayr spread and ashes upon her head, in the towne, in the frosty weather, to the astonishment of many'.[88] It was a sign, a symbolic re-enactment designed to communicate to a sinful people the prophetic judgement that they were all sinners who should repent.[89] Nayler's entry into Bristol begins to fit into a pattern of Simmonds's participation in symbolic re-enactments. Simmonds was imprisoned in Colchester. One of the Quakers there, James Parnell, commended her actions: 'the Lord hath shown his power much by her since she came here, she is A faythful hearte in her measure'.[90]

Fox and other men who were recognised as leaders were suspicious of some of these wilder manifestations. They believed that unorthodox behaviour discredited the whole church. It was better if women spoke in meetings only when there were no qualified men present. Thus from the early 1650s there was a question of authority: who was to judge who

173

spoke in the truth? These male leaders determined the qualifications: they believed that they, the men, should judge who spoke in the power of the Lord and who spoke in will. This issue of who could lead in a new religious movement was one which was always raised and always needed to be resolved. Every new church which formed had basic questions to decide: who were members? who was to be admitted? how was worship to be conducted? who was to sit where? Inevitably, these issues concerned the place of women in the church. Hints of conflict were frequent. Evidence about the disputes between women and men such as we have for the Nayler incident is exciting because it is rare.

By mid-1656, when Martha Simmonds was in London, Fox was away, and Nayler was commanding widespread interest. Gentlemen of the Cromwellian court and their wives were talking with him, and he was gaining popularity.[91] Meanwhile, Simmonds started speaking at London meetings. She also sang, a singing which was probably a certain sustained chanting – a melodious buzzing, as it is sometimes described – which silenced other people.[92] The leading men in London – Francis Howgill, Richard Hubberthorne and Edward Burrough – began to weary of her and told her in harsh terms to be quiet: 'This is the truth from ye Lord God concerning thee Martha Simmonds: thou and whoe followes thy spirit. ye are out of ye truth, out of ye way, out of ye power, out of ye wisdom, & out of the Life of God . . . ye true power of God you have lost.'[93] Simmonds complained of injustice, and turned to Nayler to right her.

Simmonds left no account of her own of the events of 1656. The accounts which survive are reports by others of what she said. It is from these sources, which are hostile to Simmonds, that a history of her struggle can be constructed. Simmonds denied the authority of the male leaders. She could not be quiet as Burrough told her without denying the Lord. She was willing to respect and love the leaders, 'as being men of pure life', but since her message was from God, she could not obey them. 'I was moved by *the power*, I could not stay though they sometimes denied me, yet I was forced to go, and *my word did prosper.*'[94] This was a not unfamiliar experience for those who had claimed a mystical experience over the centuries: an individual who believed that her or his vision was true could come into conflict with authority. Simmonds was confronted with the choice of denying either 'the power' which moved her, which she believed was from God, or the authority of the group. Like other mystics and visionaries, she knew that she apprehended the divine, and so she held to her truth. This put the leaders of the Quaker movement into an authoritarian position in relation to her, one which they would adopt towards Nayler as well later. Meanwhile, in 1656, Simmonds knew that she had a following: 'my word did prosper'. The Quaker leaders were aware that she did too.

When Simmonds turned to Nayler, his response was the conventional one: he told her that she was seeking to exercise her authority which was unwarranted, and that she ought to behave like a submissive woman. He 'told her that she sought to have the dominion & charged her to goe home & follow her calling'.[95] Martha Simmonds was not the only woman told to follow her calling, to observe the conventional division of labour between the sexes during this revolutionary period. The women who petitioned Parliament in 1649 for the release of Lilburne were told 'to goe home, and look after your own business, and meddle with your huswifery'. They were not crushed, and no more was Martha Simmonds. Women's domain was the household and 'huswifery', the private sphere, but their own sense of their responsibilities as Christians took them into conflict in the public political sphere, the men's domain.

The key question was whether public politics and the control of the sacred were to remain male preserves. The women who challenged the conventional boundaries aroused great fear and anxiety in men, for if the fundamental distinction between the two sexes and the gender divisions of labour disappeared, then the world would be truly turned upside down. Responses to women's claims indicate the limits of radicalism.

Martha Simmonds had a framework of religious belief which allowed her to resist: and so she challenged Nayler's directive to confine herself to her female-specific labour. She said that 'at length these words came to me to speak to him, which I did and struck him down: How are the mighty men falen.' Simmonds claimed that she found over the next three days that 'the power arose in me'. She did not communicate with Nayler again, but at the end of those three days, it was Nayler who came to Simmonds. He confessed that he had wronged her.[96] It was a triumph for Simmonds: her religious authority was accepted.

Fox believed that from this time, when Nayler accepted Simmonds's message, Nayler turned from the light into darkness. Quaker historians have recognised this moment as a crisis. Charitably, they now suggest that Simmonds was misguided rather than deliberately wicked, although Fox did not give her the benefit of that doubt.[97] Although Nayler was later reconciled to Fox, Simmonds never was. Hence Quaker historiography depicts her as 'out of the way' and divisive. Other historians have seen her as hysterical, gaining psychological domination over Nayler which led him astray. Certainly it was a crisis, but what has been insufficiently recognised – because it seemed even more radical than later commentators expected – was that Martha Simmonds was, for a brief period, one of the leaders of the Quaker movement.

After Nayler acknowledged that Simmonds's power was from the Lord, he left London, journeying to see Fox who was in Cornwall, via Bristol. Simmonds and others travelled to Bristol too. At some stage she had a confrontation with Fox, for in a letter found on Nayler when he was arrested, Fox complained to Nayler that Martha Simmonds, 'which is called your Mother', denounced him, Fox, denying his headship. 'She came singing in my Face, inventing words.' Fox berated Nayler for encouraging 'such as doe cry agst ye power & Life of Truth'.[98] Nayler was imprisoned in Exeter in August 1656. Simmonds used her contacts to get Nayler out of gaol in mid-October, through her connection with Major General Desborough, whose wife she had nursed. She then organised a small procession into Bristol as a re-enactment of Christ's entry into Jerusalem.[99]

It is difficult to gain an accurate picture of the entry into Bristol on 24 October 1656. Later engravings make it seem rather larger than do the written reports of the time. These refer to Nayler accompanied by only seven or eight named people, but others may have joined them.[100] Certainly the crowd was large when it was depicted in a Dutch engraving nearly fifty years later.

Among the group of seven or eight who accompanied Nayler and Simmonds were Hannah Stranger, the wife of a comb-maker, who led the procession, with Martha Simmonds and Dorcas Erbury. The group entered Bristol leading Nayler's horse, singing and strewing garments – some gloves, handkerchiefs – before him. The Bristol magistrates imprisoned the entire group, examined them, and sent them to the Parliament in London.[101]

It is worth considering why Simmonds did not claim the role of the Messiah herself, if the boundaries between the two sexes were to be redrawn in the times of the coming of the holy spirit. Sex reversals were not uncommon among the Quakers. Priscilla Cotton and Mary Cole when told by ministers that women should be silent in church, answered with the statement 'you your selves are the women that are forbidden to speak in the church, that are become women'.[102] Another, 'Mistris Williams at Appleby', had earlier claimed to be the Messiah, 'to which some presently replied that she was a woman, and therefore could not be *the eternal son of God*'. She simply reversed the situation by a new definition: '*no, you are all women, but I am a Man*'.[103] Reversals were not

des Qvackers
IACOB NAYLORS Einzug in BRISTOL.

Der tolle Hauffe schwermet in düstrer Raserey,
daß dieser Rittersmann der Christ des Herren sey
Zwo Weiber leiten's Pferd, die andern müssen streuen,
die Kleider auf den Weg, und Heilig, Heilig schreyen.

Figure 11. A continental view of James Nayler's entry into Bristol, 24 October 1656. From *Anabaptisticum et Enthusiasticum, 1702* (Library of the Religious Society of Friends).

unique to the Quakers. Other radicals such as Richard Coppin also shifted the traditional boundaries between God and man, man and woman. Coppin identified the woman as the 'Earthy part of man', while those who had the Lord's spirit were the man, irrespective of their sexual identity. Thus he told the ministers that they were the woman, 'in the weak womanish lustful nature of mankind, as you are now without Christ', and all priests, lawyers, sheriffs and committee men that they were the woman, Jezabel. Only the power and spirit of Christ gave a masculine identity, which allowed any believer, irrespective of sex, 'to become a man in Christ'. Hence 'a woman creature' could speak and answer as freely as a man, if she brought forth Christ.[104] Freedom from selfhood also allowed Quaker men to speak in the language of femininity.[105] It is signficant that the man remains the positive in these reversals, the woman the negative. In Simmonds's case, there was no sex reversal. She was probably concentrating on re-enacting a sign, which required a certain literalness. She accepted that the role of Christ was indeed a male role. But since she was directly inspired by God, 'in obedience to the power on high',[106] it did not matter what role she adopted. The weak role of a female was also a glorious one.

It was accepted by many of his contemporaries that Nayler was not literally claiming to be Christ, but that he was worshipped as Christ by some women. The evidence suggests that the women, too, had a theological position and were not the simple-minded literalists that contemporaries assumed. The women's language to Nayler was interpreted at the time as showing their literal belief that he was Christ: they hailed him as the fairest of ten thousand, my love, etc. But this too needs to be interpreted in the context of language common at the time: many Quakers were writing to Fox in similar terms, but it was not intended literally, nor in the interpretation of Fox's position has it been taken so.[107]

Simmonds was next heard of around February 1657 when she was still trying to influence the pattern of Quaker worship. She went to the meeting at the Bull and Mouth tavern in mid-1657 with seven or eight women and apparently took a Bible and read a psalm. To the men leading the movement, she was introducing formalism in worship. When the people at the meeting joined in singing after her, 'as they do in the steeplehouses', Hubberthorne stopped them. Simmonds then tried to read a chapter of Ezekiel, one of the prophetic books, but was cried down. This, too, was against the movement's reliance on direct inspiration, although Simmonds claimed that 'the Lord had sent that chapter to be read unto us'.[108] Even more challengingly, at another meeting

178

Simmonds not only took on the role of preacher and leader of worship, but also annihilated the boundary between priest and believer and offered the sacrament. She was part of a group of ten who 'broke bread & drunk drink and gave to the rude multitude'.[109] This is a clear instance of a woman actually participating in the administration of the Lord's Supper, although there were rumours earlier in the 1640s of women taking on sacred roles. Edwards reported that one preached and also baptised, 'but thats not so certain', and a minister had told him that some women at Brastead, in Kent, besides preaching, 'break Bread also'.[110] Baptism by women was permitted in Catholicism, but only among heretical movements was there ever talk of women administering the sacrament of the Lord's Supper. Among the Lollards in England, for example, Margaret Aston has found some evidence which suggested that there was at least theoretical discussion of women priests and of women administering the sacrament.[111]

The Quakers did not offer either of the two Protestant sacraments of the Lord's Supper or baptism.[112] Interestingly, while Simmonds's *interventions* in worship were in themselves radical, her *ideas* about worship were more conventional than those which the Quakers generally accepted: psalm singing, Bible reading and the Lord's Supper would not have been out of place in the Anglican, Presbyterian or Independent churches. Again, the distinction between radical and conservative needs qualification.

Simmonds disappears from the Quaker records after this date. She died in 1665.[113] Quaker historians have interpreted her behaviour at the Bull and Mouth as a deliberate attack to destroy worship, and her silence thereafter as defeat. But perhaps she disappeared from the records because she ceased to need the Quakers. She may have moved on to another church, or joined with like-minded people.

The Nayler story thus shows a power struggle in the Quaker movement in which gender played a significant role. Despite a rhetoric of equality before the Lord, the Quaker leaders did not always accept this in practice. What has not been appreciated is the extent of the women's challenge and its theological base. Simmonds was not accepted as one of the Quaker leaders, but her actions came out of her sense of the divine. She was certain that God spoke in her and through her. For her the outcome was perhaps less significant than the process: she apprehended the Lord's power directly, from which she gained her individual sense of autonomy.

It has often been observed that women belonged to the private sphere, men to the public. While these were conceptualised as two separate areas, the Nayler story is another example of how women's activities in the private sphere could bring them into public conflict. What was public and what was private was under constant negotiation as men and women disputed what was woman's proper sphere. The men in the radical Quaker movement – one which truly horrified nearly all their contemporaries – shared some of the conservative assumptions of their society. Whatever the radical Quakers said, in practice they showed that they did not believe that the sacred sphere was one in which a woman could appropriately exercise authority. Granted, the men who led the Quaker movement did not like the direction in which Simmonds's leadership tended. But they were imbued with contemporary stereotypes, and these influenced their attitudes to a woman's attempt to exercise a spiritual authority which conflicted with the views of the majority.

Keith Thomas has argued that in the long run the sectarian experience was less significant for the emancipation of women than the liberal tradition. He has seen emancipation in terms of concessions won from men.[114] But if we look at women's experiences in the sects in the context of the 1640s and 1650s, we can argue that the sectarian experience was an extraordinarily empowering one for some women. Religious experience and apprehensions of God gave women self-confidence and a sense of autonomy.

QUAKER WOMEN'S SPIRITUALITY

So far, I have explored the attractions of Quakerism to women in terms of greater freedom from social constraints of gender. Quaker spirituality gave women a new view of themselves, their social position and their relationship to the divine.

Quakerism offered transcendence. It was a mystical and ecstatic religion. Inspiration from the holy spirit moved the believer away from anthropomorphic conceptions of God.[115] Women could seek to transcend both class and gender. They could refuse social deference, bowing only to the Lord, and they could, by working through their female nature, as they understood it, be at one with the divine, where difference of sex was immaterial. As Phyllis Mack has argued, when Quaker women gave themselves to the power of the Lord, they accepted their passivity, which allowed the Lord to act through them.[116] From this abnegation of self came their possession by the divine: 'brought thither by the living God . . . [I] was moved', as Rebecca Travers expressed it.[117] Jane Withers experienced her bondage to the Lord's message as a physical one, as if chains were around her body.[118] Both men and women, Mack suggests, 'liquified' gender, and spoke and acted with the traditional attributes of both sexes. Thus in their private spiritual lives, both sexes spoke in terms of infancy, maternity and wifehood, while in their public roles they both spoke with the voice of Old Testament prophets. In a fascinating exploration of the meaning of difference of sex for these relationships to the divine, Mack suggests that men found more freedom from their customary family bonds and more emotional relief, while women, whose spiritual self-abnegation more closely resembled their social situation, unified the Quaker movement with their ability to hold both spiritual and temporal concerns together.[119]

Women experienced dreams, visions and trances, and were frequently in ecstatic states. An ordinary Quaker woman such as Mary Harris might declare 'I am filled, as it were, with Marrow and Fatness; I have seen his Glory, and tasted his Precious Truth.'[120] There are suggestions that the ability to trance was induced in part by fasting. Critics suggested that as women and children were weaker, they 'are most subject to Fascination'.[121] Contemporaries suspected also that those in the power of the Lord were in some trance-like state, but as Mack points out, women denied this, and claimed that they moved in the power of the Lord in full consciousness of their surroundings and actions. In the power of the Lord, women gained strength. They came from darkness into light: 'I saw things unutterable.'[122]

Suffering had a more prominent place in Quaker women's spirituality than that of other religious groups. Women rejoiced in confrontations with hostile groups, in imprisonment, and injustice. When Margaret Newby was put in the stocks at Evesham in 1655, 'I was moved to sing', to the astonishment of the 'heathen' standing by.[123] Frequently women seemed impervious to pain. Barbara Blagdone was whipped, but said that even if she had been whipped to death 'in the State she then was, she should not have been terrified or dismay'd'.[124]

Gender affected the punishments of women for their activities such as preaching, challenging established ministers and refusing to conform. On the one hand, they were protected from some offences. They were not, unlike men, expected to appear with their heads uncovered, and so they escaped the wrath of courts against those with hats on.[125] However, their defiance and disobedience was thought more shocking than that of their male counterparts. Conventional views of women also affected attitudes to Quaker women's sufferings. The cruelty of individuals and magistrates to women was documented in detail which dwelt upon its inappropriateness for women, who were weak and tender. Besse, for example, included many accounts of mothers taken to prison leaving behind unweaned babies, or families of children 'the eldest not able to dress it self'.[126] As Mack perceptively observed, women suffered more theatrically than men. The sight of a woman stripped to the waist for a whipping had a 'different social and sexual resonance' from that of a man in the same position.[127] Punishments and sufferings were likely to be influenced by class: gentlewomen were not stripped and whipped, although they were treated violently.

Quaker spirituality was intense. Some women had extraordinary faith. Sara Pearson attempted to raise a young man from the dead in Worcester in 1657, without success.[128] Quaker women gloried and exulted in the power of the Lord. For those whose social situation encouraged weakness, dependence and subordination, it was a stunning reversal. Quaker women shared some common elements with women in other religious groups. Depending on their social level, like other pious women, they set aside time for prayer, for Bible reading, and for attending public worship. Many were personally ascetic. But there were major differences. Quakerism encouraged transcendence, possession by the divine. Social relationships were less significant. In particular, Quaker women's relationship with male leaders differed from those of women in other radical religious movements. Women were followers of Lodovic Muggleton; they were disciples of their messianic leader. Women Baptists depended upon the ministers who recorded and categorised women's spiritual experiences.[129] Quaker women experienced an intense spirituality. Teaching, preaching, writing and bearing witness, they were more willing to challenge and transcend the constraints of sex and gender.

Part IV

Restoration to toleration 1660–1720

9

Anglicans, Catholics and Nonconformists after the Restoration 1660–1720

RESTORATION TO TOLERATION

After the Restoration, religious enthusiasm was suspect. Increasingly, those who refused to conform to the Anglican church became more sober and respectable in their religious practices so that they could gain the right to worship in peace. After 1670, Quaker women who had been prominent in some of the wilder religious manifestations of the Interregnum found that a Quaker committee censored their writings for publication. At the upper social levels, increased emphasis on scientific explanations of the world and on reasoned belief enhanced the difference between the two sexes. As elite men turned away from revealed religion, and adopted deism, or worse, the cultural gap between elite men and women widened. Enthusiastic religion was no longer a common cultural ground between men and women, and elite men distanced themselves from lower-class men as well as from women. The notion of woman as a creature of emotion remained unaltered after 1660. Indeed, the idea of woman as weak, unstable, and easily led astray was confirmed by the experiences of the revolutionary years. Men said that piety was especially good for women as a means of keeping them virtuous. Religion, in so far as it involved belief rather than reason, seemed natural to the less reasonable sex. From here it was easy to argue that women were naturally religious. By the eighteenth century, therefore, the role of religion in supporting the ideology of the good woman was enhanced. This chapter discusses some of these changes.

The restoration of Charles II in 1660 effected a major alteration in the religious situation in England. Even while the Convention debated the religious settlement, Anglican squires were removing Puritan ministers from their livings. The Anglican church was formally re-established by the Parliament which met in 1661. Legislation restored its hierarchy and institutions, minus the court of High Commission, and imposed penalties on all who refused to conform.[1] However, in practice the Anglican church abandoned the belief that there was only one true church. Dissenters were persecuted but they were not burnt as heretics.

Different religious groups were variously affected. For the first time, the Presbyterians found themselves among the Nonconformists. After their attempts to be included in the Anglican church failed, they were forced to relinquish their belief in one church, to accept a position among the hated sects and to tolerate their fellow Nonconformists. The Independents either conformed or continued their separate worship in persecuted congregations. For them, no change of theology was necessary for they had always supported a degree of toleration and liberty of conscience. Nor were the Baptists or Quakers forced to alter their theology. The Baptists were once again persecuted, as they had been before 1640. For the Quakers, who had challenged the powers of the state during the 1650s, persecution was not a new experience, but the Restoration government was more committed to the eradication of Quaker views than Cromwell's government had been. Legislation singled out the Quakers, so Quaker women as well as men suffered more persecution after 1660.

Although Antonia Fraser suggests that the Restoration was a happy time for women – 'the female clamour of the Commonwealth, both sonorous and serious, gave way to the merry prattle of the ladies of King Charles II's England'[2] – its legislation had serious consequences for the admittedly small minority of women involved in sectarian activity. After 1660 few new converts were made. Public religious activity for women was even more difficult, for there were widespread fears through the community that female disorder and rebellion went hand in hand. Women's public writings diminished sharply, even more than those of men.[3]

Ironically, the sects themselves, especially the Quakers, and the women prominent therein, contributed to the impetus toward the Restoration. The rapid growth of the Quakers in the 1650s and the amount of attention their activities received in the localities, in the news reports and tracts, all meant that many people looked to a restoration of the monarchy and the known ways as the only means of checking Quaker religious excesses.[4] Even an ejected Presbyterian minister celebrated the anniversary of Charles II's restoration two years later as 'a stop to Anabapt[ists and] Quakers & others that were grown very high'.[5]

Nonconformists have labelled the period from the Restoration to the accession of William and Mary as 'the great persecution'.[6] The legislation was harsh, although its enforcement varied depending on local circumstances. The attempts of Charles II to introduce toleration by royal prerogative were unsuccessful. The persecution was at its worst from 1681 to 1685. James II's accession to the throne in 1685 brought the very real danger to the Protestants of a pro-Catholic policy, which ultimately precipitated a better understanding between the Anglicans and Nonconformists.

The public situation of Dissenters altered in 1689. In 1688 prominent politicians invited King William of Orange to invade England on behalf of the Protestant religion. By the terms of the Toleration Act of 1689, Dissenters who took the oaths of allegiance and supremacy were allowed to worship freely in licensed meeting places. They were legally permitted to own property for religious purposes and to build chapels and meeting houses. Ministers who subscribed to thirty-six of the thirty-nine articles were no longer in danger of persecution. The historian Michael Watts has concluded that 'The "Glorious Revolution" thus gave orthodox Dissenters statutory freedom to worship in their own way, but it did not give them civil equality.'[7] However, the Revolution affected Nonconformist men more than their female counterparts. All women, however orthodox their religious views, lacked certain civic rights. They could not serve on juries, or on the bench as JPs, nor could they hold legal offices. By the late seventeenth century none could vote for Parliament, and they were certainly never elected as members.[8] A few women who held public offices, such as courtiers, midwives or searchers for the plague, were required to take the oaths.[9] It can be argued that the position of women even worsened after the Glorious Revolution.[10] The language in which ideas of liberty were discussed was androcentric. Furthermore, as Mary Astell pointed out in 1700, '*If all Men are born free*, how is it that all Women are born slaves?'[11] Nevertheless, even if women's gains were non-existent compared with those of propertied men's, there were some benefits. After the Toleration Act of 1689 women as well as men were able to worship openly in religious congregations of their own choosing and were free to witness to their faith in their daily lives.

Yet because women's lack of civil equality remained constant, in women's religious history the whole period from the Restoration to the early eighteenth century can be discussed as one. More important than the Glorious Revolution for women was the process of what has been called denominationalisation, as the churches' need to survive in the world necessitated organisation, clear membership qualifications and rules for group behaviour.[12] The transition from sects to denominations affected women, household religion and personal piety.

ANGLICANS, NONCONFORMISTS AND CATHOLICS

The majority of women in England probably thought the restoration of the Anglican church a blessing. John Morrill's work has shown 'the passive strength of Anglican survivalism' during the years of its persecution from 1646 to 1660.[13] Women had helped the Anglican faith to survive through the 1640s and 1650s. They had sought out Anglican ministers for the baptism of their children and for their marriages, and in many cases had attended Anglican services wherever possible. These services allowed women to participate more largely in corporate worship than did the Catholic church. Women used the Prayer Book for their private devotions, and kept Anglican faith alive in their households.[14] The spontaneous celebration of Easter in 1660 even before the Declaration of Breda and the restoration of the King was a sign of popular support for the Anglican church.[15]

Anglican ministers preached personal piety and morality. As one eighteenth-century commentator explained, all the best writers of the Anglican church tried 'to turn the Minds of People to the Practice of Moral Duties, and to cure them of that Madness and Enthusiasm into which they had been led ... during the Times of Anarchy and Confusion'.[16] Preachers urged gentlewomen to show a proper awareness of their social rank, to demonstrate 'that one may be a Gentlewoman, or a Lady, & yet Elect'. Women's role as mothers of pious children was stressed: the future of the church 'in succeeding generations, is contained in these Infants yet un-borne'.[17] Piety and religious conformity were the virtues emphasised for everyone after 1660. They had always been commended for women.

In later seventeenth-century England, a number of well-educated Anglican women gained the respect of their male contemporaries for their learning and piety. Ladies such as Anne Conway wrote theological treatises which orthodox Anglican divines admired.[18] Women encouraged each other in godly conversation and behaviour. The writings of Dorcas Bennet, for example, were published in the 1670s, in the hope that women would heed one of their own sex. 'Preachers may say what they will', she alleged, but women refused to reform.[19] In the 1690s Mary Astell gained public recognition for her defence of the Anglican church.[20]

After 1660, the Anglican church resumed the task of disciplining the laity through the church courts. A woman who was excommunicated was refused the rite of churching if she gave birth.[21] However, many aspects of personal and sexual morality were increasingly controlled by the parish, and the church courts declined in importance later in the seventeenth century. Increasingly, the church courts prosecuted recusants and Dissenters, but failed to eradicate either.[22]

The burden of the legislation after 1660 fell heavily on the Presbyterian and Independent ministers who had accepted Anglican livings in the 1640s and 1650s. Unable to swear the oaths required in 1662, an estimated 2,029 ministers were ejected in 1662.[23] What followed was twenty-eight years of hardship of varying degrees. The Nonconformists accepted a Christian framework which made their sufferings bearable: 'No Cross, No Crown' was a comforting text. But it was still a bleak, bitter and unhappy time. Ministers had gifts which they could not exercise, and their surviving diaries bear witness to their frustration. As the ejected minister Philip Henry wrote in September 1663 of himself and other ministers: 'Candles under a Bushel, lord set us up again yt wee may give light in thy house.'[24] Dissenters were not able to preach openly until 1689. Teaching was difficult too, and it was impossible to plan for the future of God's kingdom on earth. Nonconformists were forced to concentrate on survival.

Nonconformist historiography has focused more on the sufferings of ministers than on those of women or laymen.[25] Yet women continued to outnumber men in adherence to Dissent. Throughout the second half of the seventeenth century, women comprised 62 per cent of all members of Baptist churches, and 61 per cent of Congregational churches. In London women made up 68 per cent of both types of congregation.[26]

The wives of Nonconformist ministers suffered at the Anglican restoration. Women's private losses – of former homes, of friends and neighbours, of income and of social status and respect – have been little acknowledged. A wife did not make the decision about whether a minister could conform, but she could make it easy or difficult for her husband to follow his conscience by her attitude. One of the Baptists condemned at Aylesbury temporarily recanted, prevailed on by the tears and entreaties of his wife.[27] Poverty was more unbearable for married ministers, as Richard Baxter observed:

> it pierceth a Man's Heart to have Children crying, and Sickness come upon them for want of wholsom Food, or by drinking Water, and to have nothing to relieve them. And Women are

usually less patient of Suffering than men; and their Impatience would be more to a Husband than his own wants.[28]

Baxter's sympathy was deep for the poor man 'that was fain to Spin as Women do' to help support his family. Clearly the reversal of sex-specific work roles added to the man's humiliation. Yet many ejected ministers found support from their wives. Ellen Astey's cheerfulness when her husband laid down his living was commended in her funeral sermon in 1681: 'in stead of repining, she said she was glad they had such a house'.[29] Similar testimony came from William Kiffin, a Baptist minister. His wife never uttered 'the least discontent under all the various providences'.[30] A few months after his ejection, Philip Henry found comfort in his home: 'my wife is much my helper, present, absent, & my heart doth safely trust in her, the lord's most holy name bee blessed & praysed'.[31]

When their Nonconformist husbands were in gaol, wives tried to assist them. Wives of prisoners kept families and business going, and also visited, and supported their husbands. For example, when John Davis, a General Baptist linen merchant, was imprisoned, his wife had the shop and three children to look after and suffered personal ill-health. Yet all the time that he was in gaol, she visited him, 'During which time her affections carried her sometimes beyond her ability, to come and see me, when she was so weak I was forced to carry her upstairs in my arms.'[32] Women worked for the reprieve and release of prisoners. At the Restoration Margaret Fell 'was mov'd of the Lord' to go to London to speak with Charles II about the Quaker sufferers in gaol.[33] John James was sentenced to death for preaching to the Baptist meeting in Bulstake Alley. His wife petitioned Charles II for his reprieve. Other women, who had been present at his sermon, testified on his behalf. They denied hearing the words of which he was accused. Nevertheless, James was executed on 26 November 1662.[34] Other women friends and supporters, former members of the congregation, also supported the morale of the ejected clergy. For example, when Philip Henry and Mr Thomas and their wives dined with a Mrs Hassell in 1663, Philip told her 'tis much she is not asham'd of such poor Outcasts . . . & shee answer'd they were ye best guests yt come to her house'.[35]

Family piety became more important to Dissent after 1662. When the public ministry became impossible for some Presbyterians and Independents, the household became the one place where a man could exercise his gifts. For their wives and daughters the change after 1662 was less marked. Women had no public roles in the church during the

Civil Wars and Interregnum to lose. What changed was that their husbands needed their support more than before. Furthermore, in so far as the future was bleak, the work of a good Protestant wife and mother in bearing and rearing children was vital in providing for the time to come. As women tended their households, educated their children, catechised their servants and generally ensured that the family was a godly one, so they developed the ethos of family piety which was so important in later Nonconformity and ultimately in nineteenth-century English society. When the public ministry was persecuted, the role of wives and mothers in the family and household was correspondingly more important. By doing the work that the Lord had prescribed for women, they were serving the Lord in the present and providing for a godly future.[36]

Dissent still involved social disadvantages. Margaret Spufford has written of the isolating effect of religious Nonconformity in Cambridgeshire villages during the seventeenth century.[37] After 1689 the social isolation affected the two sexes differently. Like the male Nonconformist laity, women came to be seen as a separate group, distinct from the remainder of the population. No Dissenting wife or daughter could be a member of the town's social elite. Nonconformist women experienced social ostracism. Since women in communities depended on the support of members of their own sex in their daily household tasks and domestic emergencies, the loss of neighbourliness was a handicap. Increasingly, the rules of their own Dissenting congregations set them apart further. Standards of dress, for example, especially among the Quakers, were strict, and contempt for fashion and vanity excluded them from an important part of female culture. Many separatist churches frowned on social intercourse with outsiders, and the Quakers enforced endogamous marriage. By the early eighteenth century, Dissenters were a narrow community, consisting, it has been estimated, of perhaps only 5 per cent of the total population.[38] Endogamy further restricted women's sociability. Nonconformist women experienced the effects of outbreaks of public indignation against them at the times of riots, such as those associated with the trial of Sacheverell in 1710. As a consequence, the bonds between women in their own denominational churches may have been more intense.

For Catholic women, the period after 1660 signalled some alleviation from persecution. Catholics continued to suffer limitations on the practice of their faith, but the sympathy of Charles II and James II meant that Catholics might look to the monarch for some assistance with personal hardships. Charles and James were anxious to remove the disabilities upon Catholics and did what they could to help individuals. However, the monarchs' attempts to alter public policies so as to allow toleration of Catholicism had contrary effects, and aroused anti-Catholic hysteria, especially in 1679 when it was claimed that there was a Popish Plot. One Catholic woman, the prominent London midwife, Elizabeth Cellier, was attacked for her pamphleteering and her support of the Duke of York.[39]

Records of the activity of Catholic women are fewer than for those of the Protestant Dissenters. Catholics tried to keep their worship secret, out of the public eye. We know that missionary activity by nuns continued. In 1669, one of the Sisters of Mary Ward's Institute, Frances Bedingfield, established a Catholic girls' school at Hammersmith. A few years later another was set up near York. Although several of the sisters were imprisoned at the time of the Popish Plot, the sisters continued their work in England. In 1686 Bedingfield purchased a house near Micklegate Bar, York. There, at what became known as the Bar Convent, about twenty young women were accommodated to receive a Catholic education. The Bar and the sister-house at Hammersmith were the only two convents in England until the time of the French Revolution. Susan O'Brien suggests that despite the discontinuities in the history of the Institute, Mary Ward's educational ideals were known and upheld.[40] In the counties, Catholic women continued to shelter priests, hear mass and try to avoid being presented for recusancy. As earlier, they kept their families loyal to their faith, and created an environment in which many sons and daughters found that their religious vocation was fostered. Women who wanted to become nuns still had to travel abroad, so only the wealthier families could allow their daughters to profess their faith. Among those presented for recusancy, women were a majority. While gentlewomen continued to marry within the Catholic elite, Catholic women of lower social status increasingly married Protestants. In Lancashire, Galgano calculates that at least a quarter of Catholic brides married out of their faith.[41]

Some Nonconformist women's sufferings were public. Quaker meetings and historians noted the Quaker women who were pilloried, whipped or imprisoned.[42] Since the Restoration legislation singled out the Quakers, they were more likely to be imprisoned than other Nonconformists. Thus the experiences of women of different persuasions varied after 1660.

FROM RELIGIOUS MOVEMENT TO DENOMINATION: THE QUAKERS

Women's role in the Quaker movement changed after the first two decades, as Quakerism itself altered. Initially a dynamic movement, by about 1670 proceedings were more formalised, organisation increased, and Quaker religion became more concerned with discipline and less with mysticism and ecstasy.[43] A number of factors may explain the changes in the nature of the Quaker movement. Sociologists of religion argue that most religious movements must come to terms with the world in order to survive.[44] After the Restoration, Quakers faced ruinous fines and imprisonments. Although they endured heroically, worship and religious meetings became very difficult. In addition, as the movement enlarged, the Quakers themselves were more vulnerable to the disorder of individuals, and so sought greater control. By the 1670s, the Quakers believed that 'the Enemy', Satan, was at work undermining the truth and the light, and sought to counter his attacks by a more intense public printed campaign and by the imposition of stricter discipline.

Women's visibility declined in the Quaker movement. From the first, Quakers had developed a policy about replying to printed attacks upon them, and of proselytising through the press. In 1672 an all-male censoring committee was established, known as the Second Day Morning Meeting, whose purpose was to examine all proposed publications. Increasingly, the Friends chose to play down the prophetic element in their movement. By the 1690s, women's publications which had been numerous in this area were fewer.[45] Judith Bowlbie, for example, submitted several manuscripts in the 1690s which were returned to her as unsuitable for publication.[46] Meetings testified against those who published against the truth. The Upperside meeting of Buckinghamshire witnessed against Susannah Aldridge's publications.[47] Not all women accepted this censorship. In 1703 Abigail Fisher, whose papers were returned, protested because she said that some of the meeting's laws 'do stopp the Passage of the Spirit'.[48] She was right. All this censorship was far from the days of the early 1650s when women had spoken or published their messages as the spirit of the Lord moved them.

Quaker discipline of members became stricter. Women were in trouble more for offences relating to dress, 'back biting' and gossip, men for drunkenness and violence. Records of meetings indicate that women's economic activities were scrutinised. For example, the Upperside meeting in Buckinghamshire advised a widow how to settle up 'to yield up & deliver al she hath' to be divided among her husband's creditors.

In 1674 the Upperside meeting reproved a female shopkeeper who had accumulated debts, but also resolved to purchase wood to help her husband to gainful employment.[49] The Swathmore women's meeting reproved two of its members for selling lace 'which is needlesse'.[50] Women's meetings also objected to their members selling ale.[51]

Religious belief could make a single woman's economic circumstances even more difficult, even though some of the penalties affected men rather than women. Prior to the Toleration Act, goods could be seized in lieu of fines for attendance at religious meetings, and more men owned goods than did women. Nevertheless, single women might own property, and seizure of goods could threaten their livelihoods. In 1678 a widow in the Vale of the White Horse refused to pay tithes. Her livelihood was jeopardised when a quarter of her hemp was seized.[52] A servant maid in the Vale was transferred to parish relief in 1678, but she was forced to conform '(contrary to her conscience) for mere necessity of outward, needful things'.[53] While men, too, were likely to experience poverty, the wages paid to women and the expectation of their economic dependence meant that they were more likely to be in poverty. Women needed more poor relief, and so Quaker women experienced more economic hardship for their faith. Quaker meetings provided supplementary relief, although their main aim was to make the poor independent.[54]

Quaker beliefs restricted women's occupations. Meetings tried to prohibit participation in the luxury trades. Lace-making was judged to be unlawful in the 1690s. Both the Leeds and Brighouse meetings, for example, advised their members to forbear from those who persisted in the trade.[55] Since lace-making, millinery, and fancy sewing were largely female occupations, these restrictions bore especially harshly on them. By 1728 the Friends' School at Saffron Walden was objecting to girls learning sewing. The Friends supporting the school wanted girls to be servants, not to get an independent living.[56] What had started in the 1650s as a desire for simplicity and an avoidance of waste and scandal in dress became a rigid code later. Again, women bore the brunt of this: 'Away with your short black Aprons. . . . Away with your *Vizzards*, whereby you are not distinguished from bad Women', wrote George Fox.[57] Ornamental dress for men was also disapproved of, but did not carry the same danger of sexual immorality.

The place of women in Quakerism became contentious in the 1670s. Three main issues were involved; separate women's meetings, marriage procedures and women's speaking. Each issue involved women's exercise of authority over men, and thereby threatened male power.

The separate meetings of women Friends which had begun in the 1650s continued and expanded. The Society recognised that women's experiences and behaviour were different from men's. Since in their daily lives women were closer to people in their communities and knew who was in need of relief, they could advise the men's financial meetings of suitable recipients of the Society's charity. Moreover, women's knowledge about young people made it appropriate for marriage proposals to be referred to the women's meetings. Although Quaker historiography has credited Fox with a major role in the development of separate women's meetings, it is more likely that he was responding to women's initiatives.[58] Certainly Fox was sympathetic to the idea of different roles for women and was supportive of their separate meetings. He argued in 1676 in defence of women's activities. Fox recognised that men felt threatened, fearing that women in the power of the Lord would be 'too high'. Even so, he knew that Moses and Aaron did not tell women to stay home and wash dishes 'or such Expressions'.[59] However, Fox still thought that women served the Lord in different ways from men, because they were fitter to look after families and to train children, and to be 'mothers in Israel'.[60] John Storey, one of the strongest antagonists of the women's meetings and of Fox, claimed that the whole notion of a separate women's meeting was monstrous among Christians. Others added that it was 'ridiculous'.[61]

Increasingly by the 1670s, Quaker meetings emphasised 'orderly way of proceeding' in marriage.[62] Exogamy was not allowed, a policy which was more of a hardship to women because they outnumbered men in the Society. Meetings around the country censured those who married 'out' to persons described as a 'man of ye world' or a 'Lass of the world'.[63] Even for those who wanted to marry other Quakers, there was strict control. A couple who hesitated between the two meetings held to consider their marriage were to be 'investigated' by five men. Another pair was instructed to delay their proposed marriage until they were more settled in 'the truth'.[64] Marriage procedure required that the couple appear three times before the Men's and Women's Monthly Meetings.[65] Meetings disowned those who married according to the standard English legal form. Since the civil courts recognised only those marriages performed by priests of the Anglican church, the requirement that all Quakers marry according to the way of the Society was a severe test of faith.

Male fears of the collective power of women can be seen in their printed attacks on women's participation in the marriage procedures.

William Mucklow complained that if the women's meeting were allowed a veto, they could deprive a man of a person 'whom he most dearly loves'.[66] It was, said William Mather, 'a very hard trial' for men to submit to female authority in matters of marriage. His arguments were contradictory: on the one hand, he thought that women were incapable of independent action. They were merely pawns in the male power struggles: their meetings were set up by men. On the other hand, Mather was haunted by the fear of female power, of the inappropriateness of women 'ruffling' to the seat of counsel.[67] In 1680 Rogers mocked women who 'pry' into marriages. He too saw the issue as one of female rule, and ridiculed the role of the women's meeting in relieving the poor as mere pretence.[68]

Women's speaking was also contentious. Since many women were inhibited in mixed meetings, separate meetings allowed women to speak more freely among themselves. But many believed that if the spirit moved through male and female alike, women should still speak in mixed meetings. Others sought to confine women's speaking to the extraordinary. Preaching and bearing witness were difficult to distinguish. Female modesty might inhibit both speaking before a large audience and talking of sexual matters in relation to proposed marriages. The issue was one of power: if women spoke in the power of the Lord, or if they decided to veto marriages, they were exercising authority over men, and some men found this intolerable.

Storey and his ally Wilkinson also objected to women's speaking in the mixed meetings. Margaret Fell had earlier defended the theoretical rights of women to speak. God himself had manifested 'his Will and Mind concerning Women'. Since the Quakers believed that those who lived under the gospel were in a pre-lapsarian state of freedom, Fell argued that it was only those under the law who should not prophesy. For others, the Lord had shown his power 'without respect of Persons'.[69] Opponents of women's speaking agreed that women who 'received a Revelation from God' might speak. It was the old question of who had the power to label what was from the Lord, and what was mere will. Rogers' objection to the disorderly women who were 'so rude in their Opposition' suggests that he at least had no difficulty in deciding which women were in the power of the Lord and which were troublemakers.[70] Allegations of sexual promiscuity featured, as always, in the debates about female participation. Mucklow alleged that there was 'scandalous familiarity of the Prophets and Prophetesses' and wanton behaviour generally.[71] Other comments revealed straight misogyny: women's singing, for example, was said to be 'like caterwauling'.[72]

All these issues relating to women's place in the Society of Friends – separate women's meetings, women's role in marriage procedures and women's speaking – were central to a division in the Quaker movement in the 1670s. Some men objected to the women's meetings because they conferred unscriptural authority on women over men. Some alleged that women's meetings were a kind of separation. Others argued that if the women's meetings were an accepted part of Quaker organisation, then organisation had triumphed over inspiration. Although the Society survived the Wilkinson–Storey split, and separate women's meetings continued, preaching was more regulated by 1700. The Box Meeting expressed concern at unlicensed women preaching, and there were complaints in London that women's speaking took up too much time.[73] Procedures developed whereby those who wished to speak were required to leave their names. Modesty Newman put her name down, but the London Morning Meeting put it out.[74] In 1702 and 1703 the London Morning Meeting told Mary Obee that she appeared too frequently at public meetings. The Meeting also vetoed her papers to Queen Anne, telling her 'to be still and quiet in her mind'.[75]

Thus by the early eighteenth century, Quakerism was more organised, and less open to active female participation. There was some compensatory development of protective impulses towards women. For example, if a man gained a woman's affections, or had had sexual relations with her, Quaker meetings pressed him to marry her.[76] Meetings also reinforced the conventional norms of married life. The Vale meeting disciplined a man who struck his wife and caused her to miscarry.[77]

During the later seventeenth century, the women's meetings in various areas gained assurance and confidence. They issued yearly letters from their meetings, admonishing and advising from their own experiences.[78] But although the women's meetings continued, female rights to participate in preaching and witnessing in the mixed meetings were diminished. Individual women still became preachers, but they travelled in a more circumscribed manner, and preached to meetings of Friends, rather than to outsiders. By the early eighteenth century, the movement had lost much of its dynamism and was more concerned with formal piety rather than spirituality. It was a more pietistic, quietist spirituality that the Quaker movement offered to women.

THE PARTICULAR AND GENERAL BAPTIST CHURCHES

After the Restoration, members of the Baptist churches were set apart from the rest of society, as were other Nonconformists. The intensification of discipline affected women as well as men. Even during the 1650s, as we have seen, congregations assumed a supervisory role over many aspects of personal and family life and economic activity. In Baptist churches a higher proportion of people were excommunicated for their misdemeanours than their counterparts in the Anglican church. In the General Baptist church at Fenstanton, for example, Watts calculated that of 178 members who were baptised between 1645 and 1656, 53 were excommunicated at some time during the same period. In one Congregational church from 1690 to 1714, 795 members were added, of whom 199 were excommunicated.[79] While not all Nonconformist churches were so severe, the majority felt obliged to bear a strong witness to their gospel profession through the perfection of their personal lives.

Those who had power to discipline women in the church had power over their social roles. It is thus important to discover whether discipline was exercised by men over women, or whether women participated as members of congregations. The Baptist churches allow an exploration of this question. Unlike the Presbyterian churches, where discipline was normally exercised by the ministers, and thus fewer records survive, among the Baptists discipline was an important part of the congregation's collective duty. Baptist records were voluminous.

The records of the Maze Pond Particular Baptist church from the 1690s show something of the contradictions and conflicts between theories about the ideal church and women's place in it, and actual practice.[80] Maze Pond formed after the church at Horsleydown divided over the issue of singing. Congregational singing, according to the minority, was formal, not 'inspired' worship, in that it involved set words and a known tune. A minority of members resolved to forbear from fellowship, adding among their grievances that Horsleydown allowed a large role to women:

> you suffer Women to speake and sing, to teach and admonish in the Worship and servis of God in his Church, contrary to the Word of God, which commands women not to speak, nor to teach, but to learne in Silence 1 Cor. 14.34 1 Tim. 2.11, 12.[81]

Benjamin Keach, the Horsleydown pastor, insisted on discussing the issues with the minority group one at a time, coming last to 'several sisters'. The account of his discussion with Mary Leader, wife of one of the most prominent dissidents, raises in direct and vivid terms some of the issues which church members were forced to confront. Keach mocked Mary Leader's religious knowledge and then treated her as a puppet of her husband,

> saying to her, what have you to say . . . she replyed she could pass by all offences, but she would not keep Communion while they were in that way of singing, then he replyed quick upon her, and looking earnestly at her saying you have learnt a fine peace [sic] of Relidgion [sic] ha'nt you, I confess I am troubled to see that you that are but a Babe should pretend to such knowledg above others or to that effect, and then turning to her Husband Bro[the]r Luke Leader he said you have finely dragg'd her up . . .[82]

Keach both resented a woman having views and blamed her husband for teaching them to her, although Leader swore that he was not responsible for her views. The irony is that although Keach's side gave a large public participatory role to women, allowing them to bear witness, when Mary Leader opposed his views he dismissed her as a mere adjunct of her husband. Horsleydown excommunicated the nine men. The thirteen women decided they would continue attending, perhaps to see what would happen. They pointed out that Horsleydown's attitudes to them were contradictory:

> you seemed not to look upon us as your Members or concerned with you, bidding us some times withdraw from you that you might doe your business without us, and at another time when we were come by your . . . desire, you named us to withdraw.[83]

Although the women were perfectly able to assert their views, they were not theoretical defenders of the rights of women to speak and teach as was the Horsleydown congregation.

When the newly separated group made a covenant to form Maze Pond church, six men and thirteen women signed as witnesses, in separate lists.[84] Women were in a different category of membership from men. By 1694, the congregation had expanded enormously, to 52 men and 126 women. At this date, when women formed more than two-thirds of the congregation, the question of their participation in church business became contentious. Around December 1694 'the Liberty of the Sisters in the Church was largely discoursed' and after further dispute, resolved upon.[85] The church decided that women could neither speak 'in the immediate worship of God in his Church', nor could they debate 'equally as the men have power to do', nor be church officers. Nevertheless, women had the right to vote:

4. We doe beleive [sic] the Sisters being equaly with the Brethren members of the misticall Body of Christ, his Church they have equall right Liberty and Previledge to voate with them by lifting up of their hands or as the Church sees meet, to shew their Assent or dissent for or against any matter or thing that is moued in the Church.
5. We doe believe that a Sister haveing signified her dissatisfaction in a voate may give the reasons for her dissatisfaction.

The church was not to proceed to a resolution until a woman had given her reasons for her dissent, which she might do by a brother, unless the necessity of the case required her 'to deliver her minde her selfe'.[86] Thus in addition to voting, a woman could argue her case. Maze Pond may have been unusual, and Murdina Macdonald, in her study of the London Calvinist Baptists, concluded that it was.[87] Nevertheless, it shows how even in the most liberal of churches, there were practical confusions and theoretical inconsistencies inherent in women's membership of separatist churches.

In the selection of a pastor, the consent of the whole congregation was desired. The Cripplegate Baptist Church book recorded explicitly that if any men or women were dissatisfied with the nomination of David Crosley as their pastor in 1703, they were to hold up their hands.[88] But democracy could be limited, and class as well as gender could influence the politics. When the congregation voted in 1713 on Brother Mathews becoming an elder, there was a big majority against him, but because most of 'the Antient and ruleing brethren' were not present, the business was deferred.[89] In 1714 there was a rumour that the church had passed an act that only those who contributed to the church's finances were to have a vote. Presumably it caused disquiet because it would have disenfranchised most of the women.[90]

Women's acquiescence in the proceedings of the Baptist church was required, but their independent views were not. Sister Hopkins of the Cripplegate church thought that the congregation was too severe in their censure of a wife in a domestic dispute, so she stayed away. Questioned, she said that she had consulted both her father and a minister at Abingdon who blamed the church for its proceedings. The church admonished her.[91] In another case, female criticism of a minister was disallowed. Honour Gould applied to Maze Pond in 1694 for admission because she was dissatisfied with the conduct of Hercules Collins as her minister: 'his Preaching in her Judgment not being agreeable to the word of God, ner [nor] her owne expereirance [sic], neith can she profit thereby'. She was not admitted, because Collins denied her allegations.[92]

One formal office was specific to women in the Baptist church: that of deaconess, based on 1 Timothy 5.9 and 11. From 1656 widows assisted deacons in looking after the poor and sick. Bristol church appointed their first deaconess in 1662. On her death in 1673, another widow succeeded. In 1679, four widows over 60 years of age were asked to consider becoming deaconesses. Only three were willing to serve, for on the basis of 1 Timothy 5.11, the church required the women not to marry. Thus, for the only church office open to women, celibacy was required. Since their duties were to visit the sick, and they could even speak a word of comfort, the Bristol church book noted that this was probably the reason 'why they must be 60 yeares of age, that none occasion may be given; and as in 1 Timo. v.14'.[93] Apparently Baptists shared the conventional assumption that women were insatiable for sex until well after the menopause. However, concern for propriety did not operate in the same way when women were to be visited. Churches sent two brothers to admonish sisters, without a hint that this could compromise the women.

The Baptist churches upheld conventional views of women and the family. Since personal morality affected the public reputation of a church, the Baptist church books of the later seventeenth century show congregations seriously concerned about domestic sins 'whereby the name of God was greatly dishonored and our holy profession reproached'.[94]

A discussion of the disparate standards employed to judge the marital and social conduct of men and women reveals the role of the Dissenting church in enforcing traditional norms of social behaviour. Baptists were to be respectful to parents. A woman's admission to the Baptist church at Maze Pond was delayed until she acknowledged her fault in speaking unadvisedly of her mother.[95] Several churches punished husbands for cruelty to their wives. For example, in 1697 the Cripplegate Baptist Church disciplined Brother Simon, a journeyman shoemaker who lived near Clare Market, 'for inhumanly beating his wife and giving himselfe to much idlenes not minding to be diligent in his calling and employment'. He had gone into debt and failed to provide for his family. Since he refused to repent, the church cast him out.[96] In 1699 the Cripplegate church disciplined Brother Leeson who was in debt to his father-in-law among others, and treated his wife, who was a nurse, 'not in a loving but after an imperious scoffing rate'. On the precedent cited from 2 Timothy 3.5, the church cast him out. The case also shows that the Baptist church did not tolerate wifely insubordination. Leeson had complained of his wife's 'very uncivill and barbarous language' to him. The church found that the story was an unhappy one: 'shee had been very badly and inhumanely treated by her husband, That deep distressing poverty had afflicted her through his incapacity or negligence to gett a livelyhood or subsistence'. Even though the church recognised that her husband had failed in his duty as a provider, they expected conformity to the ideals of uncomplaining womanhood. They admonished her, and refused her communion 'till by a carefull meek conversation there may be seen a reall reformation'.[97]

The more conventional sexual sins were also disciplined. The story of Brother Benjamin, a baker's servant who promised marriage to a maidservant and then had sexual relations with her was 'publike to the neighbours to the great scandal and reproach of his holy profession'. Benjamin admitted his offence, but complained 'that he was unhappily drawn to it by the importunity of that wicked woman'. The church cast him out.[98]

The church scrutinised the economic activities of both sexes. Although the lists of members of the Baptist Cripplegate church give few clues as to economic status, the cases of discipline recorded from 1689 to 1699 occasionally mention occupations. These included shoemaker, waterman, chambermaid and coachman. Women as well as men were expected to work for their living. In 1694 Sister Cooke was excluded for a series of offences. Her case demonstrates the complex interlocking of women's financial affairs. Cooke persuaded one Mrs Green, the nurse in her child bed, to lend £40 to Sister Webb on the promise that Webb would improve it to great advantage. After a long time the money was not repaid 'though the poore woman was in great distress for want of it'. As this was all the money which Mrs Green had saved 'to help her when her strength in labour might fayl her', she was completely undone when Webb failed to repay the money. Webb was repentant, but unable to meet her creditors. The church disowned Cooke, recording that her actions had dishonoured the name of God 'and our holy profession reproached'.[99] Although many Baptists paid poor rates, congregations undertook to supplement this relief.[100] Soon after the Maze Pond church was formed in February 1694, arrangements were made for money to be collected for the poor, and a book to be kept for accounts.[101]

All denominations sought to practise endogamy. Surviving church books show that all were concerned about suitable marriage partners, to various degrees. Members of the General Baptist Assembly of 1668 resolved that while they would not call 'marrying out' a fornication – that is, they would not totally deny that it was a marriage – nevertheless they saw it as 'a marrying out of the Lord or out of the Church'.[102] Again, women were more likely to offend because they outnumbered men in Baptist churches.

The churches usually acted to support the interests of masters against undisciplined servants. Records of the Cripplegate Baptist Church in the 1690s show that servants were disciplined for disorderly behaviour.[103] Neighbourly reputation was also important: two brothers were directed to enquire of a man's neighbours about his behaviour before he could be admitted to the church.[104]

The relationship between a Nonconformist congregation and their pastor was frequently a close one, as the church books show. When it was suggested that Keach should be forbearing with the Dissidents in his Particular Baptist congregation, he replied 'you had as good take a knife and stab me in the heart'.[105] Sexual immorality was central to the dismissal of a Baptist pastor, David Crosley, from the Cripplegate church in 1709. Complaints brought to light a series of incidents involving drunkenness and offences with a number of women. To the sins of drink he confessed, but the sexual sins he denied. These, more serious because he was married, ranged from his kissing a woman in a tavern, being seen with a strumpet and going into a house of ill repute, propositioning various women, tongue kissing and exposing himself. Since Crosley was reputed to be the largest man in his county, his behaviour may have been especially offensive and menacing to women. Needless to say, there were counter-allegations, particularly relating to the last two alleged offences: one of the young women was said to be of dubious character – a liar, a drunkard and a thief and not to be trusted. The church was reluctant to conclude without consensus, but Crosley's subsequent actions led them to conclude his guilt. The whole case produced 'abundance of heat, and disorder'.[106]

To sum up, women's position in the Baptist churches remained ambiguous, although there were attempts to define it. As members of a congregation, women possessed certain freedoms and rights which they could choose to exercise if they wished. Their assent to the business of the church was necessary, and they could put items on the church's agenda for discussion. They had the numerical strength, had they chosen to vote as a group, but they appear never to have done so. It should not be forgotten when we look at the records, as it must have been impossible to forget in the congregations, that women usually outnumbered men by two to one. This being the case, the exercise of discipline was not a simple case of men controlling women. Women had absorbed so many of the conventional norms of female behaviour that they shared in the enforcement of these norms.

THE FEMINISATION OF RELIGION

By the beginning of the eighteenth century, a process was observably under way in the American colonies by which the church became a more feminine institution. Ministers there observed with sorrow that male piety had declined and women in the congregrations outnumbered men. Gender differentiation in religious life increased. Women's virtues were described in family terms, so that to be a good woman was to be a good Christian, while to be a good man was to be a good citizen. Mary Dunn has argued that such gender differentiation was a stage in the separation of church and state.[107]

Several factors mark the feminisation of religion in England. A broad general movement away from emotional and intense belief followed the revolutionary period. Divines of the Anglican church after the Restoration emphasised the importance of morality and sought to direct their congregations away from the religious enthusiasm which was blamed for the disorders of the Civil Wars and Interregnum. Increasingly, faith and reason were seen to be in binary opposition, as female and male always had been. Belief was for women, reason for men. Educated men sought to guide their conduct by the light of reason. Religion, based on emotion, was desirable for women as well as for men of lower status. This trend increased the separation between the sexes and the classes. Virtuous middle-class women became the good conscience of the family. Religion was for the household, where women taught their children personal morality. In the public sphere, educated men deemed secular values and virtues more appropriate.

By the later eighteenth century, it was claimed that women's actual natures made them more susceptible to religion. As John Gregory argued in his *Father's Legacy to his Daughter*, women's 'superior delicacy', modesty, and education preserved them from vice, while 'the natural softness and sensibility of [their] dispositions . . . along with the natural warmth of [their] imaginations' made women especially susceptible to the feelings of devotion. Gregory advised his daughter to avoid perplexing works of theology and to concentrate on those books which

The Excellent Woman

Printed for Joseph Watts

Figure 12. A wealthy, devout woman of the 1690s. From Jacques du Bosc, *The Excellent Woman, 1692* (British Library, London).

were addressed to the heart, for 'Religion is rather a matter of sentiment than reasoning.'[108] But if religion was a matter of feeling, by the early eighteenth century, extremes of feeling, such as religious enthusiasm, were deeply suspect in both men and women.

Among the Anglicans, Presbyterians and Congregationalists, emphasis on family virtues for women, on their 'relative duties' as daughters, wives, and mothers, influenced the patterns of female piety. Among some of the Dissenting churches, where women continued to outnumber men, the influence of female piety on the churches' morality was powerful, as mothers reared their children in the fear of the Lord. Household religion remained important for Nonconformists early in the eighteenth century. Yet there was a price to be paid for respectable piety. Nonconformists lost a missionary zeal and a widespread popular appeal. Converts were comparatively few in the eighteenth century, and the churches relied heavily upon the children of believers to continue the denominations. In this context, Nonconformist women could see religion as something especially their own. They could impose a regime of piety upon their households and educate their children in their beliefs.[109]

Women's numerical preponderance in Nonconformist congregations was a continuing feature of post-Restoration Dissent. Women may have outnumbered men in regularity of attendance at Anglican services, but I know of no evidence to test this hypothesis. Intriguingly, married women in the congregations were few, and single or widowed women were in the majority.[110] This, perhaps, accounts for the fact that the highest proportion of women in Baptist and Congregational churches was in London, where the increasing demand for servants attracted women to work in the capital. Historians have suggested a range of explanations for women's numerical predominance. Men risked more by Nonconformity, because of the civic disabilities imposed on Dissenters; men had less time for active religious commitment; attendance at the Anglican church placed fewer demands on them.[111] Yet the puzzle remains. Women's own statements from the earlier period speak of their determination to find spiritual satisfaction. In the smaller group of a Nonconformist congregation, the religious and social needs of some women may still have been better met.

An important shift had taken place by the eighteenth century. Religion was no longer what politics was all about, which is not to say that religion was no longer significant in politics. But the establishment of God's kingdom on earth had ceased to be the politicians' goal. Men were busy with public concerns, and religious belief was increasingly a private matter, or even a household matter, something for women and children. Men allowed women to be responsible for religion and piety in the home, but religion lost its prominence in English culture.[112] In so far as religion was a matter of public concern, it was as a means of improving the behaviour of the masses.

Early in the eighteenth century, those who were disturbed at the relative decline of religious practices organised movements for reform. They established educational foundations to improve the morality of the public. In 1698 a number of prominent clegymen and laymen founded the Society for Promoting Christian Knowledge, and established fifty-four charity schools before 1704.[113] The curriculum of these schools was sex-specific. Boys were to learn arithmetic, writing, spelling and reading, while girls were instructed 'generally to knit their Stockings and Gloves, to mark, sew, make and mend, their Cloathes', and some to 'learn to write and to spin their Cloathes'.[114] Women's participation in subscribing and fund-raising was important for the success of the schools. The school for thirty poor girls at Chelsea was governed by female trustees and directed by Mary Astell.[115]

Within the Quaker churches, women preachers seemed unnatural even to women by the 1700s. Even so, some women's testimonies show how they experienced the call to preach. They overcame the objections of their families and society as well as their own. Margaret Lucas (1701–70), reared by a Presbyterian aunt and uncle, converted to Quakerism and ultimately became a minister, although she recorded 'I had in my nature a great aversion to women's preaching.'

> The first time I ever heard a woman preach, from a prejudice imbibed from my companions, and probably an aversion in my own nature, I thought it very ridiculous; and the oftener I had opportunities to witness it, the more I secretly despised it.[116]

During the later seventeenth and early eighteenth centuries, many women followed mystics such as Bourignon and Jane Lead.[117] The prophet Anne Bathurst and Joanna Oxenbridg 'were Two Principal Persons' who carried on the work of Lead's Philadelphian Society.[118] Early in the eighteenth century, women were part of a religious movement known as the French Prophets. Women predominated among the prophets and leaders of this movement, but men as well as women prophesied when in trance. Schwartz, the historian of the group, has argued that men retained control by insisting upon judging the truth of an inspiration, and by restricting sacerdotal functions to men.[119] As in the 1650s, in 1707 a congregation of these worshippers was said to be shocked when a woman stripped naked. She stood at the altar, and 'did hold forth in a Powerful manner' for a quarter of an hour, and told them 'she was come to Reform the People, and bring them to a right understanding'.[120] Although the French Prophets numbered only around 400 in 1708 in London, 20,000 people assembled to witness a raising of a man from the dead.[121] Like many other religious groups, the French Prophets are known from the work of their enemies rather than from their own records. The opposition to the prophets, however, differed from earlier reactions to prophecies. There was more emphasis on the deception allegedly practised by the prophets, and more explanations were offered in terms of madness.[122] Even so, the same sexual slanders as earlier were made.[123]

The most significant of the movements of religious enthusiasm and revival was that initiated by the Wesley brothers in the 1730s. Although Methodism is outside the scope of this book, it is worth noting that one of its characteristics in its early phase was the presence of women preachers. As a religion of enthusiasm, Methodism recognised that some women had special spiritual gifts, and the tradition of women preachers among some of the Dissenting churches served as an example to Methodist women.

The supposedly natural religiosity of women was a powerful part of the ideology of the eighteenth century. Female religious enthusiasts were marginalised, but still professed their faith, and participated in new religious movements. Within the established Anglican church, and the Catholic and Nonconformist churches, many women continued to worship and find spiritual comfort. Many continued to find in religion a space of their own, a set of beliefs which were uniquely theirs, which provided comfort in their lives on earth and dreams and visions of a glorious life to come. Knowing God for themselves, they believed that they had found the most important thing in life.

10

Conclusion

Religion was of central importance in the lives of women in England in the early modern period. Women found spiritual satisfaction from their beliefs and a meaning for life. Frequently contemporaries recognised the intensity of female spirituality, and saw that it differed from male religiosity. Female spirituality was affected by assumptions about the two sexes and the consequent constraints upon women. Women's religious experiences were different from men's. Even when they attended the same worship, and received the same theological messages as men, they experienced the gender symbols in religion differently.[1]

How to explain the greater religiosity of women remains a challenge, but several factors should be borne in mind. Women's religious lives and experiences were affected by their different social levels. Women at upper and middling social levels had more time to concentrate on devotion. In addition to cultivating their faith by prayer and devotional reading, they made an individual regime of piety out of their household and family matters. At lower social levels, it is difficult to speculate because of limited evidence, but the testimonies of women in separatist churches speak of a powerful desire to find an immediate sense of God, and a church which would provide spiritual satisfaction. Although it has been widely observed that women were more numerous in the sects than men, they may also have attended the established church in greater numbers than did men. A woman's own family background, whether godly or not, could influence her, as could the specific religious faith, Catholic or Protestant, to which that family subscribed. Ultimately, however, women made their own choices in spiritual matters.

During the 1640s and 1650s, English men and women debated religious issues fiercely, as they struggled to establish the ideal church. Women from a wide range of social levels were involved. Women's opportunities for participation during the Civil Wars and Interregnum were unequalled at any other time during the early modern period, including during the Reformation. Some women took advantage of the greater religious freedom, and engaged in a range of public activity. They preached, proselytised, debated and published on an unprecedented scale. Women participated in religious life in ways which had not been possible earlier. The significance of the radical experience for women was considerable.

The strength of the sects by the end of the Interregnum meant that those shaping the settlements of 1660 and 1689 were forced to acknowledge a Dissenting presence. Because of the numbers of Dissenters, and the degree of their conviction about their beliefs, it was futile to argue that the church was one. A measure of religious toleration was permitted in England by the end of the seventeenth century. Women's participation in the sects during the revolutionary years meant that they had played a part in the establishment of an alternative religious tradition. They had increased everyone's religious options, their own included.

More difficult is the question of the effects of the sectarian experience on religious belief and on gender relations. Of course there was a conservative backlash after 1660, and religious enthusiasm was suspect. Judging from the persecution experiences of Quaker women, they do not seem to have been deterred from religious activity. They continued to express their views, even if their ideas were not always endorsed by the men ruling the Society. Perhaps because women suffered from civil disabilities at all times, they had less to lose for their religious enthusiasm than did Dissenting men. Although ideally wives were to obey their husbands, in practice women were freer to follow the dictates of their own consciences. Not all women were married, and for those who were wives, religious faith could justify disobedience. Divines of the Anglican church disapproved of women's enthusiasm in religion, but some women continued to seek ecstatic religious experience. The Flanders mystic Antonia Bourignon had a widespread following, and Jane Lead's mystical visions led to the founding of the Philadelphian church. Had it not been for the strength of the Dissenting tradition, Lead may have been in trouble with the ecclesiastical authorities.

On gender relations, it can be argued that the self-confidence gained by a few women made a difference. By engaging in public speaking and publishing, women challenged the bounds which had limited them. Religion was their most powerful justification for activity which was outside their conventional roles. Even though the actors themselves participated as individuals, they were gendered beings. Women's spirituality, which differed from men's, led to them challenging conventional gender roles in the spiritual sphere. Radical women could also be led by their beliefs to challenge conventional expectations of the sexes in the secular sphere as well. Thus, as a sex, women made gains.

Finally, religion empowered a few women with a feminist consciousness, albeit rudimentary, which was expressed most strongly in response to opposition. Because women's religious beliefs mattered to them, this in turn led to public action in defence of those beliefs. The male refrains of 'attend to the spindle and distaff', and 'go home and wash your dishes' led women to formulate positions which justified female political action. As the women petitioners declared to Parliament in May 1649, 'we are assured of our Creation in the image of God, and of an interest in Christ, equal unto men, as also of a proportional share in the Freedoms of this Commonwealth'.[2] Justified by Christian teachings, the women petitioners refused to accept the view that the secular political sphere was an exclusively male domain.

Belief made for contradictions. And this is where I think the sectarian experience was so important for women and the history of the 1640s and 1650s. The sects gave them an opportunity to experience the power of the Lord in a less restricted way than at any other time during the century. Other women fasted, prayed, and apprehended God. Some women in the sects were so moved by the power of the Lord that they were prepared to challenge the conventional roles apportioned to them as women: they claimed the temple and the altar – the sacred – were open to them, and in so doing they challenged male propriety and the boundaries between priest and believer, public and private, men and women. Women's participation at many levels during the revolutionary decades affected the history of the sects and the course of events during the mid-seventeenth century. Men at the time could not ignore women's presence; neither should historians.

Glossary

Antinomians believed that Christians were by grace set free from the need to observe any moral law.

Baptists From the sixteenth century, there were two Baptist communities. The **General** or Arminian Baptists believed that Christ died for all, and that there was 'general redemption'. The **Particular**, or Calvinistic Baptists believed that Christ died only for the elect.

Brownists A group of Elizabethan separatists who believed that the church consisted only of the worthy. The magistrate had no power over congregations, who were autonomous.

Barrowists Followers of Henry Barrow, Elizabethan separatists.

Churching of women The form of thanksgiving which Christian women made after childbirth.

Familists Followers of the doctrine of the defunct sect, the Family of Love, who believed that the divine spirit could raise people to perfection, beyond all sin.

Feme covert The legal term used to refer to a woman 'under the protection of her husband', a married woman.

Fifth Monarchists believed that the four kingdoms of the earth would pass away and that the fifth, that of Christ, was imminent.

Independents Also known as Congregationalists, they believed in the autonomy of congregations. In England they were prepared to allow liberty of conscience to separatists.

Ordinances Those religious practices authoritatively enjoined or prescribed. While most agreed that the Lord's Supper was an ordinance of the church, different groups disagreed about whether other matters, such as the priesthood or eldership, were church ordinances.

Presbyterians believed in a united national church with presbyters rather than bishops having authority to discipline.

Quakers   The term popularly used to refer to members of the Society of Friends. A central doctrine was the sense of the divine and direct working of Christ by which people were freed from sin and united to Christ. From the Quaker doctrine of the inner light arose different ideas about the established church and worship.

Recusants   Strictly, those who refused to attend the services of the Church of England. After 1570 the term was frequently applied to Catholics in general.

Sectaries   A pejorative term used to refer to those who did not subscribe to the established church.

Transubstantiation   The doctrine of the Catholic church that at the mass the priest changed the bread and wine into the body and blood of Christ.

For further references, see F. L. Cross, *The Oxford Dictionary of the Christian Church*, Oxford, 1947; J. S. Purvis, *Dictionary of Ecclesiastical Terms*, 1962.

Notes

Introduction

1 M. Emmanuel Orchard (ed.), *Till God Will. Mary Ward Through her Writings*, 1985, 58.
2 For a valuable discussion of this issue, see Joan Wallach Scott, *Gender and the Politics of History*, New York, 1988, 1–11.
3 For studies of unbelief, see Gerald Aylmer, 'Unbelief in seventeenth-century England', in Donald Pennington and Keith Thomas (eds), *Puritans and Revolutionaries. Essays in Seventeenth-Century History Presented to Christopher Hill*, Oxford, 1978; Michael Hunter, 'The problem of "atheism" in early modern England', *Trans. R. H. S.*, 5th series, 35, 1985, 135–57.
4 Clifford Geertz, 'Religion as a cultural system', in *The Interpretation of Cultures. Selected Essays*, New York, 1973, 87–125.
5 Caroline Walker Bynum, 'Introduction: the complexity of symbols', in Caroline Walker Bynum, Steve Harrell and Paula Richman (eds), *Gender and Religion: On the Complexity of Symbols*, Boston, 1986.
6 Patrick Collinson, 'Towards a broader understanding of the early dissenting tradition', in *Godly People. Essays on English Protestantism and Puritanism*, 1983, 527–62; William M. Lamont, *Richard Baxter and the Millennium. Protestant Imperialism and the English Revolution*, 1979, 20–2.
7 Bob Scribner, 'Review article: interpreting religion in early modern Europe', *European Studies Review*, 13, 1983, 85–105.
8 Lyndal Roper, '"The common man", "the common good", "common women": gender and meaning in the German Reformation commune', *Social History*, 12, 1987, 1–21.
9 See Merry E. Wiesner, 'Beyond women and the family: towards a gender analysis of the Reformation', *Sixteenth Century Journal*, 18, 1987, 311–21.
10 Gail Malmgreen (ed.), *Religion in the Lives of English Women, 1760–1930*, Beckenham, 1986, 1–9.
11 Max Weber, *The Sociology of Religion*, 1966.
12 For a summary of Hill's arguments, which were developed over a number of years, see Christopher Hill, *The Century of Revolution, 1603–1714*, 3rd edn, 1980.

13 J. C. Davis, *Fear, Myth and History. The Ranters and the Historians,* Cambridge, 1986.

14 J. C. Davis, 'Fear, myth and furore: reappraising the "Ranters"', *Past & Present,* 129, 1990, 79–103.

15 Joan Kelly, 'Did women have a Renaissance?', in Renate Bridenthal and Claudia Koonz (eds), *Becoming Visible. Women in European History,* Boston, 1977. The debate about the English Revolution was stimulated by the work of Christopher Hill.

16 For a recent criticism of the concept of the English Revolution, see J. C. D. Clark, *Revolution and Rebellion. State and Society in the Seventeenth and Eighteenth Centuries,* Cambridge, 1986. For a reaffirmation of his thesis, see Geoff Eley and William Hunt (eds), *Reviving the English Revolution. Reflections and Elaborations on the Work of Christopher Hill,* 1988.

17 Lotte Mulligan and Judith Richards, 'A "Radical" problem: the poor and the English reformers in the mid-seventeenth century', *Journal of British Studies,* 29, 1990, 119, n. 4.

18 Keith Thomas, 'Women and the Civil War sects', in Trevor Aston (ed.) *Crisis in Europe, 1560–1660,* 1965, 338–40.

19 Max Weber, *The Protestant Ethic and the Spirit of Capitalism,* 1965.

20 R. H. Tawney, *Religion and the Rise of Capitalism,* 1926. For a recent discussion of the debates on poverty, see Paul Slack, *Poverty and Policy in Tudor and Stuart England,* 1988; and for a review of the debate on Protestant social thought, Margo Todd, *Christian Humanism and the Puritan Social Order,* Cambridge, 1987, 1–9.

21 For a valuable introduction see Keith Wrightson, *English Society 1580–1680,* 1982.

22 For a general discussion of this theme, see Linda Woodbridge, *Women and the English Renaissance: Literature and the Nature of Womankind, 1540–1620,* Brighton, 1984.

23 Keith Thomas, *Religion and the Decline of Magic. Studies in Popular Beliefs in Sixteenth and Seventeenth Century England,* 1971, 38–9; Patricia Crawford, 'Attitudes to menstruation in seventeenth-century England', *Past & Present,* 91, 1981, 61–2.

24 Ian Maclean, *The Renaissance Notion of Woman. A Study in the Fortunes of Scholasticism and Medical Science in European Intellectual Life,* Cambridge, 1980, 28–46; Crawford, 'Attitudes to menstruation', 52–4.

25 Patricia Crawford, 'The construction and experience of maternity in seventeenth-century England', in Valerie Fildes (ed.), *Women as Mothers in Pre-Industrial England,* 1990, 6–7.

26 F. J. Cole, *Early Theories of Sexual Generation,* Oxford, 1930; P. J. Bowler, 'Preformation and pre-existence in the seventeenth century: a brief analysis', *Journal of the History of Biology,* 4, 1971, 221–44.

27 Margaret Bowker, *The Henrician Reformation. The Diocese of Lincoln under John Longland 1521–1547,* Cambridge, 1981, 7.

28 Crawford, 'Attitudes to menstruation', 61–3

29 Sara Heller Mendelson, *The Mental World of Stuart Women. Three Studies,* Brighton, 1987, 1.

30 Edmund Tilney, *A brief and pleasant discourse of duties in mariage,* 1568, sig. [C 5v.].

31 Geoffrey Grigson (ed.), Thomas Tusser, *Five Hundred Points of Good Husbandry*, 1573, Oxford, 1984, 159.

32 There is an extensive literature on women's work in early modern England. Alice Clark, *Working Life of Women in the Seventeenth Century*, 1919, 1982, 1992; Lindsey Charles and Lorna Duffin (eds), *Women and Work in Pre-Industrial England*, 1985.

33 Caroline Walker Bynum, *Holy Feast and Holy Fast. The Religious Significance of Food to Medieval Women*, Berkeley, California, 1987.

34 Geoffrey Elton, *England under the Tudors*, 1955, 262. This view of Thatcher was expressed by Chancellor Kohl. For a discussion of some ambiguities of a female Prime Minister, see Wendy Webster, *Not A Man to Match Her*, 1990.

35 Etienne Binet, *The admirable life of S. Aldegond*, 1632, 216. Binet also referred to 'a tender, & masculine devotion', 244.

36 For a contemporary account of the legal status of women at the common law, see T. E., *The Lawes Resolutions of Womens Rights*, 1632, Eng. Exp., Amsterdam, 1979. There is a growing literature on the subject of women and the law: Carol Z. Weiner, 'Sex roles and crime in late Elizabethan Hertfordshire, *Journal of Social History*, 8, 1975, 38–60; J. M. Beattie, *Crime and the Courts in England, 1660–1800*, Oxford, 1986.

37 Maria Cioni, 'The Elizabethan chancery and women's rights', in D. J. Guth and J. W. McKenna (eds), *Tudor Rule and Revolution. Essays for G. R. Elton from his American friends*, Cambridge, 1982; Amy Louise Erickson, 'Common law versus common practice: the use of marriage settlements in early modern England', *Economic History Review*, 43, 1990, 21–39.

38 Weiner, 'Sex roles and crime', 38–60.

39 Carole Levin, 'John Foxe and the responsibilities of Queenship', in Mary Beth Rose (ed.), *Women in the Middle Ages and the Renaissance. Literary and Historical Perspectives*, Syracuse, 1986, 129; Carole Levin, 'Power, politics, and sexuality: images of Elizabeth I', in Jean R. Brink, Allison P. Coudert and Maryanne Horowitz (eds), *The Politics of Gender in Early Modern Europe*, vol. 12, *Sixteenth Century Essays and Studies*, 1989.

40 Christopher Hill, *The World Turned Upside Down. Radical Ideas during the English Revolution*, 1972, 257.

41 Mary Maples Dunn, 'Saints and Sisters. Congregational and Quaker women in the early colonial period', *American Quarterly*, 30, 1978, 584–5.

42 *The Works of that emininet servant in God . . . John Bunyan*, ed. G. Offor, 3 vols, Glasgow, 1855, ii.438.

43 Alison Wall, 'Elizabethan precept and feminine practice: the Thynne family of Longleat', *History*, 243, 1990, 23–38.

44 Denise Riley, *'Am I That Name?' Feminism and the Category of 'Women' in History*, 1988.

45 Orchard (ed.), *Till God Will*, 58.

46 Ibid.

47 For further details, see Amy Erickson, Introduction to the 1992 edn of Alice Clark, *Working Life of Women*.

48 Daniel N. Maltz, 'The Bride of Christ is filled with his spirit', in Judith Hoch Smith and Anita Spring (eds), *Women in Ritual and Symbolic Roles*, New York, 1978.

49 Edmund Morgan, *The Puritan Family*, 1944, rev. edn, New York, 1966, 161–86.

50 Ben Barker-Benfield, 'Anne Hutchinson and the puritan attitude toward women', *Feminist Studies*, 1, 1972, 65–96.

51 Caroline Walker Bynum, *Jesus as Mother. Studies in the Spirituality of the High Middle Ages*, Berkeley, California, 1982.

52 Natalie Zemon Davis, *Society and Culture in Early Modern France*, Stanford, 1975; Lyndal Roper, *The Holy Household. Women and Morals in Reformation Augsburg*, Oxford, 1989.

53 Peter Hausted, *Ten Sermons preached upon severall Sundayes and saints dayes*, 1636, 173. In a case in 1683 the parishioners of Moulton, Lincoln, were prosecuted for setting up various statues and the Holy Ghost 'in the Form of a Dove' over them; Thomas Barlow, *Several miscellaneous & weighty cases of conscience*, 1692, 4.

54 [Charles Barecroft], *A letter to a lady*, 1688, 52; Laurence Clarkson and John Aubrey quoted in Barry Reay, 'Popular religion', in Barry Reay (ed.), *Popular Culture in Seventeenth-Century England*, 1985, 99.

55 S. R. Gardiner, *A History of England 1603–1642*, 10 vols, 1901, vii.254–8

56 *CSPD, 1634–5*, 537–9.

57 Roger Hutchinson, *The Image of God*, 1550, in *The Works of Roger Hutchinson*, ed. John Bruce, Parker Society, Cambridge, 1842, 18–23.

58 Ranew and Penington quoted in Mendelson, *Mental World of Stuart Women*, 106.

59 Margaret Claridge, *Margaret Clitherow (1556–1586)*, 1966, 103.

60 Sir Thomas Herbert quoted in Gertrude Scott Stevenson (ed.), *Charles I in Captivity. From Contemporary Sources*, 1927, 278.

61 John Taylor, *Ranters of both sexes, male and female*, 1651, 1.

62 'The Hubbard-How-More Church', *Transactions of the Baptist Historical Society*, 2, 1910–11, 44.

63 R. A., *Heaven Opened*, 1646, 29.

64 *OED*, meaning 7.

65 Stephen Marshall, *The strong helper*, 1645, 30, reprinted in *Fast Sermons to the Long Parliament*, vol. 16, 402.

66 John Bastwick, *Independency not Gods ordinance*, 1645, 11, 98.

67 John Mayer, *A patterne for women*, 1639, 119.

68 Mary Cary, 'A dialogue betwixt the soule, and the body', Bodl., MS Rawl. D 1208, 11 Feb. 1649, 126.

69 Fildes (ed.), *Women as Mothers in Pre-Industrial England*.

70 John Brinsley, *The sacred and soveraigne church-remedie*, 1645, 62.

71 Ephraim Pagitt, *Heresiography*, 6th edn, 1661, 87.

72 Diary, 8 May 1673 quoted in Mendelson, *Mental World of Stuart Women*, 107.

73 Samuel James, *An Abstract of the Gracious Dealings of God with several eminent Christians*, 1760, 73, 84.

74 Anne Bradstreet, 'As weary pilgrim', in J. R. McElrath and A. P. Robb (eds), *The Complete Works of Anne Bradstreet*, Boston, 1981, 211.

75 Mary Cary, 'A dialogue', 120.

76 John Mush, 'A true report of the life and martyrdom of Mrs Margaret Clitherow', in John Morris (ed.), *The Troubles of Our Catholic Forefathers*, 1877, iii.393.

77 'Ann Bathurst's rhapsodies', 1693–6, Bodl., Rawl D 1262, ff. 45–6.

78 Ibid., 12 Sept., ff. 49–50.

79 Ibid., 27 July: 'I saw myself sett as a little child at the feet of my dear Jesus'; f. 82.

80 For defamation cases, see Martin Ingram, *Church Courts, Sex and Marriage in England, 1570–1640*, Cambridge, 1987, ch. 10. Also, Susan Amussen, *An Ordered Society. Gender and Class in Early Modern England*, Oxford, 1988, 101–4.

81 [John Bale], *The huntyng and fyndyng out of the Romysche foxe*, 1543, 16; Christopher Lever, *The History of the Defenders of the Catholique Faith*, 1627, 246–7.

82 Thomas Grantham, *Christianismus Primitivus*, 1678, iv.36.

83 *The Church of England as by law established*, 1685.

84 Articles against Cosin, 1630, in *The Correspondence of John Cosin D. D., Lord Bishop of Durham*, ed. G. Ornsby, Surtees Society, 52, 1869, 177.

85 Dennis Hollister, *The skirts of the whore discovered*, 1656. See also Dennis Hollister, *The harlots veil removed*, 1658, 3.

86 Walter Rosewell, *The serpents subtilty discovered*, 1656, 16.

87 Robert Read, *Fiery change*, 1656, 19.

88 *The triumphs of Rome over despised Protestancy*, 1667, 1.

89 Edmund Gurnay, *Gurnay redivivus*, 1661, 20.

90 *A parte of a register*, 1593, 7.

91 *Booke of Discipline*, Amsterdam, 1621, sig. [Bv.].

92 Hendrik Niclas, *An epistle sent unto two daughters of Warwick . . . With a refutation . . . by H. A[insworth]*, Amsterdam, 1608, 13.

93 Examples quoted in Crawford, 'Attitudes to menstruation', 57–8.

94 Various female (and male) witnesses in 1651 testified that John Robbins was God Almighty and that Christ was now in the womb of Joan Robbins; *The Ranters creed*, 1651; *All the proceedings at the sessions of the peace holden at Westminster*, 20 June 1651.

95 Elizabeth Poole, *A prophecie touching the death of King Charles*, 1649, sig. [A3].

1 The Reformation

1 [Bathsua Makin], *An Essay to revive the antient education of gentlwomen*, 1673, 28.

2 Roland H. Bainton, *Women of the Reformation*, 3 vols, Minneapolis, Minnesota., 1971–7.

3 A. G. Dickens, *The English Reformation*, 1964; 2nd edn, 1989.

4 Merry E. Wiesner, 'Beyond women and the family: towards a gender analysis of the Reformation', *Sixteenth Century Journal*, 18, 1987, 311–21; Lyndal Roper, '"The common man", "the common good", "common women": reflections on gender and meaning in the Reformation German Commune', *Social History*, 12, 1987, 1–21.

5 Lyndal Roper, *The Holy Household. Women and Morals in Reformation Augsburg*, Oxford, 1989; Retha M. Warnicke, *Women of the English Renaissance and Reformation*, Westport, Connecticut, 1983; Diane Willen, 'Women and religion in early modern England', in Sherrin Marshall (ed.),

Women in Reformation and Counter-Reformation Europe. Public and Private Worlds, Bloomington, Indiana, 1989.

6 Patrick Collinson, 'The role of women in the English Reformation illustrated by the life and friendships of Anne Locke', *SCH*, 2, 1965, 258–72; Patrick Collinson, *The Religion of Protestants. The Church in English Society 1559–1625*, Oxford, 1982; Claire Cross, '"He-Goats before the Flocks": a note on the part played by some women in the founding of some Civil War churches', *SCH*, 9, 1972, 195–202; Claire Cross, *Church and People 1450–1660. The Triumph of the Laity in the English Church*, 1976. More recently, there have been a number of important studies of the Reformation in particular counties including Christopher Haigh, *Reformation and Resistance in Tudor Lancashire*, Cambridge, 1975; Peter Clark, *English Provincial Society from the Reformation to the Revolution: Religion, Politics and Society in Kent, 1500–1640*, Hassocks, 1977; Diarmaid MacCulloch, *Suffolk and the Tudors. Politics and Religion in an English County 1500–1600*, Oxford, 1986; Susan Brigden, *London and the Reformation*, Oxford, 1989; Graham Mayhew, *Tudor Rye*, Falmer, 1987.

7 For monasticism, see David Knowles, *The Religious Orders in England*, 3 vols, Cambridge, 1959–1961.

8 Eileen Power, *Medieval English Nunneries, c. 1275–1535*, Cambridge, 1922, 1.

9 David Knowles and R. Neville Hadcock, *Medieval Religious Houses. England and Wales*, 1953, 233–324.

10 A. G. Dickens, *The English Reformation*, 2nd edn, 1989, 74. An estimated 9,300 monks and nuns amounted to ·26 per cent of an estimated population of 3.5 million; Carlo M. Cipolla, *Before the Industrial Revolution. European Society and Economy, 1000–1700*, 2nd edn, 1974, 82.

11 Margaret Bowker, *The Henrician Reformation. The diocese of Lincoln under John Longland 1521–1547*, Cambridge, 1981, 25–7.

12 Claire Cross, 'The religious life of women in sixteenth-century Yorkshire', *SCH*, 27, 1990, 308–16.

13 Rotha Mary Clay, *The Hermits and Anchorites of England*, 1914; Ann K. Warren, *Anchorites and their Patrons in Medieval England*, Berkeley, California, 1985.

14 Norman P. Tanner, *The Church in Late Medieval Norwich, 1370–1532*, Toronto, 1984, 57–64.

15 Ibid., 64–6.

16 Donald E. Weinstein and Rudolph M. Bell, *Saints and Society. The Two Worlds of Western Christendom, 1000–1700*, Chicago, 1982, 223, 232–5.

17 Caroline M. Barron, 'The parish fraternities of medieval London', in Caroline M. Barron and Christopher Harper-Bill (eds), *The Church in Pre-Reformation Society. Essays in Honour of F. R. H. Du Boulay*, Woodbridge, Suffolk, 1985, 13.

18 V. Reinburg, 'Popular prayers in late medieval and Reformation France', unpublished Ph.D. thesis, Princeton University, 1985, ch. 2 and 3.

19 *Here begynneth a shorte treatyse of contemplacyon taken out of the boke of Margerie kempe*, [1501], SCT 14924.

20 Ronald C. Finucane, *Miracles and Pilgrims. Popular Beliefs in Medieval England*, 1977, 142–3.

21 Ann Crawford, 'The piety of late medieval English Queens', in Barron and Harper-Bill (eds), *The Church in Pre-Reformation Society*.

22 *The Accounts of the Wardens of the Parish of Morebath, Devon 1520–1573*, ed. J. E. Binney, Exeter, 1904. See also Bishop Hobhouse (ed.), *Church Wardens Accounts of Croscombe . . . 1349 to 1560*, Somerset Record Society, 4, 1890, 6. In Kilmington, Devon, there were female church-wardens on at least six occasions during the Elizabethan period; J. Charles Fox (ed.), *Churchwardens Accounts*, 1913, 7. Fox also cited the records of St Brideaux, Devon, where women were churchwardens on several occasions up to 1699.

23 Margaret Aston, 'Iconoclasm at Rickmansworth 1522: troubles of church-wardens', *J. Eccles. H.*, 40, 1989, 536. The inventory of the chapel of St Mary of the Bridge, Derby, in 1488 listed a number of items such as coral beads, and a gilt girdle, all of which were gifts from women; Fox (ed.), *Churchwardens Accounts*, 147–8. In Morebath, Devon, Joan Rumbelow, widow, bequeathed money for a new image of our lady; one woman left a pair of beads and a girdle to St Sidwell, another, her best gown; Binney (ed.), *The Accounts of the Wardens of the Parish of Morebath*, 7, 24, 26.

24 Charles Kerry (ed.), *A History of the Municipal Church of St Lawrence Reading*, Reading, 1883, 108. For further examples, see Cross, 'The religious life of women in sixteenth-century Yorkshire', 317.

25 J. E. Foster (ed.), *Churchwardens' Accounts of Great St Mary's Cambridge, 1504–1635*, Cambridgeshire Antiquarian Society, 35, 1905, 13.

26 *Letters and Papers, Foreign and Domestic of the Reign of Henry VIII, vol. 10, Visitation of the Monasteries*. Among the items lent were listed the girdles of St Bernard, of St Mary and St Alred (p. 139), a finger of St Stephen (p. 140) and a ring of St Ethelred (p. 143).

27 Keith Thomas, *Religion and the Decline of Magic. Studies in Popular Beliefs in Sixteenth and Seventeenth Century England*, 1971. Susan Brigden, 'Religion and social obligation in early sixteenth-century London', *Past & Present*, 103, 1984, 67–112.

28 Thomas N. Tentler, *Sin and Confession on the Eve of the Reformation*, Princeton, 1977, 162–232.

29 Christina Larner, *Witchcraft and Religion. The Politics of Popular Belief*, Oxford, 1984, 60–3. See further chapter 5 in this volume.

30 For the different theological emphases of Lollardy and Calvinism, see Michael R. Watts, *The Dissenters. From the Reformation to the French Revolution*, Oxford, 1978, 7–14.

31 Margaret Aston, 'Lollard women priests?', in *Lollards and Reformers. Images and Literacy in late Medieval Religion*, 1984, 49–70; see also Claire Cross, '"Great Reasoners in Scripture": the activities of women Lollards 1380–1530', *SCH*, 2, 1965, 258–72; Anne Hudson, *The Premature Reformation. Wycliffite Texts and Lollard History*, Oxford, 1988, 99, 137.

32 R. A. Knox, *Enthusiasm. A Chapter in the History of Religion with Special Reference to the xvii and xviii Centuries*, Oxford, 1950, for an unsympathetic account.

33 Malcolm Lambert, *Medieval Heresy. Popular Movements from Bogomil to Hus*, New York, 1976.

34 A. G. Dickens, *The English Reformation*, rev. edn (pbk), 1967, 46–56.

35 Derek Plumb, 'The social and economic spread of rural Lollardy: a reappraisal', *SCH*, 23, 1986, 129.
36 For earlier fourteenth-century trials, see Norman P. Tanner (ed.), *Heresy Trials in the Diocese of Norwich, 1428–31*, Camden Society, 4th series, 20, 1977.
37 John Strype, *Ecclesiastical Memorials*, Oxford, 1822, 1(2), p. 61 (doc. 21).
38 *The Acts and Monuments of John Foxe*, ed. S. R. Cattley, 8 vols, 1939, iv.238.
39 Ibid., 549.
40 Ibid., 239.
41 Philip Hughes, *The Reformation in England*, 1, 1950; P. Heath, *The English Parish Clergy on the Eve of the Reformation*, 1969; J. J. Scarisbrick, *The Reformation and the English People*, Oxford, 1984.
42 A. G. Dickens suggests that Haigh, by attributing to him the simple view that the Reformation was inspired from below, has unwarrantedly polarised the debate: A. G. Dickens, 'The Early Expansion of Protestantism in England, 1520–1558', *Archive for Reformation History*, 78, 1987, 187–222; C. Haigh, 'The recent historiography of the English Reformation', *Historical Journal*, 25, 1982, 995–1007.
43 Peter Brown, *The Cult of the Saints. Its Rise and Function in Latin Christianity*, Chicago, 1981, 20.
44 Jean Delumeau, *Catholicism between Luther and Voltaire: A New View of the Counter-Reformation*, 1987.
45 Foxe, iv.232.
46 The translation used was that of Miles Coverdale; Dickens, *English Reformation*, rev. edn. (pbk), 1967, 183–8.
47 Eric Ives, *Anne Boleyn*, Oxford, 1986, 302–31; Margaret Patterson Hannay (ed.), *Silent But for the Word. Tudor Women as Patrons, Translators and Writers of Religious Works*, Kent, Ohio, 1985; Maria Dowling, 'Anne Boleyn and reform', *J. Eccles. H.*, 35, 1984, 30–46.
48 Elaine V. Beilin, *Redeeming Eve. Women Writers of the English Renaissance*, Princeton, 1987, 3–28
49 This account of Elizabeth Barton is based on the *DNB*; Thomas Wright (ed.), *Three Chapters of Letters relating to the suppression of the Monasteries*, Camden Society, 1st series, 26, 1843, 13–34; L. E. Whatmore (ed.), 'The Sermon against the Holy Maid of Kent and her Adherents. . .', *EHR*, 58, 463–75; Clark, *Religion, Politics and Society in Kent*, 32–5.
50 Alan Neame, *The Holy Maid of Kent. The Life of Elizabeth Barton, 1506–1534*, 1971.
51 G. R. Elton, *Reform and Reformation. England 1509–1558*, 1977, 180–1.
52 Judith C. Brown, *Immodest Acts: The Life of a Lesbian Nun in Renaissance Italy*, New York, 1986.
53 In her speech at her death, Barton said that she 'thought I might feign what I would'; A. D. Cheyney, 'The Holy Maid of Kent', *Trans. R. H. S.*, new series, 18, 1904, 119. Neame, *The Holy Maid of Kent*, claims her as a martyr, which Knowles, *Religious Orders in England*, iii.190, denies, concluding that she 'had more than a touch of hysteria and fantasy'. Elton, *Reform and Reformation*, 180, dismisses her as 'an hysterical girl'. Clark, *Religion, Politics and Society in Kent*, 35 argues that she was 'never quite the

innocent country maid that her more recent Catholic apologists would have us believe'.

54 Cromwell complained to Bishop Fisher that the testimonies of various godly men on her behalf were unsatisfactory evidence; Wright (ed.), *Three Chapters of Letters*, 28–31.

55 Elizabeth Alvilda Petroff (ed.), *Medieval Women's Visionary Literature*, New York, 1986.

56 John Poynet, *An apologie*, [1556], 48.

57 Retha M. Warnicke, *Women of the English Renaissance and Reformation*, 68–9.

58 *The Complete Works of St Thomas More*, 6, Yale, New Haven, 1981, 93–4. See also MacCulloch, *Suffolk and the Tudors*, 143–5.

59 G. A. J. Hodgett (ed.), *The State of the Ex-Religious and Former Chantry Priests of the Diocese of Lincoln, 1547–1574*, Lincoln Record Society., 53, 1959, xvi–xxi.

60 Joyce Youings, *St Nicholas Priory*, Exeter, 1960, 15.

61 Dickens, *English Reformation*, 2nd edn, 1989, 246.

62 Of sixty or so Protestant martyrs in the reign of Henry VIII, only four or five were female, although among those questioned for heresy earlier in Henry's reign, about one-third were women; Warnicke, *Women of the English Renaissance*, 68, 71.

63 Anne Askew, *The first examinacyon of Anne Askewe, . . . with elucydacyon of J. Bale*, Marpurg, 1546, STC 848; *The lattre examinacyon of Anne Askewe, with the elucydcyon of J. Bale*, Marpurg, 1547, STC 850. Both works were reprinted several times.

64 Beilin, *Redeeming Eve*, 29–47; see also John N. King, *English Reformation Literature. The Tudor Origins of the Protestant Tradition*, Princeton, 1982, 71–5.

65 Susan Brigden, 'Youth and the English Reformation', *Past & Present*, 95, 1982, 61–4. See also Robert Whiting, *The Blind Devotion of the People. Popular Religion and the English Reformation*, Cambridge, 1989, 146–7.

66 Foxe, quoted in Brigden, 'Youth', 58.

67 Mary Prior, 'Reviled and crucified marriages: the position of Tudor bishops' wives', in Mary Prior (ed.), *Women in English Society, 1500–1800*, 1985.

68 King, *English Reformation Literature*, 104–6.

69 Strype, *Ecclesiastical Memorials*, 2(1), 335.

70 John Davis, 'Joan of Kent, Lollardy and the English Reformation', *J. Eccles. H.*, 33, 1982, 225–33.

71 A. Th. van Deursen, 'Holland's experience of war during the revolt of the Netherlands', in A. C. Duke and C. A. Tamse (eds), *Britain and the Netherlands*, 6, The Hague, 1977, 23–5.

72 D. M. Loades, *The Reign of Mary Tudor. Politics, Government and Religion in England, 1553–1558*, 1979, 332–5.

73 Brigden, *London and the Reformation*, 559–60.

74 Dickens, *English Reformation*, rev. edn (pbk), 1967, 364–5.

75 When Foxe's work appeared with illustrations, there were several woodcuts depicting the martyrdom of women, including one of the burning of a pregnant woman, whose baby was depicted bursting out into the flames; Foxe, *Acts and Monuments*, 1576, p. 1850.

76 Foxe, viii.541.
77 Richard Bernard, *A guide to grand jury men*, 1630, 214–15; Matthew Hopkins, *The discovery of witches*, 1647, 4; John Stearne, *A confirmation and discovery of witchcraft*, 1648, 42–50; C. L'Estrange Ewen, *Witch Hunting and Witch Trials*, 1929, 62, 267; thanks to Stuart Clark for these references.
78 Dickens, *English Reformation*, rev. edn (pbk), 1967, 365; Warnicke, *Women in the English Renaissance and Reformation*, 74. The marital status of six was unclear.
79 Foxe, viii.495.
80 Ibid., vii.191–2.
81 Ibid., viii.537.
82 Strype, *Ecclesiastical Memorials*, 2(1), 335.
83 Prior, 'Tudor bishops' wives', in Prior (ed.), *Women in English Society*.
84 T. Marten, *A treatise*, 1554, sig. [Riiiv.].
85 A. G. Dickens, 'The Marian reaction in the Diocese of York', in *Reformation Studies*, 1982, 93–157.
86 Marten, *A treatise*, sig. p.
87 John Harington, *A briefe view of the state of the Church of England*, 1653, 4.
88 Thomas Becon, *The Supplication, in Prayers and other Pieces of Thomas Becon*, ed. J. Ayre, Parker Society, 1844, 227.
89 John Knox, *The first blast of the trumpet against the monstruous regiment of women*, 1558, Eng. Exp., Amsterdam, 471, 1972.
90 Strype, *Annals*, 1(2), 406.
91 Robert Parsons, *An answere to the fifth part of Reportes lately set forth*, 1606, 49, 76.
92 Richard Challoner, *Memoirs of Missionary Priests*, ed. J. H. Pollen, 1924, 140.
93 *The works of that famous and worthie minister of Christ, . . . William Perkins*, 1603, 743.
94 C. W. Foster (ed.), *The State of the Church in the reigns of Elizabeth and James I*, Lincoln Record Society, 23(1), 1926, 370.
95 Anthony Stafford, *The femall glory: or, the life and death of our blessed lady*, 1635, 20–3.
96 A. F. Mitchell and J. Struthers, *Minutes of the Westminster Assembly of Divines*, 1874, 128.
97 *Certain Sermons or Homilies Appointed to be Read in Churches in the Time of Queen Elizabeth*, 1908, 179–283; Eamon Duffy, 'Holy maydens, holy wyfes: the cult of women saints in fifteenth- and sixteenth-century England', *SCH*, 27, 1990, 175–96; Margaret Aston, *England's Iconoclasts*, 1, Oxford, 1988, 107–9.

2 The social teachings of the Protestant church: women, marriage and the family

1 *Certain Sermons or Homilies appointed to be read in Churches in the time of Queen Elizabeth*, 1908, 539–40.
2 Karl Marx and Frederick Engels, *Collected Works*, 4, New York, 1974, 196. Lise Vogel, *Marxism and the Oppression of Women. Toward a Unitary Theory*, New Brunswick, New Jersey, 1983, 42 and 183 n. 2, points out that

Fourier's point was a different one, namely that the improvement of the condition of women was the cause, not the index, of social progress. Earlier, some writers of the Scottish enlightenment had made a similar claim.

3 Thomas Becon, *A New Catechism*, in *The Catechism of Thomas Becon*, ed. John Ayre, Parker Society, Cambridge, 1844. For further discussion of domestic advice manuals, see Chilton Latham Powell, *English Domestic Relations 1485–1653*, New York, 1917.

4 William Perkins, *Christian Oeconomie*, 1590, trans. 1609; John Dod and Robert Cleaver, *A godly form of household government*, 1630.

5 Papal power to annul an invalid marriage disappeared, but the bishops took over this power. The number of prohibited degrees of kinship between the Catholic and Anglican churches differed; Martin Ingram, *Church Courts, Sex and Marriage in England, 1570–1640*, Cambridge, 1987, 145–6.

6 Becon, *Catechism*, 339.

7 [John Bale], *The huntyng and fyndyng out of the Romysche foxe*, 1543, sig. [Evi v.].

8 Kathleen Davies, 'Continuity and change in literary advice on marriage', in R. B. Outhwaite (ed.), *Marriage and Society: Studies in the Social History of Marriage*, 1981, 58–80.

9 Margo Todd, *Christian Humanism and the Puritan Social Order*, Cambridge, 1987.

10 Patrick Collinson, *The Birthpangs of Protestant England: Religious and Cultural Change in the Sixteenth and Seventeenth Centuries*, Basingstoke, 1988, 92–3.

11 Lawrence Stone, *The Family, Sex and Marriage in England 1500–1800*, 1977, 135–42; Ralph A. Houlbrooke, *The English Family 1450–1700*, 1984.

12 Levin L. Schücking, The *Puritan Family. A social study from the literary sources*, 1929, trans. 1969, 88–9, 94.

13 Edmund Morgan, *The Puritan Family*, 1944, rev. edn, New York, 1966.

14 Merry E. Wiesner, 'Nuns, wives and mothers: women and the Reformation in Germany', in Sherrin Marshall (ed.), *Women in Reformation and Counter-Reformation Europe*, Bloomington, Indiana, 1989; Lyndal Roper, *The Holy Household. Women and Morals in Reformation Augsburg*, Oxford, 1989; Retha Warnicke, *Women in the English Renaissance and Reformation*, Westport, Connecticut, 1983, 78–86; Diane Willen, 'Women and Religion in early modern England', in Marshall (ed.), *Women in Reformation and Counter-Reformation Europe*. I am most grateful to Professor Willen for allowing me to read her chapter before publication.

15 Foxe, viii.541, 498.

16 John Dod, *Bathshebaes Instructions to her sonne*, 1614, 61–2; Keith Thomas, 'Women and the Civil War sects', in Trevor Aston (ed.), *Crisis in Europe 1560–1660*, 1965, 331n points out also that religious women in the Middle Ages were usually urged to return to the distaff.

17 George Gifford, *A dialogue betweene a Papist and a Protestant*, 1582, sig. [I–2v.], 53.

18 [Robert Wilkinson], *The Merchant Royall*, 1607, 23.

19 [*Two sermons preached at the funerals of Mrs Elizabeth Montfort and of Dr Montfort*, 1632], 15.

20 [Wilkinson], *The Merchant Royall*, 18.
21 Hannah Wolley, *The gentlewoman's companion*, 1675, 1.
22 *Sermons by Hugh Latimer*, ed. G. E. Corrie, Parker Society, Cambridge, 1844, 14.
23 Samuel Clark, *The lives of sundry eminent persons*, 1683, 154.
24 John Bale, *The huntinge*, sig. [F v v.] claimed that Catholics said that if there were no stews in London, then there would be violence against merchants' wives in the streets.
25 Lyndal Roper, 'Discipline and respectability: prostitution, and the Reformation in Augsburg', *History Workshop*, 19, 1985, 3–28.
26 Keith Thomas, 'The double standard', *Journal of the History of Ideas*, 20, 1959, 195–216.
27 *Homilies*, 123.
28 Patricia Crawford, 'The construction and experience of maternity in seventeenth century England', in Valerie Fildes (ed.), *Women as Mothers in Pre-Industrial England*, 1990, 9–11.
29 Ian W. Archer, *The Pursuit of Stability. Social Relations in Elizabethan London*, Cambridge, 1991, 211–15; I. W. Archer, 'Governors and governed in late sixteenth-century London, c. 1560–1603: studies in the achievement of stability', unpublished D. Phil. thesis, University of Oxford, 1988, 305–30.
30 Keith Thomas, 'The Act of 1650 reconsidered' in Donald Pennington and Keith Thomas (eds.), *Puritans and Revolutionaries. Essays in Seventeenth-Century History Presented to Christopher Hill*, Oxford, 1978.
31 Lyndal Roper, 'Drinking, gorging and whoring: brutish indiscipline and the development of Protestant identity', unpublished paper. Thanks to Dr Roper for allowing me to cite her unpublished paper.
32 *The whole workes of W. Tyndall, John Frith and Doct. Barnes*, 1573, 317. For this discussion of clerical marriage I am indebted to the kindness of Vanessa Webster who allowed me to consult her unpublished B.A. dissertation, 'Clerical marriage in England c. 1547 to c. 1580', University of Cambridge, 1989.
33 John Poynto, *An Apologie*, [1556], 37.
34 John Poynet, *A defence for mariage of priestes*, 1549, sig. [C viii v.].
35 In the 1590s Richard Allison, *A confutation of Brownisme*, 69, reported that 'relievers or widows' were to be over 60 years of age.
36 Roger Hayden (ed.), *The Records of a Church of Christ in Bristol, 1640–1687*, Bristol Record Society, 27, 1974, 208–9.
37 Carole Levin, '"Would I Could Give You Help and Succour": Elizabeth I and the politics of touch', *Albion*, 21, 1989, 191–205.
38 Clarissa W. Atkinson, '"Precious balsam in a fragile glass": the ideology of virginity in the later Middle Ages', *Journal of Family History*, 8, 1983, 131–43.
39 Latimer, *Sermons*, 392.
40 *The Arminian Nunnery*, 1641, 4. The treatise was a printing of the copy of a letter to Sir Tho. Herley, King's Sergeant-at-Law, Bodl. MS Ashmol. 800, ff. 28–37.
41 Bishop Hacket, *Memoirs of the Life of Archbishop Williams*, 1715, 154.
42 Bridget Hill, 'A refuge from men: the idea of a Protestant nunnery', *Past & Present*, 117, 1987, 107–30.

43 Carlo Ginzburg, *The Cheese and the Worms. The cosmos of a sixteenth-century miller*, trans. J. & A. Tedeschi, 1980, 122.

44 William Perkins, *The works*, 1603, *A Reformed Catholicke*, preface, 721, 743.

45 Barnaby Rich, *The true report of a late practise. . . with a yong maiden in Wales*, 1582, sig. [Ei–iiv.].

46 For female literacy, see David Cressy, *Literacy and the Social Order; Reading and Writing in Tudor and Stuart England*, Cambridge, 1980; Margaret Spufford, 'First steps in literacy: the reading and writing experiences of the humblest seventeenth-century spiritual autobiographers', *Social History*, 4, 1979, 407–35; Keith Thomas, 'The meaning of literacy in early modern England', in G. Baumann (ed.), *The Written Word: Literacy in Transition*, Oxford, 1986.

47 Gouge, *Domesticall Duties*, 18–19, sig. 2v..

48 For a general discussion of fear of disorder, see Amussen, *An Ordered Society*, ch. 1.

49 Statute of Artificers, 5 Eliz. c. iv.

50 Paul Slack, 'Poverty and social regulation in Elizabethan England', in Christopher Haigh (ed.), *The Reign of Elizabeth I*, 1984, 238. In Southampton there was concern about 'young women and maidens which keep themselves out of service and work for themselves in divers men's houses' or who 'take chambers and so live by themselves masterless'; David Underdown, *Revel, Riot and Rebellion*, 1985, 36–7.

51 DRO, MS C1/61, Minute book of the sessions of the peace, 1618–21, 339. There are numerous cases in the Mayor's court book in Norwich.

52 Judith M. Bennett, 'Review Essay', *Feminist Studies*, 14, 1988, 269–83.

53 Merry E. Wiesner, *Working Women in Renaissance Germany*, New Brunswick, New Jersey, 1986.

54 Alice Clark, *Working Life of Women in the Seventeenth Century*, 1919.

55 Joan Thirsk, *Economic Policies and Projects. The Development of a Consumer Society in Early Modern England*, Oxford, 1978, 3.

56 For an important recent discussion of this theme, see Kevin Sharpe, 'A commonwealth of meanings', in *Politics and Ideas in Early Stuart England. Essays and Studies*, 1989, 3–71.

57 Gouge, *Domesticall duties*, 1626, preface sig. [A 3v.]–4.

58 Ste B., *Counsell to the Husband: to the wife instruction*, 1608, 43–50.

59 Ibid., 73–4, 78.

60 Amussen, *An Ordered Society*, 34–66.

61 Gouge, *Domesticall duties*, 18–19, preface sig. [2v.]; 1627, 10–11. For further discussion of women's public duties, see Patricia Crawford, 'Public duty, conscience and women in early modern England', in John Morrill, Paul Slack and Daniel Woolf (eds), *Public Duty and Private Conscience. Festschrift for G. E. Aylmer*, Oxford, forthcoming.

62 The Marprelate controversy in the late Elizabethan period bandied about accusations against the chastity of Bishop Cooper's wife. The counter-attack on a Protestant female supporter, Margaret Lawson, was for her abusive tongue; *The Marprelate Tracts*, ed. W. Pierce, 1911, 268–9.

63 For further discussion, see chapter 3.

64 Felicity Heal, *Of Prelates and Princes: A Study of the Economic and Social Position of the Tudor Episcopate*, Cambridge, 1980, 240.

65 Patrick Collinson, '"A Magazine of Religious Patterns": an Erasmian topic transposed in an English Protestantism', *SCH*, 14, 1977, 240–1.
66 S. R. Gardiner, *History of England*, 10 vols, 1901–7, iv.145 (I have been unable to trace Gardiner's source, Bradford's Dialogue in *Young's Chronicles*, 446).
67 See chapter 7.
68 Like a father, a minister was unwilling 'to have his children stollen from him'; Thomas Edwards, *Reasons against the Independent Government of Particular Congregations*, 1641, 51.
69 John Bunyan, *Grace Abounding to the Chief of Sinners*, dedication.
70 Injunctions, 1559, in Edward Cardwell (ed.), *Documentary Annals of the Reformed Church of England*, 2 vols, Oxford, 1844, i.228.
71 Samuel Clarke, *A Collection of the Lives of Ten Eminent Divines*, 1662, 506.
72 *HMC D'Lisle*, vi.561–2.
73 John Bale, *Select Works*, ed. Henry Christmas, Parker Society, Cambridge, 1849, 199, 237–8.
74 Becon, *Catechism*, 340–1.
75 Gouge, *Domesticall duties*, 1634, 193–6. The 1622 edition leaps from sig. [N4] to sig. [O3], indicating the suppression of four pages.

3 Anglicans, Puritans and Catholics 1558–1640

1 James Oxley, *The Reformation in Essex to the Death of Mary*, Manchester, 1965, 65.
2 Christopher Haigh, 'Puritan evangelism in the reign of Elizabeth I', *EHR*, 92, 1977, 30–58; J. J. Scarisbrick, *The Reformation and the English People*, Oxford, 1984, 61.
3 In addition to Oxley, local studies include Christopher Haigh, *Reformation and Resistance in Tudor Lancashire*, Cambridge, 1975; Peter Clark, *English Provincial Society from the Reformation to the Revolution: Religion, Politics and Society in Kent, 1500–1640*, Hassocks, 1977; Diarmaid MacCulloch, *Suffolk and the Tudors: Politics and Religion in an English County 1500–1600*, Oxford, 1986; Susan Brigden, *London and the Reformation*, Oxford, 1989.
4 John White, *A defence of the way to the true church*, 1614, 55.
5 J. S. Purvis (ed.), *Tudor Parish Documents of the Diocese of York*, Cambridge, 1948, 94.
6 John Morris (ed.), *The Troubles of Our Catholic Forefathers*, 1877, iii.248. Morris prints several pages of records relating to female refusal to attend church. A standard plea recorded was 'because her conscience will not serve her'.
7 Purvis (ed.), *Tudor Parish Documents*, 175–6.
8 Morris (ed.), *The Troubles of Our Catholic Forefathers*, iii.255, 256.
9 Purvis (ed.), *Tudor Parish Documents*, 79.
10 Ibid., 67.
11 Ibid., 5 (1576 Articles), 176.
12 *CSPD, 1547–1580*, 271, 273.
13 Patrick Collinson, *The Elizabethan Puritan Movement*, 1967, 82.
14 S. R. Gardiner, *History of England*, 10 vols, 1901–5, vii.255–8.

15 Martin Ingram, *Church Courts, Sex and Marriage in England, 1570–1640*, Cambridge, 1987, 108.

16 Keith Thomas, *Religion and the Decline of Magic. Studies in Popular Beliefs in Sixteenth and Seventeenth Century England*, 1971, 59–61; William Coster, 'Purity, profanity, and puritanism: the churching of women, 1500–1700', *SCH*, 27, 1990, 377–88.

17 J. P. Wilson and J. Bliss (eds.), *Works by Lancelot Andrewes*, 9 vols, Oxford, 1841–54, v.121.

18 F. G. Emmison, *Elizabethan Life. Morals and the Church Courts*, Chelmsford, 1973, 159–61.

19 Leland H. Carlson (ed.), *The Writings of Henry Barrow, 1590–1591*, 1966, 76–8.

20 Katherine Chidley, *The justification of the Independent churches of Christ*, 1641, 57.

21 Roger Hayden (ed.), *The Records of a Church in Bristol, 1640–1687*, Bristol Record Society, 27, 1974, 88.

22 Jeremy Boulton, *Neighbourhood and Society. A London Suburb in the Seventeenth Century*, Cambridge, 1987, 196–7. Of those whose babies died, 70 per cent were churched, showing that the ceremony was linked to childbirth, not baptism.

23 Christopher Durston, '"Unhallowed wedlocks": the regulation of marriage during the English Revolution', *Historical Journal*, 31, 1988, 45–59.

24 John Calvin, *A Compend of the Institutes of the Christian Religion*, ed. H. T. Kerr, Philadelphia, 1939, Bk 4, ch. 24, 193–4.

25 *The Booke of Common Prayer*, 1588, sig. B4–4v.

26 William Barlow, *The summe and substance of the conference*, 1604, 8; Frederick Shriver, 'Hampton Court re-visited: James I and the Puritans', *J. Eccles. H.*, 33, 1982, 58.

27 Thomas, *Religion and the Decline of Magic*, 38. In a Nonconformist sect at the end of the seventeenth century, a female so polluted the sacred place by giving birth to a bastard there that the meeting was to be moved 'for the present'; FHL, Vale of White Horse Minutes, 1673–1722, transcribed B. Snell, 140:

28 Churchwardens accounts, 1628–66, All Hallows Barking, Inventory by John Shaw, 1629, f.10.

29 Hester Shaw, widow of a citizen and turner of London, made an annual payment of £8 out of private benevolence from 1643; Hester Shaw, *A plaine relation of my sufferings*, 1653, 7.

30 Churchwardens accounts, Guildhall, St Margaret, Westminster, 1650, E.30: 'to Goodwife Browne for mending of the church Cloaths'; 'to widdow Browne for washing the Church Lynnen quarterly, xs for the whole year'; 'to her for more sweeping the church quarterly iis'. Thanks to David Cressy for these references.

31 Mary Ellen Lamb, 'The Cooke sisters: attitudes toward learned women in the Renaissance', in Margaret Patterson Hannay (ed.), *Silent But for the Word. Tudor Women as Patrons, Translators and Writers of Religious Works*, Kent, Ohio, 1985, 107–25.

32 [Bathsua Makin], *An essay to revive the antient education of gentlewomen*, 1673.

33 Arthur Searle (ed.), *Barrington Family Letters 1628–1632*, Camden Society, 4th series, 28, 1983.

34 Michael Finlayson, *Historians, Puritanism and the English Revolution: The Religious Factor in English Politics Before and After the Interregnum*, Toronto, 1983. An alternative designation by contemporaries was frequently 'the godly'. Peter Lake, *Anglicans and Puritans? Presbyterianism and English Conformist Thought from Whitgift to Hooker*, 1988, 7 suggests that the term 'puritan' refers to a broad span of advanced Protestants who regarded themselves as godly, a minority of genuinely true believers. Finlayson doubts the utility of the term.

35 G. E. Aylmer, 'Collective mentalities in mid seventeenth-century England: 1. The Puritan outlook', *TRHS*, 5th series, 36, 1986, 24–5.

36 Nicholas Tyacke, 'Puritanism, Arminianism and counter-revolution', in Conrad Russell (ed.), *The Origins of the English Civil War*, 1973; *Anti-Calvinists. The Rise of English Arminianism c. 1590–1640*, Oxford, 1987.

37 For a reassessment of Charles's role, see Julian Davies, 'The growth and implementation of "Laudianism" with special reference to the Southern Province', unpublished D.Phil. thesis, University of Oxford, 1987.

38 *The Correspondence of John Cosin, D. D. Lord Bishop of Durham*, Surtees Society, 52, 1868, 174.

39 Alfred Heales, *The History and Law of Church Seats and Pews*, 1872, i.73.

40 Sister Joseph Damien Hanlon, 'These be but women', in Charles H. Carter (ed.), *From Renaissance to the Counter-Reformation*, 1966, 371–400. See also Retha Warnicke, *Women of the English Renaissance and Reformation*, Westport, Connecticut, 1983, ch. 9.

41 J. C. H. Aveling, *The Handle and the Axe. The Catholic Recusants in England from Reformation to Emancipation*, 1976, 87–103; J. J. Scarisbrick, *The Reformation and the English People*, Oxford, 198, 150–9.

42 John Bossy, *The English Catholic Community 1570–1850*, 1975, 153–8.

43 A. L. Rowse, *The England of Elizabeth. The Structure of Society*, 1950, 456.

44 Marie B. Rowlands, 'Recusant women 1560–1640', in Mary Prior (ed.), *Women in English Society 1500–1800*, 1985, 149–80.

45 The following paragraph is based largely on Rowlands, 'Recusant women', 150–6, 161–2.

46 Bossy, *The English Catholic Community*, 157–8.

47 Claire Cross, *The Puritan Earl. The Life of Henry Hastings, Third Earl of Huntingdon, 1536–1595*, 1966, 234–5.

48 J. Payne Collier (ed.), *The Egerton Papers*, Camden Society, 12, 1840, 453–4.

49 Bossy, *The English Catholic Community*, 152–7.

50 J. T. Rutt (ed.), *Diary of Thomas Burton Esquire, Member in the Parliaments of Oliver and Richard Cromwell*, 4 vols, 1828, i.6.

51 Adam Hamilton (ed.), *The Chronicle of the English Augustinian Canonesses Regular of the Lateran at St Monica's in Louvain*, 2 vols, Edinburgh, 1904, i.253–6.

52 R. Simpson (ed.), *The Lady Falkland her Life*, 1861, 27–37.

53 Rowlands, 'Recusant women', 150–1; Philip Caraman, *The Other Face. Catholic Life under Elizabeth I*, [1960], 36–58.

54 Purvis (ed.), *Tudor Parish Documents*, 67, 80.

55 Roger B. Manning, *Religion and Society in Elizabethan Sussex*, Leicester, 1969, 158–61.
56 Much of this discussion of harbouring priests is based on Rowlands, 'Recusant women', 156–60.
57 Ann M. C. Forster, 'Ven. William Southerne: another Tyneside martyr', *Recusant History*, 4, 1957, 206–7.
58 *The Life of Mrs Dorothy Lawson of St Anthony's near Newcastle-on-Tyne*, 1855, 19–20.
59 Mary C. E. Chambers, *The Life of Mary Ward (1559–1645)*, 2 vols, 1882, i.243.
60 Bossy, *The English Catholic Community*, 157. For some examples of maternal influence, see Anthony Kenny (ed.), *The Responsa Scholarum of the English College, Rome*, Catholic Record Society., 54, 1962, i.76, 108, 118, 142; 55, 1963, ii.395, 420, 466–7, 628–9. Thanks to Claire Walker for these references.
61 H. Foley (ed.), *Records of the English province of the Society of Jesus . . . in the sixteenth and seventeenth centuries*, 7 vols, 1882, iv.19.
62 Ibid., 547.
63 *Life of Lawson*, 25.
64 Richard Smith, *The life of . . . the Lady Magdalen Viscountess Montague*, 1627, 27–31.
65 *Life of Lawson*, 21–2; Sister Dorothea's narrative, in Chambers, *Life of Mary Ward*, ii.28.
66 Rowlands, 'Recusant women', 156–60.
67 PRO, SP 12/173/26 (1), examination of Joane Morley, 1584.
68 J. H. Pollen (ed.), *Unpublished Documents relating to the English Martyrs*, 2 vols, *CRS*, 5, 1908, i.327.
69 Alan Davidson, 'Roman Catholicism in Oxfordshire from the late Elizabethan period to the Civil War (*c.* 1580 to *c.* 1640)', unpublished Ph.D. thesis, University of Bristol, 1970, 584. I am grateful to Dr Davidson for lending me his thesis and for discussions on the subject.
70 *Life of Lawson*, 19–20.
71 Ibid., 25.
72 Sister Dorothea's Narrative, in Chambers, *Life of Mary Ward*, ii.29.
73 Archives of St Monica's, Louvain MS CS. Thanks to Claire Walker for this reference.
74 *Life of Lawson*, 33.
75 Katharine Longley, *Saint Margaret Clitherow*, Wheathampstead, 1986. See also John Mush, 'A true report of the life and martyrdom of Mrs Margaret Clitherow', in John Morris (ed.), *The Troubles of Our Catholic Forefathers, 1877*. Mush's 'True report' exists in various versions.
76 Unpublished paper by Inez Alfors, 'Elizabethan women martyrs'. I am most grateful to Dr Alfors for allowing me to cite her paper.
77 Foley, *Records of the Society of Jesus*, i.414–15
78 Rowlands, 'Recusant women', 159.
79 Alfors, 'Elizabethan women martyrs'.
80 Warnicke, *Women of the English Renaissance and Reformation*, 169–70; Godfrey Anstruther, *Vaux of Harrowden. A Recusant Family*, Newport, 1953, 191, 461 and passim.
81 Foley, *Records of the Society of Jesus*, ii.316.

82 Chambers, *Life of Mary Ward*, i.47. I am grateful to Claire Walker for discussing nuns with me. Her forthcoming thesis on English nuns abroad should extend our knowledge of this largely neglected group of women.

83 J. C. H. Aveling, *The Handle and the Axe. The Catholic Recusants in England from Reformation to Emancipation*, 1976, 90. Between 1598 and 1642, 5,000 people entered orders abroad; ibid., 98.

84 The main source for Mary Ward is the biography by Chambers, *The Life of Mary Ward*. See also Warnicke, *Women of the English Renaissance and Reformation*, ch. 9; Rowlands, 'Recusant women', 168–74; Ruth Liebowitz, 'Virgins in the service of Christ: the dispute over an active apostolate for women during the Counter-Reformation, in Rosemary Radford Reuther (ed.), *Women of Spirit*, New York, 1979, 140; M. Emmanuel Orchard, *Till God Will. Mary Ward Through her Writings*, 1985, 34.

85 Aveling, *The Handle and the Axe*, 95; Chambers, *Life of Mary Ward*, ii.97.

86 Chambers, *Life of Mary Ward*, i.375–85.

87 Sir Dudley Carlton, 1625, quoted in Anstruther, *Vaux of Harrowden*, 459.

88 Lewis Owen, *The running register*, 1626, 108.

89 Chambers, *Life of Mary Ward,* ii.403ff.

90 Susan O'Brien, 'Women of the "English Catholic Community": nuns and pupils at the Bar Convent, York, 1680–1790', in Judith Loudes (ed.), *Monastic Studies*, 1, forthcoming, 267–8. I am most grateful to Dr O'Brien for allowing me to consult her paper prior to publication.

91 Haigh, 'Puritan evangelism', 56; Carol Weiner, 'The Beleaguered Isle. A study of Elizabethan and Early Jacobean Anti-Catholicism', *Past & Present*, 51, 1971, 27–62.

92 Caroline Hibbard, *Charles I and the Popish Plot*, Chapel Hill, [1983]; Erica Veevers, *Images of Love and Religion: Queen Henrietta Maria and Court Entertainments*, Cambridge, 1989.

93 Gardiner, *History of England*, x.128.

94 Rowlands, 'Recusant women', 175.

95 Foley, *Records of the Society of Jesus*, i.416.

96 Foxe, viii.543.

97 Mush, 'Clitherow', in Morris (ed.), *The Troubles of Our Catholic Forefathers*, iii.420, 422, 425.

98 Ibid., 377, 381–2.

99 Ibid., 392, 401.

100 Foxe, viii.495.

101 Mush, 'Clitherow', iii.414, 427, 433, 426.

102 Longley quotes Clitheroe's words from the Morris transcript, *Saint Margaret Clitherow*, 135. These precise words are not in the Morris version of Mush, nor in Mush's *Abstract* of 1619, sig. [C5].

103 Luther was a monk, Edward VI a child, Elizabeth a woman, but with God as the agent, great things were done; Thomas Hall, *A practical and polemical commentary*, 1658, 469–70.

104 Guildhall MS 20,228/IA, Turners Hall Meeting, c. 1664–1727, 3/1/1672.

105 Elliot Rose, *Cases of Conscience. Alternatives Open to Recusants and Puritans under Elizabeth I*, Cambridge, 1975, 29, 39.

106 Bodl., MS Top Oxon c. 124, ff. 14–15.

107 Robert Sanderson, *Eight cases of conscience*, 1674, 20–4.
108 Alfors, 'Elizabethan women martyrs', 7.

4 Piety and spirituality

 1 Richard Sibbes, *The hidden life*, 1639, 128.
 2 Cotton Mather, *Ornaments for the daughters of Zion*, 1694, 57.
 3 For a classic statement, see John Gregory, *A Father's Legacy to His Daughter*, 1774, 9–25.
 4 Bryan S. Turner, *Religion and Social Theory. A Materialist Perspective*, 1983, 3–4, 109–33.
 5 For a later period, see Gail Malmgreen, Introduction to the collection she edited, *Religion in the Lives of English Women, 1760–1930*, Beckenham, 1986.
 6 Lawrence Stone, *The Crisis of the Aristocracy 1558–1641*, Oxford, 1965, 738; Richard L. Greaves, *Society and Religion in Elizabethan England*, Minnesota, 1981, 742.
 7 Caroline Walker Bynum, '". . . And Woman His Humanity": female imagery in the religious writing of the later Middle Ages', in *Fragmentation and Redemption. Essays on Gender and Human Body in Medieval Religion*, New York, 1991, 154.
 8 Sara Mendelson, 'Stuart women's diaries', in Mary Prior (ed.), *Women in English Society, 1500–1800*, 1985, 194.
 9 Keith Thomas, 'Women and the Civil War sects', in Trevor Aston (ed.), *Crisis in Europe, 1560–1660*, 1965, 321. Patrick Collinson, *The Birthpangs of Protestant England. Religious and Cultural Change in the Sixteenth and Seventeenth Centuries*, 1988, 74–7, follows similar ideas.
10 Natalie Zemon Davis, *Society and Culture in Early Modern France*, Stanford, 1975, 77.
11 Michael G. Finlayson, *Historians, Puritanism, and the English Revolution: The Religious Factor in English Politics Before and After the Interregnum*, Toronto, 1983.
12 Margo Todd, *Christian Humanism and the Puritan Social Order*, Cambridge, 1987, 1–21
13 J. Sears McGee, *The Godly Man in Stuart England. Anglicans, Puritans and the Two Tables, 1620–1670*, New Haven, 1976, 169-70. See also Charles E. Hambrick-Stowe, *The Practice of Piety. Puritan Devotional Disciplines in Seventeenth-Century New England*, Chapel Hill, 1982. Studies of female piety include Claire Cross, '"He-goats before the flock": a note on the part played by some women and the founding of some Civil War churches', *SCH*, 8, 1972, 195–202; Patrick Collinson, 'The role of women in the English Reformation illustrated by the life and friendships of Anne Locke', in *Godly People. Essays on English Protestantism and Puritanism*, 1983; Peter Lake, 'Feminine piety and personal potency: the "emancipation" of Mrs Jane Ratcliffe', *The Seventeenth Century*, 2, 1987, 143–65.
14 B. Spencer, *A dumb speech; [Funeral Sermon for Mrs Mary Overman]*, 1646, 54.
15 *The vertuous . . . life and death of the late Lady Letice, Vi-Countess Falkland*, 1653, 3.
16 Anthony Walker, *The holy life of Mrs Elizabeth Walker*, 1690, 96–7.

17 T. Crofton Croker (ed.), *Autobiography of Mary, Countess of Warwick*, Percy Society, 2, 1848, 24; Sara Mendelson, *The Mental World of Stuart Women. Three Studies*, Brighton, 1987, 80–110.

18 J. H. Turner (ed.), *The Rev. Oliver Heywood, B.A., 1630–1702: His Autobiography, Diaries, Anecdote and Event Books*, 4 vols, Brighouse, 1882–5, i.59–60.

19 DWL, Baxter MS V, f. 216.

20 Ibid., ff. 3, 28.

21 John Mush, 'A true report of the life and martyrdom of Mrs Margaret Clitherow', in John Morris (ed.), *The Troubles of Our Catholic Forefathers*, 1877, iii.378–82; *The Life of Mrs Dorothy Lawson of St Anthony's near Newcastle-on-Tyne*, 1855, 42.

22 Patrick Collinson, *The Birth-pangs of Protestant England*, 1988, 75–6 discusses this spiritual intimacy ('one is tempted to call them affairs'). In an unpublished paper he argues that these relationships were 'not sexual in the ordinary sense'.

23 Examples in Richard Greaves, 'The role of women in early English nonconformity', *Church History*, 52, 1983, 303–4; Claire Cross, 'The genesis of a godly community: two York parishes, 1590–1640', *SCH*, 23, 1986, 218.

24 Susan Wabuda, 'Shunamites and nurses of the English Reformation: the activities of Mary Glover, niece of Hugh Latimer', *SCH*, 27, 1990, 335–44.

25 Thomas Taylor, *The pilgrims profession. Or a sermon preached at the funerall of Mris Mary Gunter*, 1622, 125–32

26 Mendelson, 'Stuart women's diaries', 207, n. 56.

27 There is limited evidence about attendance at Anglican worship. At Earls Colne in 1679–80, 76 per cent of thirty-three communicants were women, and in the eighteenth century more men than women in the diocese of Chester were presented for non-attendance. For this information, and the reference from Edward Weston, *A letter to the Right Reverend the Lord Bishop of London*, 3rd edn, 1760, I am grateful to Dr Clive Field.

28 Samuel Clark, *The lives of sundry eminent persons*, 1683, 146.

29 Edmund Calamy, *The happinesse of those who sleep in Jesus*, 1662, 28.

30 John Kettlewell, *Five Discourses . . . of Practical Religion*, 2nd edn, 1708, 102.

31 East Sussex RO, Dunn MS 51/54, Anna Temple to her daughter, 16 Jan [1641]. I am grateful to Ann Hughes for this reference.

32 Mary Cary, 'A Dialogue', Bodl., MS Add B 58, 91–3. This was not the prophet of the same name.

33 Mush, 'Clitherow', iii.388.

34 [John Mayer], *A patterne for women*, 1639, sig. [A.5].

35 F. G. Emmison, *Elizabethan Life: Morals and the Church Courts*, Chelmsford, 1973, 97–9.

36 C. Stuart, *The Life of the Lady Halket*, Edinburgh, 1701, 55.

37 David Cressy, *Literacy and the Social Order. Reading and Writing in Tudor and Stuart England*, Cambridge, 1980, 176–7.

38 William Harrison, *Deaths advantage little regarded*, 1602, 79.

39 BL, Harleian MS 382, f. 180.

40 Nathaniel Parkhurst, *The Faithful and Diligent Christian described*, 1684, 49.

41 Edward Reynolds, *The churches triumph over death*, 1662, 33.
42 Translators included Margaret Roper, Anne Prowse, and Anne Cooke.
43 Edward Rainbowe, *A sermon . . . Susana, Countess of Suffolk*, 1649, 12.
44 Edmund Calamy, *The godly mans ark . . . preached at the funeral of Elizabeth Moore*, 1658, 233–54; Reynolds, *The churches triumph*, 36.
45 See F. B. Williams, *Index of Dedications and Commendatory Verses in English Books before 1641*, 1962.
46 For a list of those godly books directed to women published before 1640, see Suzanne W. Hull, *Chaste, Silent and Obedient. English Books for Women 1475–1640*, San Marino, 1982.
47 Thomas Bentley, *The monument of matrones: concerning seven seuerall lamps of virginitie*, [1582], iii.1, 127.
48 David Crane, 'English translations of the Imitatio Christi in the sixteenth and seventeenth centuries', *Recusant History*, 13, 1976, 79–100; see also Josephine Evetts Secker, 'Henry Hawkins, S. J., 1577–1646: a recusant writer and translator of the early seventeenth century', *Recusant History*, 11, 1972, 237–52.
49 [Antonio Molina], *A treatise of mental prayer*, trans., [St Omer], 1616, 159–92.
50 John Bucke, *Instructions for the use of the beades*, Louvain, 1589 [ERL, vol. 77].
51 Etienne Binet, *Life of S. Aldegonde*, Paris, 1632, 216 [ERL, vol. 29].
52 Francis de Sales, *A treatise of the love of God*, Douai, 1630, [ERL, vol. 252]; Luis de la Puente, SJ, *Meditations upon the mysteries of our faith*, 1624 [ERL, vol. 295]. John Fisher, *A treatise of prayer*, Paris, 1640 [ERL, vol. 11]. For these and other references to dedications to women in the English Recusant Literature series I am grateful to Claire Walker.
53 [Ann Bathurst], Bodl., MS Rawlinson Qe27, 'The fourth Boke of my daily observations on my self', 1680; 5th book, 9 Jan. 1680, ff. 31, 1–25.
54 Chester City RO, Diary of Sarah Savage, see especially the entry for 24 Nov. 1687; Patricia Crawford, 'Attitudes to pregnancy from a woman's spiritual diary, 1687–8', *Local Population Studies*, 21, 1978, 43–5.
55 Anne Venn, *A wise virgins lamp burning*, 1658.
56 Susanna Bell, *The legacy of a dying mother*, 1673, 38.
57 Jane Turner, *Choice experiences*, 1653, sig. [B8].
58 Pakington papers, Bodl., MS Add. B 58, f. 133.
59 Mary Cary, 'A Dialogue', Bodl., MS Add. B 58, 146.
60 Bell, *Legacy*, 45–57; see also Mendelson, 'Stuart women's diaries', 195–7.
61 Mary Cary, 'A Dialogue', 176.
62 Mendelson, 'Stuart women's diaries', 186.
63 Elspeth Graham, Hilary Hinds, Elaine Hobby and Helen Wilcox (eds), *Her Own Life. Autobiographical Writings by Seventeenth-Century English-women*, 1989, 150–63.
64 Mary Cary, 'A Dialogue', 36.
65 A. L. W., 'Obituary notices of the nuns of the English Benedictine Abbey of Ghent in Flanders. 1627–1811', *CRS Miscellanea*, 11, 1917, 25–6.
66 Ibid., 5.
67 C. S. Durant, *A Link betwen Flemish Mystics and English Martyrs*, 1925, 272–305.

68 For examples of monastic rules for women, see *The rule of the most blissed Father saint Benedict*, trans. Alexia Gray, Gant, [1632], [ERL, vol. 278]; [Mary Gouge], *A pious collection of several profitable directions fitted for the English Poor Clares*, Douai, 1684.

69 *Rule of saint Benedict*, 72.

70 J. Gillow and R. Trappes-Lomax (eds), 'Diary of the "Blue Nuns"', *CRS*, 8, 1910, 285.

71 Gertrude More, *The Holy Practices of a Divine Lover*, ed. Dom H. Lane Fox, Edinburgh, 1909, ix. More's work was edited by Fr. Augustine Baker.

72 'Obituary notices of the nuns of the English Benedictine Abbey', 67.

73 More, *The Holy Practices of a Divine Lover*, 108.

74 Ibid., 28, 14, 70.

75 Ibid., 19, 47.

76 Joseph Gillow, 'Registers of the English Poor Clares at Gravelines . . . 1608–1837', *CRS Miscellanea*, 9, 1914, 34, 39.

77 Quoted in David Lunn, *The English Benedictines 1540–1688. From Reformation to Revolution*, 1980, 207.

78 Mary C. E. Chambers, *The Life of Mary Ward (1559–1645)*, 2 vols, 1882, i.180.

79 M. Emmanuel Orchard (ed.), *Till God Will. Mary Ward Through her Writings*, 1985, 34–8, 52–3, 60–1.

80 Chambers, *Mary Ward*, i.357–62.

81 George Herbert, 'The Elixir', in F. E. Hutchinson and Helen Gardner (eds), *The Poems of George Herbert*, Oxford, 1961, 175–6.

82 Walker, *Life of Mrs Elizabeth Walker*, 88. The minister was Robert Bolton.

83 BL, Add. MS 27351, 8 June, 29 July, 24 Dec. 1668; Mendelson, *Mental World*, 5–6.

84 John Bunyan, *Grace Abounding to the Chief of Sinners*, 1928, 16.

85 Tessa Watt, *Cheap Print and Popular Piety, 1550–1640*, Cambridge, 1991, 178–253.

86 Kathleen M. Davies, 'Continuity and change in literary advice on marriage', in R. B. Outhwaite (ed.), *Marriage and Society: Studies in the Social History of Marriage*, 1981, 58–80; Todd, *Christian Humanism*.

87 Norfolk RO, *Mistris Shaws Tombstone*, [died 1657], 23.

88 Clark, *Lives of sundry eminent persons*, 154.

89 Walker, *Life of Mrs Elizabeth Walker*, 69.

90 Patricia Crawford, 'Katharine and Philip Henry and their children: a case study in family ideology', *Transactions of the Historic Society of Lancashire and Cheshire*, 134, 1984, 39–73.

91 Gerald Strauss, *Luther's House of Learning. Indoctrination of the Young in the German Reformation*, Baltimore, 1978, 108–9.

92 Elizabeth Joceline, *The mothers legacie to her unborne child*, 1624, preface.

93 Walker, *Life of Mrs Elizabeth Walker*, 66, 69–70.

94 Margaret Spufford, 'First steps in literacy: the reading and writing experiences of the humblest seventeenth-century spiritual autobiographers', *Social History*, 4, 1979, 407–35.

95 Kettlewell, *Five Discourses*, 98.

96 Samuel James, *An Abstract of the Gracious Dealings of God with several eminent Christians*, 1760, 74.

97 John Duncon, *The returns of spiritual comfort*, 1649, 166.

98 Calamy, *The happinesse of those who sleep*, 29–30; Edward Rainbow, *A sermon preached at the funeral of . . . Anne, Countess of Pembroke, Dorset and Montgomery*, 1677, 40.

99 Nathaniel Parkhurst, *The faithful and diligent Christian described*, 1684, 59.

100 Elizabeth Burnet, *A Method of Devotion*, 2nd edn, 1709, 383–8.

101 Clark, *Lives of sundry eminent persons*, 155.

102 Thomas Kenn, *A sermon at the funeral of . . . Lady Margaret Mainard*, 1688, 22; Duncon, *The returns of spiritual comfort*, 158–60.

103 BL, Add. MS 27, 352, Diary of Mary Rich, vol. 2, 7 & 16 March 1670. Thanks to Sara Mendelson for this reference.

104 Mary Penington, *A Brief Account of my Exercises from Childhood*, Philadelphia, 1848, 25. Another Quaker, who died in 1683, was commended as being 'of the Pure Religion, which is to visit the Fatherless and Widows'; *A testimony of the life and death of Mary*, 1683, 4.

105 W. K. Jordan, *The Charities of Rural England 1480–1660. The Aspirations and the Achievements of the Rural Society*, 1961, 96–7; W. K. Jordan, *The Charities of London. The Aspirations and the Achievements of the Urban Society*, 1960, 30.

106 'Memoir of Mrs Goodal', in W. K. Tweedie (ed.), *Select Biographies*, Edinburgh, 1847, 489; Roger Hayden (ed.), *The Records of a Church of Christ in Bristol, 1640–1687*, Bristol Record Society, 27, 1974, 85.

107 Parkhurst, *The Faithful and diligent Christian discribed*, 69–70.

108 Ibid., 69.

109 DWL, Baxter MS IV, ff. 142v., 217v.–218v.; Baxter MS V, f. 3.

110 [Matthew Henry], *The Life of Philip Henry*, 1699, 85.

111 Crawford, 'Katharine and Philip Henry', 54.

112 J. C. H. Aveling, ' Catholic households in Yorkshire, 1580–1603', *Northern History*, 16, 1980, 96–8.

113 Mary Claridge, *Margaret Clitherow 1556–1586*, 1966.

114 Mush's account exists in various versions; here, it is taken from Morris (ed.), *The Troubles of Our Catholic Forefathers*, iii.390–7.

115 Walker, *Life of Mrs Elizabeth Walker*, 33–41 ('How she spent the day').

116 Quoted in Mendelson, *Mental World*, 189; Samuel Clark published the lives of four godly women in *A collection of the lives of ten eminent divines*, 1662.

117 *Imitation and caution for Christian women*, 1659, 1; Patrick Collinson, '"A Magazine of Religious Patterns": an Erasmian topic transposed in an English Protestantism', *SCH*, 14, 1977, 240–1.

118 Kettlewell, *Five Discourses*, 118.

119 Nicholas Breton, *The good and the badde*, 1616, 27. The diet of a virgin, he said, was abstinence.

120 Philip S[tubbes], *A christal glasse for Christian women*, 1591, 2.

121 Walker, *Life of Mrs Elizabeth Walker*, 22, 39.

122 John Ley, *A pattern of piety . . . Mrs Jane Ratcliffe*, 1640, 79.

123 Ephraim Pagitt, *Heresiography*, 6th edn, 1661, 197. Mrs Traske refused her husband sexual relations telling him they were imprisoned to suffer. He recanted and was released; she died in prison in 1645. *BDBR*.

124 Mush, 'Clitherow', iii.394–5

125 R. S., *The Lady Falkland her Life*, 1861, 53–4.

126 Walker, *Life of Mrs Elizabeth Walker*, 22.
127 See chapter 6.
128 Mush, 'Clitherow', iii.375.
129 *The life of . . . the Lady Magdalen Viscountess Montague*, 1627, 5.
130 Caroline Walker Bynum, 'Bodily miracles and the resurrection of the body in the high Middle Ages', in Thomas Kselman (ed.), *Belief in History. Innovative Approaches to European and American Religion*, 1991, 68–106. Further suggestions come from conversation with Lyndal Roper, who is writing about the Reformation and attitudes to the body.
131 Chester City R. O., D/ Basten 8, Diary of Sarah Henry, 1686–8, Aug. 1686.
132 DWL, Baxter MS V, f. 28v.
133 Crawford, 'Women's published writings', 224 and passim 211–82.
134 Edith Klotz, 'A subject analysis of printing, 1480–1640', *Huntingdon Library Quarterly*, 1, 1937–8, 417–19.
135 Parkhurst, *The faithful and diligent Christian described*, 48.
136 John Batchiler, *The virgins pattern: in the exemplary life . . . of Mrs Susanna Perwich*, 1661, 25.
137 George Ballard, *Memoirs of Several Ladies of Great Britain*, Oxford, 1752, 425.
138 Rachel Speght, *Mortalities memorandum, with a dreame prefixed*, 1621, 5.
139 Elizbeth Hincks, *The poor widow's mite*, 1671; Mary Forster and others, *A living testimony from the power and spirit of our Lord Jesus Christ*, [1685], 2.
140 Aemilia Lanyer, *Salve deus rex Judaeorum. Containing, the passion of Christ*, 1611, sig. [Dv.].
141 Crawford, 'Women's published writings', 221–3.
142 For example, Margaret Fell, *Women's speaking justified*, 1666.
143 M. J. Galgano, 'Negotiations for a nun's dowry: Restoration letters of Mary Caryll, O. S. B. and Ann Clifton, O. S. B.', *American Benedictine Review*, 24, 1973, 292.
144 Ibid., 296.
145 Ibid.,292, n.34.
146 For a fuller discussion of this theme, see Sara Mendelson and Patricia Crawford, *A Social History of Tudor and Stuart Women*, forthcoming.
147 BL, Harl MS 384, f. 90.
148 Bodl., Rawlinson MS D 749, f. 158, the petition of Anne Paul, wife to Sir John Paul.
149 Robert Walmsley, 'John Wesley's parents. Quarrel and reconciliation', *Proceedings of the Wesleyan Historical Society*, 29, 1953, 50–7.
150 Ibid., 52.
151 Ibid., 52–3.
152 Ibid., 53–7.
153 *The lyf of the Mother Theresa of Jesus*, dedicatory epistle.
154 *To the Parliament: The humble petition*, 1653.
155 Mendelson, 'Stuart women's diaries', 189.

5 Dangerous beliefs: magic, prophecy and mysticism

1 Keith Thomas, 'History and anthropology', *Past & Present*, 24, 1963, 3–24; Keith Thomas, *Religion and the Decline of Magic. Studies in Popular Beliefs in Sixteenth and Seventeenth Century England*, 1971.

2 Imogen Luxton, 'The Reformation and popular culture', in Felicity Heal and Rosemary O'Day (eds.), *Church and Society in England: Henry VIII to James I*, 1977, 57–77; Peter Burke, *Popular Culture in Early Modern Europe*, 1978; Barry Reay, 'Popular religion', in Barry Reay (ed.), *Popular Culture in Seventeenth-Century England*, 1985, 91–128.

3 See Reay, 'Popular religion', 91–2.

4 Anne Llewellyn Barstow, *Joan of Arc: Heretic, Mystic, Shaman*, Lewiston, 1986, 1–19.

5 Jean Delumeau, *Catholicism between Luther and Voltaire: A New View of the Counter-Reformation*, 1977; Patrick Collinson, *The Religion of the Protestants. The Church in English Society 1559–1625*, Oxford, 1982, 189–241.

6 Hildred Geertz, 'An anthropology of religion and magic', *Journal of Interdisciplinary History*, 6, 1975, 71–89.

7 Carlo Ginzburg, *The Cheese and the Worms. The Cosmos of a Sixteenth-Century Miller*, trans. J. & A. Tedeschi, 1980.

8 Thomas, *Religion and the Decline of Magic*, 609–10, 648–9.

9 J. Britten (ed.), *John Aubrey, Remains of Gentilisme*, Folk Lore Society, 4, 1881, 24.

10 A. L. Rowse, *Simon Forman: Sex and Society in Shakespeare's Age*, 1974, 226–7.

11 Michael MacDonald, *Mystical Bedlam. Madness, Anxiety, and Healing in Seventeenth-Century England*, Cambridge, 1981, 22–32.

12 J. H. Beattey (ed.), *Calendar of the Correspondence of the Smyth Family of Ashton Courts, 1548–1642*, Bristol Record Society, 35, 1982, 192.

13 In 1697 Amy Forster was accused by the Cripplegate Baptists of going to 'a cunning man alias a conjurer' to find some misappropriated goods; *Baptist Quarterly*, 2, 1924–5, 117.

14 Patricia Crawford, 'Attitudes to menstruation in seventeenth-century England', *Past & Present*, 91, 1981, 70–1.

15 Patricia Crawford, '"The sucking child": adult attitudes to child care in the first year of life in seventeenth-century England', *Continuity and Change*, 1, 1986, 27.

16 Women's medical commonplace books, Wellcome Institute, MS 130, c. 1710, f. 30; MS 504, later seventeenth century; MS 4049, 1669, unfoliated; BL, Sloane MS 3859; Kendal R. O., Browne MS WD/TE, Box 16, Commonplace book, 1699. For other magical healing, see Thomas, *Religion and the Decline of Magic*, 177–92.

17 DWL, MS Henry 4.25, Sarah Savage to Hannah Whitton, 2 April 1734.

18 Michael MacDonald, 'Religion, social change, and psychological healing in England, 1600–1800', *SCH*, 19, 1982, 101–25.

19 Thomas, *Religion and the Decline of Magic*, 190–1.

20 William Jones, *Credulities Past & Present*, 1880, 388.

21 Thomas, *Religion and the Decline of Magic*, 192–8.

22 Ibid., 200–4.

23 J. F. Williams (ed.), *Bishop Redman's Visitation 1597. Presentments in the Archdeaconries of Norwich, Norfolk and Suffolk*, Norfolk Record Society, 18, 1946, 133–4.

24 Alan Macfarlane, *Witchcraft in Tudor and Stuart England*, 1970, 62; cp. C. L. Ewin, *Witch Hunting and Witch Trials*, 1929, 112, who estimated that fewer than 1,000 were executed.

25 H. R. Trevor-Roper, *The European Witch-Craze of the 16th and 17th Centuries*, Harmondsworth, 1969; Macfarlane, *Witchcraft*; E. W. Monter, 'Witchcraft in Geneva, 1537–1662', *Journal of Modern History*, 43, 1971, 179–204.

26 Christina Larner, *Enemies of God. The Witch-hunt in Scotland*, Oxford, 1983, 89; Christina Larner, *Witchcraft and Religion. The Politics of Popular Belief*, Oxford, 1984, Ch. 5.

27 Larner, *Enemies of God*, 89–90; Larner, *Witchcraft and Religion*, 85; see also Macfarlane, *Witchcraft*, 160.

28 Macfarlane, *Witchcraft*, 150–2; see also Thomas, *Religion and the Decline of Magic*, 520.

29 Perkins and Stearne quoted in Macfarlane, *Witchcraft*, 161.

30 Thomas, *Religion and the Decline of Magic*, 435–49.

31 Ibid., 192. Larner, *Witchcraft and Religion*, 80.

32 Larner, *Witchcraft and Religion*, 80, 84–5; Larner, *Enemies of God*, 96.

33 Macfarlane, *Witchcraft*, 170–6. There was an unusually high number of prosecutions in Essex.

34 Lyndal Roper, 'Witchcraft and Fantasy in Early Modern Germany', *History Workshop Journal*, 32, 1991, 19–43. See also R. W. Scribner, 'Sorcery, superstition and society: the Witch of Urach, 1529', in *Popular Culture and Popular Movements in Reformation Germany*, 1987, 274; J. A. Sharpe, 'Witchcraft and women in seventeenth-century England: some northern evidence', *Continuity and Change*, 6, 1991, 179–99.

35 Larner, *Witchcraft and Religion*, 85.

36 Thomas, *Religion and the Decline of Magic*, 519–26; cp. Larner, *Enemies of God*, 95: typically, the Devil promised 'that they should never want'.

37 William H. Hale (ed.), *A Series of Precedents and Proceedings in criminal causes . . . 1475 to 1640*, 1847, 254.

38 Larner, *Enemies of God*, 96; Thomas, *Religion and the Decline of Magic*, 444–5, 522.

39 Ibid., 191.

40 Ibid., 512–13. I am grateful to Susan Wabuda who drew my attention to this practice.

41 G. R. Elton, *Policy and Police. The Enforcement of the Reformation in the Age of Thomas Cromwell*, Cambridge, 1972, 57.

42 Max Weber, *The Sociology of Religion*, 4th edn, 1965; Norman Cohn, *The Pursuit of the Millennium. Revolutionary Millenarians and Mystical Anarchists of the Middle Ages*, 1972, 53-60.

43 Crawford, 'Women's printed writings', in Mary Prior (ed.), *Women in English Society, 1500–1800*, 1985, 269; Mary Douglas, *Natural Symbols. Explorations in Cosmology*, Harmondsworth, 1973, 102–18.

44 Phyllis Mack, 'Women as prophets during the English Civil War', *Feminist Studies*, 8, 1982, 24. See also Elaine Hobby, *Virtue of Necessity. English Women's Writing 1646–1688*, 1988, 26–53.

45 Crawford, 'Women's printed writings', 272

46 Cp. Hobby, *Virtue of Necessity*, 26–53, who groups together a wide range of women as prophets, including Susanna Parr, who is discussed in this book in chapter 7.

47 Mack, 'Women as prophets', 22–3.

48 Sara Wight, *A wonderful pleasant and profitable letter*, 1656, 24.

49 Elinor Channel, *A message from God . . . to his Highnes*, 1653; Elizabeth Poole, *A prophecie touching the death of King Charles*, 1649, 8.

50 *BDBR*, Eleanor Davies; More, Dialogues, *Works*, vi.94.

51 Mack, 'Women as prophets', 25–6.

52 More, Dialogues, *Works*, vi.93.

53 Caroline Walker Bynum, *Holy Feast and Holy Fast. The Religious Significance of Food to Medieval Women*, Berkeley, California, 1987. See also Rudolph M. Bell, *Holy Anorexia*, Chicago, 1985.

54 Walter N. Pahnke and William A. Richards, 'Implications of LSD and experimental mysticism', in Charles T. Tart (ed.), *Altered States of Consciousness. A Book of Readings*, New York, 1969, 416–17. Thanks to Alan Richardson for this reference.

55 Douglas, *Natural Symbols*, 112.

56 Ann Venn, *A wise virgins lamp burning*, 1658, 66, 258

57 Anna Trapnel, *A legacy for saints*, 1654, 1–7.

58 Ibid., 33, 37, 39, 41.

59 Ibid., 25–7.

60 William Lambarde, *A Perambulation of Kent*, Chatham, 1826, 171; L. E. Whatmore (ed.), 'The Sermon against the Holy Maid of Kent . . . 1533', *EHR*, 58, 1943, 464.

61 Bourignon, quoted in Mack, 'Women as prophets', 19. See also Anna Trapnel, who referred to herself as 'poor Instrument'; [Trapnel, Poem, untitled, Bodl. S. I. 42. Th].

62 Channel, *Message*, 1.

63 Sara Wight, *The exceeding riches of grace, advanced by the spirt of grace in an empty nothing creature*, 1647, 54, 56.

64 Cranmer, *Remains*, Letter 84, quoted in Alan Neame, *The Holy Maid of Kent. The Life of Elizabeth Barton, 1506–1534*, 1971, 36.

65 Pazzi (1566–1607), was canonised; Wilhelm Schamoni, *The Face of the Saints*, trans. 1948, 180–1.

66 Champlin Burrage, 'Anna Trapnel's prophecies', *EHR*, 26, 1911, 527. Wight, *The exceeding riches of grace*, 87.

67 Lambarde, *A Perambulation of Kent*, 173.

68 *CSPD*, 1628–9, 530.

69 Lambarde, *A Perambulation of Kent*, 173; [Trapnel, Poem, untitled, Bodl. S. I. 42. Th].

70 More, Dialogues, *Works*, vi.94; for Barton see chapter 2, 49–54 and footnotes.

71 Lambarde, *A Perambulation of Kent*, 171–3; E. J. Devereux, 'Elizabeth Barton and Tudor censorship', *John Rylands Library Bulletin*, 49, 1966, 91–106.

72 Elton, *Policy and Police*, 59–60. Elton thought her a wise woman and a virago, one not entirely sane. But she had been prophesying for over thirty years.

73 Mack, 'Women as prophets', 19–20; *BDBR*, Eleanor Davies.

74 Barstow, *Joan of Arc*, 1986.

75 *Anna Trapnel's report*, 1654, 22, 26–7, 49, 51. It was asserted that she could not be a witch because 'she spake many good words'.

76 John Hacket, *Scrinia Reserata*, 1693, ii.47–8.

77 Poole, *An Alarum*, 1649, preface.

78 *Clarke Papers*, ed. C. H. Firsth, 4 vols, Camden NS, 1891–1901, liv, 167–8.

79 Poole, *A prophesie*, sig. [A3].

80 Anna Trapnel, *Cry of a stone*, 1654, 14.

81 Trapnel, *Report*; *BDBR*.

82 Bodl., [Trapnel, untitled poem], 889, 741.

83 Anne Bathurst, 'Rhapsodies', Bodl., Rawl. D 1262, 1693–6, f. 1; ibid., MS Rawl. Qe28, ff. 48v.–49v.

84 Rawl. 1262, ff. 1–6?

85 Wight, *The exceeding riches*, 149.

86 Anne Bathurst, Bodl., MS Rawl. D 1262, f. 10.

87 Mack, 'Women as prophets', 37–8.

88 Poole, *Alarm*, postscript.

89 See, for example, the title of Wight's pamphlets, *The exceeding riches of grace . . . Published for the refreshing of poor souls*, 1647; *A wonderful pleasant and profitable letter . . . Published for the use of the afflicted*, 1656.

90 Gertrude More, *The spiritual exercises*, Paris, 1658, 236; see also Marion Norman, 'Dame Gertrude More and the English mystical tradition', *Recusant History*, 13, 1976, 196–211.

91 M. Emmanuel Orchard (ed.), *Till God Will. Mary Ward Through her Writings*, 1985, 53–4, 60–1.

92 Bathurst, Writings, vol. 5., Bodl., MS Rawl. D 1263, f. 1.

93 [George Garden], *An apology for M. Antonia Bourignon*, 1699, 276.

94 D. P. Walker, *The Decline of Hell*, 1964, ch. 13; John Cockburn, *Bourignianism detected*, 1698, preface sig. [A2].

95 Jane Lead, *A fountain of gardens*, 3 vols, 1696–1700, i.18; ii, epistle to reader, sig. [A2v.–A3]; Janet Todd (ed.), *A Dictionary of British and American Writers 1660–1800*, 1987.

96 Jane Lead, *The wonders of God's creation manifested*, [1695?], 8.

97 Lead, *A fountain of gardens*, i.4.

98 Lead, *A fountain of gardens*, iii, epistle, sig. [A3].

99 Nigel Smith, *Perfection Proclaimed. Language and Literature in English Radical Religion 1640–1660*, Oxford, 1989, 185–225.

100 Jane Lead, *The wonders of God's creation manifested*, [1695?], 8.

101 Jane Lead, *A living funeral testimony*, 1702, 36.

102 Walker, *The Decline of Hell*, 229.

103 Lead, *A fountain of gardens*, ii, epistle, sig. [A3].

104 James K. Hopkins, *A Woman to Deliver her People. Joanna Southcott and English Millenarianism in an Era of Revolution*, Austin, Texas, 1982.

105 Lady Dorothy Packington, Prayers and meditations, Bodl., MS Add. B. 58, f. 29.

106 Bathurst, Bodl., Rawl. D 1262, f. 66.

107 See chapter 10.

108 Elizabeth Burnet, Diary, Bodl. MS Rawl. D 1092, ff. 138v.–139.

109 B. Robert Kreisner, *Miracles, Convulsions, and Ecclesiastical Politics in Early Eighteenth-Century Paris*, Princeton, 1978.

6 Radical religion: separatists and sectaries 1558–1660

1 *The Quacking Mountebanck*, 1655, 20.
2 R. A. Knox, *Enthusiasm. A Chapter in the History of Religion with Special Reference to the xvii and xviii centuries*, Oxford, 1950, 20.
3 For circumstantial separatists, see Patrick Collinson, *The Elizabethan Puritan Movement*, 1967, 87–91.
4 Patrick Collinson, 'The English Conventicle', *SCH*, 23, 1986, 223–59.
5 Knox, *Enthusiasm*.
6 Miles Hogarde, *The displaying of the protestantes*, 1556, f. 75v.
7 Nicholas Sander, *Rise and Growth of the Anglican Schism*, (1585, with a continuation by Edward Rishton), 1877, 240.
8 *The Folger Library Edition of The Works of Richard Hooker*, Cambridge, Massachusetts, 1977, i.13 (preface ch. 3, 13).
9 Ibid.
10 John Elborow, *Evodias and Syntyche: or, the female zelots of the Church of Philippi*, 1637, 7.
11 Thomas Marten, *A traictise declaryng . . . that the pretensed marriage of priestes, is no mariage*, 1554, sig. A1.
12 Thomas White, *A discoverie of Brownisme*, 1605, 3.
13 Origins and influences are discussed in George Huntston Williams, *The Radical Reformation*, 1962; B. R. White, *The English Separatist Tradition*, Oxford, 1971. Patrick Collinson emphasises the need to study separatism in its social context; 'Towards a broader understanding of the early Dissenting tradition', in *Godly People. Essays on English Protestantism and Puritanism*, 1983, 527–62.
14 For a discussion of the term 'sect', see Bryan Wilson, *Religion in Sociological Perspective*, Oxford, 1982, 89–91.
15 Nuttall quoted in White, *The English Separatist Tradition*, xiii.
16 James Gairdner (ed.), *Three Fifteenth Century Chronicles*, Camden Society, new series, 28, 1880, 143.
17 H. Gareth Owen, 'A nursery of Elizabethan Nonconformity, 1567–72', *J. Eccles. H.*, 17, 1966, 65–76.
18 F. G. Emmison, *Elizabethan Life: Morals and the Church Courts*, Chelmsford, 1973, 97.
19 John Rogers, *The displaying of an horrible secte of grosse and wicked heretiques, . . . the Familie of Love*, 1578, sig. [Ivii–Ivii v.], sig. k. See also Rufus M. Jones, *Studies in Mystical Religion*, 1909, 429–41.
20 Christopher Marsh, '"A Graceless and Audacious Companie": the Family of Love in the parish of Balsham, 1550–1630', *SCH*, 23, 1986, 209–22.
21 Jean Dietz Moss, *'Godded with God': Hendrich Niclaes and his Family of Love*, American Philosophical Society, 71, 1981.
22 Rogers, *Familie of Love*, sig. [kii v.].
23 Moss, *'Godded with God'*, 77.
24 Rogers, *Familie of Love*, sig. [k v., kii].
25 John Robinson, *A justification of separation from the Church of England*, 1610, in Joyce L. Irwin (ed.), *Womanhood in Radical Protestantism, 1525–*

1675, New York, 1979, 163–4; John Robinson, *A just and necessary apology of certain Christians*, 1625, 52.

26 S. R. Gardiner, *History of England . . . 1603–1642*, 10 vols, 1901, iv.143–4.
27 Thomas White, *A discoverie of Brownisme*, 1605, 7–10, 17. An elder was accused of incest with his wife's daughter – presumably, his stepdaughter.
28 Ibid., 23.
29 Francis Johnson, *An inquirie and answer of Thomas White his discoverie of Brownisme*, 1606, 6, 27–8, 32.
30 For Lathrop, see *BDBR*; Bodl., MS Rawl. A 128, f. 27.
31 Ibid., f. 29v.
32 Ibid., ff. 30, 31, 33v., 36v.
33 Ibid., ff. 37, 40.
34 *Records of a Church of Christ in Bristol*, 85; Claire Cross, '"He-Goats before the Flocks": a note on the part played by some women in the founding of some Civil War churches', *SCH*, 8, 1972, 195–202.
35 Ellen S. More, 'Congregationalism and the social order: John Goodwin's gathered church, 1640–60', *J. Eccles. H.*, 38, 1987, 201–35.
36 David Hall (ed.), *The Antinomian Controversy, 1636–1638. A Documentary History*, Middletown, Connecticut, 1968; Ben Barker-Benfield, 'Anne Hutchinson and the Puritan attitude toward women', *Feminist Studies*, 1, 1972, 65–97; Lyle Koehler, 'The case of the American Jezabels: Anne Hutchinson and female agitation during the years of Antinomian turmoil, 1636–1640', *William and Mary Quarterly*, 31, 1974, 55–78.
37 Robert Baillie, *A dissuasive from the errours of the time*, 1645, 63–4.
38 James Anderson, *Memorable Women of the Puritan Times*, 2 vols, 1860, 185.
39 Emry Battis, *Saints and Sectaries. Anne Hutchinson and the Antinomian Controversy in the Massachusetts Bay Colony*, Chapel Hill, 1962, 346–8.
40 Anne Kibbey, *The Interpretation of Material Shapes in Puritanism. A Study of Rhetoric, Prejudice and Violence*, Cambridge, 1986, 93–107.
41 I. B. Horst, *The Radical Brethren. Anabaptism and the English Reformation to 1558*, Niewkoop, 1972, 20, commended Elton et al. for being fair to the radicals.
42 Collinson, 'Towards a broader understanding', 550.
43 I am deeply grateful to Professor Mack for allowing me to read some of her forthcoming book before publication, and for her friendship over the years.
44 Knox, *Enthusiasm*, 20.
45 Edwards, *Gangraena*, part i, epistle dedicatory, sig. a, sig. a2.
46 Baillie, *A dissuasive*, 110, 226.
47 John Brinsley, *The sacred and soveraigne church-remedie*, 1645, 63.
48 *A short history of the Anabaptists of high and low Germany*, 1642; *Englands warning by Germanies woe*, 1646.
49 Robert Baillie, *Anabaptism, the true fountaine of Independency, Brownism, Antinomy, Familisme*, 1647, 33. See also J. F. McGregor, 'The Baptists: fount of all heresy', in J. M. McGregor and B. Reay (eds), *Radical Religion in the English Revolution*, Oxford, 1984, 25–6.
50 Baillie, *A dissuasive*, 63–4. Baillie also reported monstrous births to Hutchinson's associate, Ann Dyer. See also Christopher Fowler, *Daemonium meridianum. Satan at noon*, [16 Feb. 1655], 105.

51 Baillie, *A dissuasive*, 140, n. kkk, 116.
52 John Brinsley, *A looking-glasse for good women*, 1645, 10–22.
53 BL, Harl. MS 4931, a collection which possibly belonged to the Archbishop of Armagh, f. 9.
54 See, for example, *The Ranters religion*, [11 Oct.] 1650.
55 Baillie, *Anabaptism*, 171.
56 M. P. Tilley, *A Dictionary of the Proverbs in England in the Sixteenth and Seventeenth Centuries*, Ann Arbor, 1950, H.778.
57 Knox, *Enthusiasm*, 20. For a fuller discussion of this theme, see Patricia Crawford, 'Historians, women and the Civil War sects', *Parergon*, 6, 1988, 19–32
58 John Morrill, 'The Church in England, 1642–9', in John Morrill (ed.), *Reactions to the English Civil War, 1642–1649*, 1982, 90, 231 n. 4.
59 Barry Reay, *The Quakers and the English Revolution*, New York, 1985, 11, 26–31.
60 Clive D. Field, 'Adam and Eve: gender in the English Free Church constituency', forthcoming, *J. Eccles. H.* I am most grateful to Dr Field for allowing me to cite his work.
61 *OED*.
62 John Locke, *A Letter Concerning Toleration*, in H. R. Penniman (ed.), *John Locke on Politics and Education*, New Haven, 1947, 33.
63 Ernst Troeltsch, *The Social Teaching of the Christian Churches*, 1931.
64 Wilson, *Religion in Sociological Perspective*, 91–2.
65 Currently, the existence of the Ranters as a group rejecting moral constraints is under debate; see J. C. Davis, *Fear, Myth and History. The Ranters and the Historians*, Cambridge, 1986, and reviews.
66 Patricia Crawford, 'Women's printed writings 1600–1700', in Mary Prior (ed.), *Women in English Society, 1500–1800*, 1985, 212–13.
67 For a discussion of the formation of churches, see chapter 7.
68 Crawford, 'Women's printed writings', 269, Table 7.3.
69 Henry Walker, *Spiritual experiences, of sundry believers*, 1653; Jane Turner, *Choice experiences*, 1653. Anne Laurence, 'Women's testimonies: some experiences of English women in the 1650s', unpublished paper. I am most grateful to Dr Laurence for allowing me to read this.
70 Some of these have been reprinted in Elspeth Graham, Hilary Hinds, Elaine Hobby and Helen Wilcox (eds), *Her Own Life. Autobiographical Writings by seventeenth-century Englishwomen*, 1989. See also Elaine Hobby, *Virtue of Necessity. English Women's Writing, 1646–1688*, 1988, and her bibliography; Val Drake, 'I Matter Not How I Appear to Man', unpublished Ph.D. thesis, Oxford Polytechnic, 1988.
71 *BDBR*.
72 Katherine Chidley, *The justification of the independent churches of Christ*, 1641, preface to readers.
73 Ibid., 67.
74 Ibid., 1.
75 Ibid., preface.
76 K. C[hidley], *Good Counsell to the Petitioners for Presbyterian Government*, [1 Nov. 1645], broadside.
77 Ian Gentles, 'London Levellers in the English revolution: the Chidleys and their circle', *J. Eccles. H.*, 29, 1978, 281–309.

78 Phyllis Mack, 'The prophet and her audience: gender and knowledge in the world turned upside down', in Geoff Eley and William Hunt (eds), *Reviving the English Revolution. Reflections and Elaborations on the Work of Christopher Hill*, 1988, 145–7.
79 Gerrard Winstanley, *The Law of Freedom*, 1651, in Leonard Hamilton (ed.), *Gerrard Winstanley. Selections from his Works*, 1944, 176.
80 Mary Cary, *The little horns doom*, 1651, 288–90.
81 Patricia Higgins, 'The reactions of women, with special reference to women petitioners', in B. Manning (ed.), *Politics, Religion and the English Civil War*, 1973.
82 Ann Venn, *A wise virgins lamp burning*, 1658, 4–5.
83 *A list of some of the grand blasphemers . . . given in to the committee for religion*, 1644.
84 *The Brownists conventicle*, 1641, 2–3.
85 *Satan deluded by feigned miracles*, 1655, 1–9; T. J., *A brief representation and discovery*, 1649.
86 *A discoverie of six women preachers*, 1641.
87 Thomas Edwards, *Gangraena*, 2nd edn, 1646, i.118–20; *BDBR*.
88 *CSPD*, 1653–4, 50–1. John Rogers himself was influenced as a child by a preacher 'stiring about, and thundring and beating the Pulpit'; John Rogers, *Ohel, or Beth-shemesh*, 1653, 415.
89 David Brown, *The naked woman*, [23 Nov.] 1652, 5–9. Brown thought the woman mad and her action monstrous.
90 Ann Hughes, 'The pulpit guarded', unpublished paper; I am most grateful to Dr Hughes for allowing me to read her paper.
91 Thomas Edwards, *Gangraena*, 2nd edn, 1646, i.111–12.
92 Christopher Fowler, *Daemonium meridianum. Satan at noon*, [16 Feb. 1655], 1–2.
93 For examples of men who disturbed worship, see E. H. B. Harbin (ed.), *Somerset Quarter Session Records*, 3, 1646–60, Somerset Record Society, 28, 1912, xxxix–xliv.
94 *BDBR*.
95 Humphery Ellis, *Psuedochristus*, 1650.
96 *BDBR*; *All the proceedings at the session of the peace holden at Westminster*, 20 June 1651, 2–3, 12. The author observed that 'if his son prove a daughter, sure his few Disciples will leave him'; 12.
97 Robert Baillie, *Anabaptism*, 30. Baillie cited Clopenburgia, Edwards' *Gangraena*, and Bullinger on the subject of women messiahs.
98 Ralph Farmer, *The great mysteries of godlinesse and ungodlinesse*, 1655, 87.
99 See chapter 8.
100 Phyllis Mack, 'Women as prophets during the English Civil War', *Feminist Studies*, 8, 1982, 19–45; see also Hobby, *Virtue of Necessity*, 26–53.
101 See Dorothy Ludlow, '"Arise and be doing": English "Preaching" women, 1640–1660', unpublished Ph.D. thesis, Indiana, 1978, ch. 4. For a discussion of the relationship of prophecy to the individual's sense of self, see Nigel Smith, *Perfection Proclaimed. Language and Literature in English Radical Religion, 1640–1660*, Oxford, 1989.
102 Patricia Crawford, '"Charles Stuart, that Man of Blood"', *Journal of British Studies* 17, 1977, 41–61.
103 *BDBR*.

104 Elizabeth Poole, *A prophesie touching the death of King Charles*, 1649, 8–9.
105 Ibid., sig. [A3].
106 Elizabeth Poole, *A vision*, 164[9], 1, [4–5].
107 Elizabeth Poole, *An alarum of war*, 1649, 3–6.
108 *BDBR*; Smith, *Perfection Proclaimed*, 45–53.
109 John Price, *The mystery and method of his Majesty's happy restauration*, 1680, 39–40.
110 Ludlow, 'English "preaching" women', 62; see also Dorothy Ludlow, 'Shaking patriarchy's foundations: sectarian women in England, 1641–1700', in Richard Greaves (ed.), *Triumph over Silence. Women in Protestant History*, Westport, Connecticut, 1985.
111 Brinsley, *Looking-glasse for good women*, sig. [A2v.], 10, 22; Katherine Chidley, *A New Years Gift, or a brief exhortation to Mr Thomas Edwards*, 1645, 13.
112 See chapter 8.
113 Joseph Besse, *An Abstract of the Sufferings of the People call'd Quakers*, 3 vols, 1733–8, i.71.
114 Dennis Hollister, *The harlots vail removed*, 1658, 28.

7 Separatist churches and sexual politics

1 For a discussion reaching similar conclusions to those argued here, see Anne Laurence, 'A priesthood of she-believers: women and congregations in mid-seventeenth-century England', *SCH*, 27, 1990, 345–63. See also Patricia Crawford, 'Historians, women and the Civil War sects, 1640–1660', *Parergon*, 6, 1988, 19–32.
2 See, for example, Christopher Hill, *The World Turned Upside Down. Radical Ideas during the English Revolution*, 1972. For the Baptists, see J. F. McGregor, 'The Baptists: fount of all heresy', in J. F. McGregor and B. Reay (eds), *Radical Religion in the English Revolution*, Oxford, 1984, 23–64.
3 John Taylor, *An anatomy of the Separatists*, 1641, 5.
4 Robert Baillie, *A dissuasive from the errours of the time*, 1645, 123.
5 Roger Hayden (ed.), *The Records of a Church of Christ in Bristol, 1640–1687*, Bristol Record Society, 27, 1974, 93.
6 John Knowles and his Socinians in Chester used a parish church. Thanks to Anne Laurence for this reference.
7 A. G. Mathews, *Calamy revised*, Oxford, 1934 (see entries for Thomas Ford III and Lewis Stucley). Trinity church in Hull was similarly divided, with Presbyterians in one half, Independents in the other.
8 G. B. Harrison (ed.), *The Church Book of Bunyan Meeting*, 1928, 15.
9 *The Records of a Church of Christ in Bristol*, 99, 102.
10 Ellen S. More, 'Congregationalism and the social order: John Goodwin's gathered church, 1640–60', *J. Eccles. H.*, 38, 1987, 223.
11 Geoffrey Nuttall, *Visible Saints. The Congregational Way 1640–1660*, Oxford, 1957, 111.
12 H. G. Tibbut (ed.), *Some Early Nonconformist Church Books*, Bedfordshire Historical Record Society, 51, 1972, 27, 23. In 1681 Mary Ball began to relate her experiences publicly, 'but could not go on', so was permitted to give her testimony privately.

13 Anne Laurence, 'Women's testimonies', forthcoming, which I am grateful to Dr Laurence for allowing me to read.
14 John Rogers, *Ohel, or Beth-shemesh*, 1653, 402–6.
15 Henry Walker (ed.), *Spirituall experiences of sundry believers*, [6 Jan.] 1653, 25–30.
16 Ibid., 68–9.
17 Ibid., 60–5.
18 More, 'Congregationalism', 222–3.
19 'Hubbard–How–More', *Transactions of the Baptist Historical Society*, 2, 1910–11, 45.
20 Named after the record keeper, Peter Chamberlen.
21 'A true and short declaration', *Baptist Quarterly*, 1, 1922–3, 154. This is a version of Bodl., Rawl. MS D 828. The printed version leaves out most of the sections relating to women.
22 DWL, MS Harmer 76.2, Transcript, Great Yarmouth Congregational Church, 1642–1815, 2–3; *Church Book of Bunyan Meeting*, vi.
23 John Bastwick, *Independency not Gods ordinance*, 1645, 99.
24 Rogers, *Ohel*, 463–75.
25 DWL, MS Harmer 76.1, Transcript of the Church Book . . . Norwich, 1643–1813, 55.
26 Ibid., 86, 87.
27 DWL, MS Harmer 76.2, Great Yarmouth, 46, 1650; 83, 1655; 99, 1658.
28 John Bunyan, *Grace Abounding to the Chief of Sinners*, preface: 'dedicated to those whom god hath counted him worthy to beget to faith . . . Children, grace be with you'.
29 Katherine Chidley, *A New-Yeares-gift*, 1645, 13.
30 Robert Baillie, *Anabaptism the true fountaine of Independency*, 1647, 118.
31 John Brinsley, *A looking-glasse for good women*, 1645, 34.
32 *Association Records of the Particular Baptists of England, Wales and Ireland to 1660*, ed. B. R. White, 3 vols, Baptist Historical Society, 1971–4, i, South Wales and the Midlands, 27.
33 Susanna Parr, *Susanna's apologie against the elders*, 1659, 10–13.
34 Edward Bean Underhill (ed.), *Records of the Church of Christ, gathered at Fenstanton, Warboys, and Hexham, 1644–1720*, Hanserd Knollys Society, 1854, 24.
35 John Tomkins, *Piety Promoted*, 1701, new edn, 1812, 359–60.
36 *Association Records*, ii.184–5.
37 Bodl., [Minutes of a Puritan Congregation], Rawl. D 828, 32.
38 Rogers, *Ohel*, 475–7.
39 Barry Reay, *The Quakers and the English Revolution*, New York, 1985, xiii. Milton said it was lawful for a wife to desert a non-believing husband, Baillie noted with horror; Robert Baillie, *A dissuasive from the errours of the time*, 1645, 116.
40 John Gee, *New shreds of the old snare*, 1624, 3.
41 Richard Baxter, *A holy commonwealth*, 1659, sig. [c4v.].
42 *Association Records*, iii.140, 157. There was contention during the early modern period over what were the prohibited degrees. The Catholic church took these further than the Protestant.
43 'A true and short declaration', *Baptist Quarterly*, i.160.
44 *Church Book of Bunyan Meeting*, f. 67.

45 Elinor Channel, *A message from God . . . to his Highnes*, 1653.
46 *Some account of the circumstances in the life of Mary Penington*, 1821, 13–14.
47 Lucy Hutchinson, *Memoirs of the Life of Colonel Hutchinson*, ed. James Sutherland, 1973, 169
48 Baillie, *A dissuasive*, 119.
49 *Association Records*, Tiverton, i.28.
50 *Records of the Church of Christ, Fenstanton*, 23.
51 Ibid., 46.
52 Ibid., 20–1. Henry Denne wrote the first volume of the Fenstanton records.
53 [Minutes of a Puritan Congregation], f. 121.
54 Ibid., ff. 41, 45–6.
55 Ibid., f. 28.
56 *Records of the Church of Christ, Fenstanton*, 42–4.
57 *The Church of Christ in Bristol recovering her vail*, 47–9.
58 Dennis Hollister, *The harlots vail removed*, 1658, 58–60.
59 Quoted in Reay, *The Quakers*, 58.
60 Tobie Allein, *Truths manifeste: or, a full and faithful narrative of all the passages*, 1658; Tobie Allein, *Truths manifest revived*, 1659; Susanna Parr, *Susanna's apologie against the elders*, 1659. An extract from *Susanna's Apology* is printed in *Her Own Life. Autobiographical Writings by Seventeenth-Century Englishwomen*, ed. Elspeth Graham, Hilary Hinds, Elaine Hobby and Helen Wilcox, 1989, 103–13. [Thomas Mall], *A true account of what was done by a Church of Christ in Exon*, [8 March] 1658; Lewis Stucley, *Manifest Truth: or an inversion of Truths Manifest*, [2 June 1658]; E. T., *Diotrophes detected, corrected, and rejected*, 1658.
61 Patrick Collinson, 'Towards a broader understanding of the early Dissenting tradition', in *Godly People. Essays on English Protestantism and Puritanism*, 1983, 562 n. 143; R. Buick Knox (ed.), *Reformation, Conformity and Dissent. Essays in Honour of Geoffrey Nuttall*, 1977, 11.
62 A. G. Matthews, *Calamy Revised*, Oxford, 1934, 469; Geoffrey Nuttall, *Visible Saints. The Congregational Way 1640–1660*, Oxford, 1957, 127–30. A local historian of the congregation also sympathised with Stucley, describing Susanna as 'a zealous, earnest, tactless woman, whose mental equilibrium was very much upset by the death of one of her children'; Walter Harte, 'Ecclesiastical and religious affairs in Exeter, 1640–62', *Report and Transactions of the Devonshire Association*, 49, 1937, 67.
63 Parr, *Susanna's apologie*, 7.
64 Ibid., 1–2.
65 Allein, *Truths manifeste*, 1–2.
66 Ibid., 4–12.
67 Mall was appointed co-minister in 1655; Matthews, *Calamy Revised*, 335.
68 The Devon ministers were not prepared to admit to their assembly any congregation which lacked the power to discipline; DRO, MS 35420/M1/1, Minutes of the Exeter Assembly, 1655–9.
69 Elizabeth Vodola, *Excommunication in the Middle Ages*, Berkeley, California, 1986. Gordon Leff, *Heresy in the Later Middle Ages*, 2 vols, Manchester, 1967, i. 42; Ralph Houlbrooke, *Church Courts and the People during the English Reformation 1520–1570*, Oxford, 1979, 48–9; Ronald

A. Marchant, *The Church under the Law: Justice, Administration and Discipline in the Diocese of York*, Cambridge, 1969, 220–2.

70 *The first and second book of discipline*, 1621, 16 explained that excommunication was 'from God, and from all the society of the Kirk'. Nuttall points out that the formula Stucley used was similar to that used in two other cases in Thomas Jollie's congregation; *Visible Saints*, 129, n. 1. Allein, *Truths manifeste*, 20–4.

71 Ibid., 14.

72 Parr, *Susanna's apologie*, 76.

73 Ibid., 76, 29.

74 Ibid., 4, 13; Stucley, *Manifest Truth*, 36.

75 Allein, *Truths manifest revived*, 89.

76 E. T., *Diotrophes detected*, 1658, 1. Nuttall, *Visible Saints*, 127, n. 2 suggests that the author was perhaps Edmund Tucker, the curate at Halwell, Devon. My arguments for suggested female authorship are contextual.

77 E. T., *Diotrophes detected*, 3–6.

78 Allein, *Truths manifeste*, 5–10. I have no evidence that Allein was excommunicated.

79 Parr, *Susanna's apologie*, 13. For a discussion of the significance of Providentialism, see Blair Worden, 'Providence and politics in Cromwellian England', *Past & Present*, 109, 1985, 55–99.

80 Allein, *Truths manifeste*, 2; Allein, *Truths manifest revived*, 76–80. Stucley was said to be a kinsman of General Monk's; Matthews, *Calamy Revised*, 469.

81 Parr, *Susanna's apologie*, 56.

82 E. T., *Diotrophes detected*, 11–12, 17–18.

83 Stucley, *Manifest Truth*, 34.

84 Ibid., 14, 34, 36–7; Allein, *Truths manifeste*, [30].

85 Ibid., 28–37; Allein, *Truths manifest revived*, sig. [D3], 31, 107, 10. Parr's husband was mentioned in 1654, but not thereafter, suggesting that she may have been widowed during the 1650s.

86 Allein, *Truths manifeste*, 10; Allein, *Truths manifest revived*, sig. [D3.]

87 Parr, *Susanna's apologie*, preface.

88 Ibid., 114.

89 Allein, *Truths manifeste*, 30–1.

90 Ibid., 4, 7.

91 Parr, *Susanna's apologie*, 21, 24–5.

8 Sex and power in the early Quaker movement: the case of Martha Simmonds

1 The name was used in 1647 of a sect of women at Southwark. The term was applied to Fox and his followers in 1651; W. C. Braithwaite, *The Beginnings of Quakerism to 1660*, 2nd edn, 1955, 57–8.

2 Michael Watts, *The Dissenters. From the Reformation to the French Revolution*, Oxford, 1978, 189.

3 Barry Reay, *The Quakers and the English Revolution*, New York, 1985, 9.

4 Bonnelyn Young Kunze, 'The family, social and religious life of Margaret Fell', unpublished Ph. D. thesis, University of Rochester, 1986.

5 William C. Braithwaite, *The Second Period of Quakerism*, 2nd edn, 1961, 270.

6 J. F. McGregor and Barry Reay (eds), *Radical Religion in the English Revolution*, Oxford, 1984, 144.

7 Phyllis Mack, 'Gender and spirituality in early English Quakerism, 1650–1665', in Elizabeth Potts Brown and Susan Mosher Stuard (eds), *Witnesses for Change. Quaker Women over Three Centuries*, New Brunswick, 1989.

8 Reay, *Quakers*, 9.

9 Richard Baxter, *The Quakers catechism*, 1655, sig. C2.

10 Reay, *Quakers*, 10.

11 Ibid., 26–31.

12 George Bishop and others, *The cry of blood*, 1656, 116.

13 Susanna Bateman, *I matter not how I appear to man*, [1657], 8.

14 Folger Library, Washington, Bennett Papers, 174, 175. I am grateful to John Morrill for sending me this reference.

15 Martha Simmonds, *A lamentation for the lost sheep*, 1655, 5–6.

16 Bishop et al., *The cry of blood*, 16–17.

17 Ibid., 114–17; Joseph Besse, *An Abstract of the Sufferings of the People call'd Quakers*, 3 vols, 1733–8, i.9; FHL, Ellis Hookes, Great Book of Sufferings, i.81.

18 Norman Penney (ed.), *Extracts from State Papers relating to Friends 1654 to 1672*, 1913, 20. For further examples, see FHL, Hookes, Great Book of Sufferings, i.421, 547–8; ii.1; Somerset, 142; Sussex, 5; Yorkshire, 8–10.

19 Braithwaite, *The Beginnings of Quakerism*, 420–31.

20 Joseph Besse, *A Collection of the Sufferings of the People called Quakers*, 1753, i.84–5.

21 Gerard Croese, *The General History of the Quakers*, 1696, 108.

22 FHL, Caton MS, vol. 3, 396–7, Hubberthorne to Margaret Fell, 13 June [1654].

23 From 1659 Friends resolved to record all sufferings; Braithwaite, *The Beginnings of Quakerism*, 315. From 1660 details were recorded centrally; Braithwaite, *The Second Period of Quakerism*, 282.

24 Sarah Cheevers and Katherine Evans, *To all the people upon the face of the earth*, 1663.

25 BDBR. Dyer was married and had six children; Emily Manners, *Elizabeth Hooton. First Quaker Woman Preacher (1600–1672)*, 1914, 30–3. See also Mack, 'Gender and spirituality', 32–3.

26 Bishop et al., *The cry of blood*, 113–14, 117.

27 Patricia Crawford, 'Women's published writings 1600–1700', in Mary Prior (ed.), *Women in English Society, 1500–1800*, 1985, 224–5, 269.

28 Mack, 'Gender and spirituality ', 58, n. 6.

29 Besse, *An Abstract of the Sufferings*, i.136.

30 FHL, Hooke, Great Book of Sufferings, i.547.

31 Bishop et al, *The cry of blood*, 98–103.

32 Norman Penney, *The First Publishers of Truth*, 1907, 259.

33 Kenneth L. Carroll, 'Early Quakers and "Going Naked as a Sign"', *Quaker History*, 67, 1978, 69–87; Richard Bauman, *Let Your Words Be Few. Symbolism of Speaking and Silence among Seventeenth-Century Quakers*, Cambridge, 1983.

34 Kenneth L. Carroll, 'Quaker attitudes towards signs and wonders', *Journal of the Friends' Historical Society.*, 54, 1977, 77.
35 Beatrice Carré, 'Early Quaker women in Lancaster and Lancashire', in Michael Mullett (ed.), *Early Lancaster Friends*, Lancaster, 1978, 44–5.
36 Mary Forster and 7,000 Hand-maids of the Lord, *These several papers was sent to the Parliament*, 1659.
37 Besse, *An Abstract of the Sufferings*, ii.252.
38 Carré, 'Early Quaker women', 45–6.
39 Braithwaite, *The Beginnings of Quakerism*, 75.
40 *From our womens meeting held at York*, 1692, 4–5.
41 Braithwaite, *The Beginnings of Quakerism*, 340–2; Braithwaite, *The Second Period of Quakerism*, 269–75.
42 Kunze, 'Margaret Fell', vi; Bonnelyn Young Kunze, 'Religious authority and social status in seventeenth-century England: the friendship of Margaret Fell, George Fox, and William Penn', *Church History*, 57, 1988, 170–86.
43 William Grigge, *The Quakers Jesus*, 1658, 3.
44 *Diary of Thomas Burton Esquire, member in the Parliaments of Oliver and Richard Cromwell*, ed. J. T. Rutt, 4 vols, 1828, i.28.
45 John Deacon, *An exact history of the life of James Nayler*, 1657, 43-5.
46 Robert Darnton, *The Great Cat Massacre and other Episodes in French Cultural History*, 1984, 78.
47 Emilia Fogelklou, *James Nayler. The Rebel Saint 1618–1660*, trans. 1931; Ronald Matthews, *English Messiahs. Studies of Six English Religious Pretenders 1656–1927*, 1936; Geoffrey Nuttall, *James Nayler. A Fresh Approach, Journal of the Friends' Historical Society Supplement*, 1954; William G. Bittle, *James Nayler, 1618–1660. The Quaker Indicted by Parliament*, York, 1986.
48 *Diary of Thomas Burton*, i.171.
49 Christopher Hill, *The World Turned Upside Down. Radical Ideas during the English Revolution*, 1972, 200–1.
50 Blair Worden, 'Toleration and the Cromwellian Protectorate', *SCH*, 21, 1984, 199–233.
51 Since this chapter was written, Christine Trevett has published an article reaching very similar conclusions to those argued here. Christine Trevett, 'The women around James Nayler, Quaker: a matter of emphasis', *Religion*, 20, 1990, 249–73.
52 R. A. Knox, *Enthusiasm. A Chapter in the History of Religion with special reference to the xvii and xviii centuries*, Oxford, 1950, 160–1; Mabel Richmond Brailsford, *A Quaker from Cromwell's Army: James Nayler*, 1927, 97; Isabel Ross, *Margaret Fell. Mother of Quakerism*, 2nd edn, 1984, 105; Bittle, *James Nayler*, 84.
53 *A true narrative of the examination, tryall, and sufferings of James Nayler*, 1657, 27.
54 Grigge, *The Quakers Jesus*, 10–11. See also Ralph Farmer, *Satan inthron'd in his chair of pestilence*, [18 Dec.] 1657, 18–19. Barry White says Dorcas Erbury was the wife, Hill says widow or daughter, of William Erbury, a New Model Army chaplain. White described Erbury as a Seeker; *BDBR*.
55 *A true narrative*.
56 Deacon, *An exact history*, 35–[6].

57 *A true narrative*, 53. The author of a *True relation*, 1657, 4–5, mocked the women who greeted Nayler when he returned to Bristol for punishment. They competed to be the nearest to Nayler's horse, were officiously busy about his food, and had 'transportations' before his punishment.

58 *Diary of Thomas Burton*, i.155.

59 Ibid., i.129.

60 Ibid., i.55, 56.

61 Ibid., i.129, 69. Sydenham reminded the MPs of an uncomfortable truth: some of the earlier Parliaments being cited for their precedents in dealing with heresy would have condemned most of the Protectorate Parliament as heretics.

62 *Diary of Thomas Burton*, 207.

63 Ibid., 247.

64 Ibid., 336, 205. MPs were not usually so sensitive about women's words, since these were of less concern than what men said.

65 Farmer, *Satan inthron'd*, 9, 22.

66 Thomas Hall, *A practical and polemical commentary . . . upon . . . Timothy*, 1658, 226. For further examples of witchcraft allegations, see Trevett, 'The women around James Nayler', 251 and n. 14.

67 Farmer, *Satan inthron'd*, 29.

68 *CSPD*, 1656–7, vol. 10, 236.

69 His wife Anne petitioned to be allowed to come to him after his imprisonment; *CSPD*, 1656–7, vol. 10, 289–90, petition 24 Feb. 1657. Hubberthorne reported that when Nayler was a close prisoner in Bridewell in February 1657, she was the only one allowed to see him; FHL, Caton MS, vol. 3, 377–9.

70 *A true narrative*, 2–3; Deacon, *An exact history*, 14–17.

71 *Diary of Thomas Burton*, 10.

72 G. F. Nuttall (ed.), *Early Quaker Letters*, 1952, Letter 315, Hubberthorne to Fell, 16 Sept. [1656]. In 1655 an anti-Quaker pamphlet accused Martha Simmonds of being 'wife to Mr Bourn the Astronomer in Morefields'; *The Quacking Mountebanck*, 1655, 19. (I owe this reference to the late C. M. Williams.) There is no evidence of her husband Thomas being disturbed by her behaviour. He went to Exeter with her in 1656, although he thought that the diversion to Bristol was a mistake, and that the Lord would have brought them to London and manifested his power there. Farmer, *Satan inthron'd*, 20–1.

73 Watts, *The Dissenters*, 210.

74 Carol Z. Weiner, 'Sex roles and crimes in late Elizabethan Hertfordshire', *Journal of Social History*, 8, 1975, 38–60.

75 Matthews, *English Messiahs*, 4, 10.

76 Fogelklou, *James Nayler*, 161, 185.

77 Geoffrey F. Nuttall, *James Nayler. A Fresh Approach*, *Journal of the Friends' Historical Society Supplement*, 1954, 15–16.

78 FHL, Caton MS, vol. 3, 364, Hubberthorne to Fell, 26 July 1656. Much of the strongest abuse of Simmonds came from Hubberthorne.

79 *A collection of sundry books, epistles and papers written by James Nayler*, 1716, viii–ix.

80 Braithwaite, *The Beginnings of Quakerism*, 246.

81 Hugh Barbour, *The Quakers in Puritan England*, New Haven, 1964, 63.

82 *BDBR*, Nayler.
83 Brailsford, *A Quaker from Cromwell's Army*, 97. Brailsford also refers to her as 'this half-crazy woman'; ibid., 106.
84 Kenneth L. Carroll, 'Martha Simmonds, a Quaker Enigma', *Journal of the Friends' Historical Society.*, 67, 1972, 31–52.
85 This view first appeared in Farmer, *Satan inthron'd*, sig. [A3v.–4]; Knox, *Enthusiasm*, 160–6. His alternative reading did not exonerate the female sex from blame. Margaret Fell, he believed, encouraged Fox in his errors.
86 *Diary of Thomas Burton*, 10.
87 Martha Simmonds, *A lamentation for the lost sheep*, 1655. This was reprinted with an additional warning in 1656; [*An Admonition*, 25 April 1655], brs.
88 H. J. Cadbury (ed.), *Letters to William Dewsbury and Others*, 1948, 41.
89 Bauman, *Let Your Words Be Few*, 84–94.
90 Cadbury (ed.), *Letters*, 41.
91 Nuttall, *James Nayler*, 11–12.
92 Hubberthorne reported that the substance of what she sang for over an hour was 'Innocency, innocency'; FHL, Caton MS, vol. 3, 364–5.
93 FHL, Markey MS, 120–2.
94 Farmer, *Satan inthron'd*, 10–11.
95 FHL, Caton MS, vol. 3, 364–5, [Richard Hubberthorne to Margaret Fell], 26 [Aug.] 1656.
96 Farmer, *Satan inthron'd*, 10–11.
97 Simmonds had directly abused Fox in 1656; FHL, Swathmore transcripts, ii.233, Fox to Nayler 1656.
98 Ibid.; part of Fox's letter published in Farmer, *Satan inthron'd*, 9–10.
99 Farmer, *Satan inthron'd*, 12–15.
100 FHL, Swathmore MS, i.188. Those named in this and other sources were Martha Simmonds, Hannah Stranger, Dorcas Erbury, James Stringer, Timothy Wedlock, Samuel Cater, Robert Crab, and Nayler.
101 Farmer, *Satan inthron'd*; Bittle, *James Nayler*, 104–12.
102 Priscilla Cotton and Mary Cole, *To the priests and people of England, we discharge our consciences*, 1655, 7–8.
103 The story was first told of one 'Williamson's wife' in Francis Higginson, *A brief relation*, 1653, 3; see also Deacon, *An exact history*, 51.
104 Richard Coppin, *Saul smitten*, 1653, 8–10; Richard Coppin, *Michael opposing the dragon*, 1659, 85, 243–4; *BDBR*.
105 Mack, 'Gender and spirituality', 43.
106 Examination of Simmonds before Bristol magistrates, quoted in Farmer, *Satan inthron'd*, 15.
107 N. Penney (ed.), *Journal of George Fox*, 2 vols, Cambridge, 1911, i.xxvi.
108 FHL, Caton MS, vol. 3, 373–4.
109 Ibid., 376.
110 Thomas Edwards, *Gangraena*, 1646, i.116, 120–1.
111 Margaret Aston, 'Lollard women priests?', in *Lollards and Reformers. Images and Literacy in late Medieval Religion*, 1984, 49–70.
112 So far as I can discover. Their enemies certainly believed that the Quakers had no sacraments; [Richard Blome], *Questions propounded to George Whitehead and George Fox*, 29 Aug. 1659, 24.
113 Carroll, 'Martha Simmonds', 51–2.

114 Keith Thomas, 'Women and the Civil War sects', in Trevor Aston (ed), *Crisis in Europe 1560-1660: Essays from Past and Present*, 1965, 339–40.

115 Thomas F. Torrance, *The Trinitarian Faith. The Evangelical Theology of the Ancient Catholic Church*, Edinburgh, 1988, 72.

116 This section owes a great deal to the insights of Phyllis Mack's essay, 'Gender and spirituality'.

117 Rebecca Travers, *For those that meet to worship*, 1659, 3.

118 James Nayler, *A discovery of the man of sin*, 1655, 44.

119 Mack, 'Gender and spirituality', 41–3.

120 John Tomkins, *Piety Promoted*, 1703, i.70.

121 Higginson, *A brief relation*, 17.

122 Travers, *For those that meet to worship*, 17.

123 FHL, Swathmore transcripts, i.651–2.

124 Besse, *An Abstract of the Sufferings*, i.67; see also Besse, *Collection*, i. 150.

125 Besse, *An Abstract of the Sufferings*, i.70.

126 Ibid., ii.48; i.76.

127 Mack, 'Gender and spirituality', 33.

128 [Blome], *Questions propounded*, 17.

129 Mack, 'Gender and spirituality', 56.

9 Anglicans, Catholics and Nonconformists after the Restoration 1660–1720

1 The main acts were as follows: the Corporation Act of 1661 debarred from office all men who did not take the Anglican sacrament. The Act of Uniformity of 1662 required all ministers to take oaths of loyalty, to accept the Book of Common Prayer and be reordained if they had not already been ordained by a bishop. The date of submission was St Bartholemew's day, 24 August 1662. On that date many ministers bade farewell to their congregations. The Conventicle Act of 1664 struck at the religious liberty of the laity: no more than five people, apart from the household, were to come together for worship. By the Five Mile Act of 1665, preachers were forbidden to come within five miles of their former congregations. This legislation, collectively but incorrectly known as the Clarendon Code, deprived people of the ease for their consciences which Charles had promised in his Declaration of Breda. Historians have debated whether this was part of a deliberate plot by the Anglicans, or the inevitable outcome of Puritan division over comprehension or toleration. For an account from the Dissenting perspective, see Michael R. Watts, *The Dissenters. From the Reformation to the French Revolution*, Oxford, 1978.

2 Antonia Fraser, *The Weaker Vessel: Woman's Lot in Seventeenth-Century England*, 1984, 263.

3 Patricia Crawford, 'Women's printed writings 1600–1700', in Mary Prior (ed.), *Women in English Society, 1500–1800*, 1985, 212, 266.

4 Barry Reay, *The Quakers and the English Revolution*, New York, 1985, 81.

5 Philip Henry, Stedman transcript of Diary, 29 May 1662 (I am grateful to Mr P. Warburton-Lee for allowing me to consult his manuscripts).

6 Gerald R. Cragg, *Puritanism in the Period of the Great Persecution, 1660-1688*, Cambridge, 1957.

7 Watts, *The Dissenters*, 259–60.

8 Rose Graham, 'The civic position of women at common law before 1800', in *English Ecclesiastical Studies*, 1929.

9 Patricia Crawford, 'Public duty, conscience, and women in early modern England', in John Morrill and Paul Slack (eds), *Public Duty and Private Conscience: Festschrift for G. E. Aylmer*, forthcoming, Oxford.

10 Ruth Perry, 'Mary Astell and the feminist critique of possessive individualism', *Eighteenth Century Studies*, 23, 1990, 445. See also Lois G. Schwoerer, 'Women and the Glorious Revolution', *Albion*, 18, 1986, 195–218, esp. 217–18.

11 Mary Astell, *Reflections upon Marriage*, 1706, in Bridget Hill (ed.), *The First English Feminist*, 1986, 76.

12 Michael Mullett, 'From sect to denomination? Social developments in eighteenth-century English Quakerism', *Journal of Religious History*, 13, 1986, 168–91.

13 John Morrill, 'The attack on the Church of England in the Long Parliament, 1640–1642', in Derek Beales and Geoffrey Best (eds), *History, Society and the Churches. Essays in Honour of Owen Chadwick*, Cambridge, 1985, 105–24. See also Patrick Collinson, *The Religion of Protestants. The Church in English Society 1559–1625*, Oxford, 1982, 192.

14 Sharon L. Arnoult, Abstract of paper, '"Deliver us and thy whole church": Anglican women during the English Civil War and Interregnum, 1640–1660', delivered at 1990 Western Conference of British Studies, 32–4.

15 Morrill, 'The attack on the Church of England', 124.

16 E. Gibson, *Observations*, 1744, in E. Neville Williams (ed.), *The Eighteenth-Century Constitution, 1688-1815. Documents and Commentary*, Cambridge, 1960, 378.

17 John Oliver, *A present for teeming women*, 1663, sig. [A5v.], [a2v.].

18 Carolyn Merchant, *The Death of Nature. Women, Ecology and the Scientific Revolution*, New York, 1983, 253–68.

19 Dorcas Bennet, *Good and seasonable counsel*, 1670, sig. [a2].

20 Joan Kinnaird, 'Mary Astell and the conservative contribution to English feminism', *Journal of British Studies*, 19, 1979, 53–75; Hill (ed.), *The First English Feminist*; Ruth Perry, *The Celebrated Mary Astell. An Early English Feminist*, Chicago, 1986, 182–231.

21 Evan Davies, 'The enforcement of religious conformity in England, 1668–1700, with special reference to the dioceses of Chichester and Worcester', unpublished M.Litt. thesis, University of Oxford, 1982, 181.

22 Martin Ingram, *Church Courts, Sex and Marriage in England, 1570–1640*, Cambridge, 1987, 372–4.

23 Watts, *The Dissenters*, 229.

24 M. H. Lee (ed.), *Diaries and Letters of Philip Henry . . . 1631–1696*, 1882, 147.

25 The tradition of the ministers' suffering began with the ministers themselves who preached farewell sermons, and was continued by Edmund Calamy with his account of the sufferings of those ejected; A. G. Matthews, *Calamy Revised*, Oxford, 1974.

26 Clive D. Field, '"Adam and Eve". Gender in the English Free Church constituency', *J. Eccles. H.*, forthcoming. I am most grateful to Dr Field for sending me his manuscript and allowing me to cite his findings.

27 Thomas Crosby, *The History of the English Baptists*, 2 vols, 1738, ii.183.

28 Richard Baxter, *Reliquiae Baxterianae*, 1696, iii.4.
29 Owen Stockton, *Consolation in life and death . . . A funeral sermon . . . Mrs Ellen Asty*, 1681, 14.
30 *Remarkable Passages in the Life of William Kiffin*, 1823, 50.
31 *Diaries of Philip Henry*, 143.
32 *The Last Legacy of Mr Joseph Davis, Senr*, 1707, 1720, printed in A. C. Underwood, *A History of the English Baptists*, 1947, 100–2.
33 Margaret Fell, *A brief collection of remarkable passages*, 1710.
34 Thomas Crosby, *The History of the English Baptists*, 4 vols, 1739, ii.165–71.
35 *Diaries of Philip Henry*, 147. Mr Thomas was probably Zechariah Thomas, ejected Aug. 1662; Matthews, *Calamy Revised*.
36 Patricia Crawford, 'Katharine and Philip Henry and their children: a case study in family ideology', *Transactions of the Historic Society of Lancashire and Cheshire*, 134, 1984, 39–73.
37 Margaret Spufford, *Contrasting Communities*, Cambridge, 1974.
38 A. D. Gilbert, 'The growth and decline of Nonconformity in England and Wales, with special reference to the period before 1850', unpublished D. Phil. thesis, University of Oxford, 1973, 153.
39 Elizabeth Cellier, *Malice defeated*, 1680. Bodl., Ashmol. 1677 contains a collection of pamphlets on her case, including *Tho. Dangerfield's answer to a certain scandalous lying pamphlet*, 1680.
40 Susan O'Brien, 'Women of the "English Catholic Community": nuns and pupils at the Bar Convent, York, 1680–1790', forthcoming in Judith Loudes (ed.), *Monastic Studies*, i.267–82.
41 Michael J. Galgano, 'Out of the mainstream: Catholic and Quaker women in the Restoration Northwest', in Richard S. Dunn and Mary Maples Dunn (eds), *The World of William Penn*, Philadelphia, 1986, 119–21.
42 Joseph Besse, *A collection of the sufferings of the people called Quakers*, 2 vols, 1753.
43 Richard T. Vann, *The Social Development of English Quakerism, 1655-1755*, Cambridge, Massachusetts, 1969, 197–208. For discussions of this theme, see T. A. Davies, 'The Quakers in Essex, 1655–1725', unpublished D.Phil thesis, University of Oxford, 1986, 189–250.
44 Michael Mullett has reservations about this typology. His article, 'From sect to denomination?', 169–91, provides useful references to the discussion.
45 Louella M. Wright, *The Literary Life of the Early Friends 1650–1725*, repr. New York, 1966, 97–107.
46 FHL, Book of Minutes of the Second days Morning Meeting, Transcript, [hereafter LMMM], ii.103, 19, 56.
47 B. S. Snell (ed.) *The Minute book of the Monthly meeting of the Society of Friends for the Upperside of Buckinghamshire, 1669–1690*, Buckinghamshire Archaeological Society, 1, 1937, 154–5.
48 FHL, LMMM, iii.124–8. Fisher was widowed in 1690.
49 Snell (ed.), *Upperside Minutes*, 34–5.
50 FHL, Swathmore Monthly Meeting, Women's minutes 1671–1700, f. 28.
51 Arnold Lloyd, *Quaker Social History*, 1950, 116.
52 FHL, Vale of the White Horse Monthly Meeting Minutes, 1673–1722, transcribed by S. & B. Snell, pt 2 (Notes), 28.
53 Vale Minutes, pt 1, 23.

54 T. A. Davies, 'The Quakers in Essex', 130–61.
55 Jean and Russell Mortimer (eds), *Leeds Friends' Minute Book, 1692 to 1712, Yorkshire Archaeological Society*, 139, 1980, 12–13n.
56 David W. Bolam, *Unbroken Community. The History of the Friends' School Saffron Walden, 1702–1952*, Cambridge, 1952, 13.
57 [William Mucklow], *Tyranny and hypocrisy detected*, 1673, 72.
58 W. C. Braithwaite, *The Beginnings of Quakerism to 1660*, 2nd edn, 1955, 340–2; W. C. Braithwaite, *The Second Period of Quakerism*, 2nd edn, 1961, 269–75; Bonnelyn Young Kunze, 'The family, social and religious life of Margaret Fell', unpublished Ph.D. thesis, University of Rochester, 1986.
59 George Fox, *This is an encouragment*, 1676, 25, 12, 20.
60 Ibid., 20, 95.
61 Storey quoted in William Rogers, *The Christian-Quaker distinguished from the apostate & innovator*, 1680, iv.12; FHL, Swathmore MS, Women's Meeting, letter from Fox, [1675], f. 12.
62 *Upperside Minutes*, 130.
63 Ibid., 108–9, 133.
64 Ibid., 126–7, 99.
65 Isabel Ross, *Margaret Fell. Mother of Quakerism*, 2nd edn, York, 1984, 294.
66 [William Mucklow], *The spirit of the hat*, 1673, 32.
67 William Mather, *A novelty: or, a government of women*, [1694?], 5, 22.
68 Rogers, *The Christian-Quaker*, i.64–6; iv.9–12.
69 Margaret Fell, *Women's speaking justified*, 1666, 3, 9, 12. Selections of this work have been reprinted in various forms.
70 Rogers, *The Christian-Quaker*, iii.52.
71 [William Mucklow], *Tyranny and hypocrisy detected*, 1673, 47–52.
72 Rogers, *The Christian-Quaker*, iv.12.
73 FHL, LMMM, iii.17.
74 Ibid., iii.332 (1709). She was required to bring a certificate from her previous meeting place.
75 Ibid., iii.79, 129, 135.
76 FHL, Vale of White Horse Minutes, 119.
77 Ibid., 18.
78 For a few yearly meeting letters, see Quaker women in my 'Provisional checklist of women's published writings', in Prior (ed.), *Women in English Society*, 254.
79 Watts, *The Dissenters*, 324.
80 Angus Library, Regent's Park College, MS 2/4/1, Maze Pond Church Book, 1691–1745.
81 Maze Pond, 44, Oct. 1691.
82 Ibid., 44.
83 Ibid., 49.
84 Ibid., 4.
85 Ibid., 105, 9 Oct. 1694.
86 Ibid., 108–9.
87 Murdina D. Macdonald, 'London Calvinistic Baptists, 1689–1727: tensions within a Dissenting community under toleration', unpublished D.Phil thesis, University of Oxford, 1982, 91.
88 Angus Library, Cripplegate Church Book 1689–1723, f. 22.
89 Ibid., ff. 69–70, 10 Dec. 1713.

90 Ibid., f. 72.

91 Ibid., ff. 86v.-88v., 1716.

92 The only concession Maze Pond gave was to record that if indeed he had been guilty of the matters as charged, she had done right to leave; Maze Pond, 100, 102.

93 *Records of a Church of Christ*, 51, 208–9; Cripplegate, f. 72v.

94 Cripplegate, f. 10.

95 Maze Pond, 101.

96 Cripplegate, f. 10.

97 Ibid., ff. 11–12; printed in *BQ*, ii.182–4.

98 *BQ*, ii.121.

99 Ibid., 113–15, 122–3.

100 Watts, *The Dissenters*, 336–41.

101 Maze Pond, f. 93.

102 W. T. Whitley (ed.), *Minutes of the General Assembly of the General Baptist Church in England*, 2 vols, 1910, i.23.

103 *BQ*, ii.119–21.

104 Maze Pond, f. 102.

105 Ibid., f. 32.

106 Cripplegate, ff. 32–6v., 47v.–49.

107 Mary Maples Dunn, 'Saints and Sisters: Congregational and Quaker women in the Early Colonial Period', *American Quarterly*, 30, 1978, 592–5.

108 John Gregory, *A Father's Legacy to His Daughter*, 1774, 9–25.

109 For a discussion of the importance of the family ideology of the good woman, see Crawford, 'Family of Philip and Katharine Henry'.

110 In 1703, there were only six couples in Heywood's Presbyterian congregation of fifty-one members; W. J. Sheils, 'Oliver Heywood and his congregation', *SCH*, 23, 1986, 268–71.

111 Field, 'Gender in the English Free Church constituency', Table 3.

112 Dale A. Johnson, *Women in English Religion 1700–1925*, Studies in Women and Religion, 10, New York, 1984, 13.

113 M. G. Jones, *The Charity School Movement. A Study of Eighteenth Century Puritanism in Action*, Cambridge, 1938, 57.

114 Craig Rose, 'Evangelical philanthropy and Anglican revival: the Charity Schools of Augustan London, 1698–1740', *London Journal*, 16, 1991, 35–65; W. O. B. Allen and Edmund McClure, *Two Hundred Years: The History of the Society for Promoting Christian Knowledge, 1698–1898*, 1898, 138. Nearly twice as many boys as girls were enrolled by 1704; ibid., 140.

115 Perry, *Mary Astell*, 239.

116 'An account of the . . . call to the ministry of Margaret Lucas', *The Friends' Library*, 13, Philadelphia, 1849, 179–201.

117 See chapter 5.

118 Desirée Hirst, *Hidden Riches. Traditional Symbolism from Renaissance to Blake*, 1964, 103–5.

119 Hillel Schwartz, *Knaves, Fools, Madmen, and that Subtile Effluvium. A Study of the Opposition to the French Prophets in England, 1706–1710*, University of Florida Monographs, 62, 1978, 19–20; Hillel Schwartz, *The*

French Prophets. The History of a Millenarian Group in Eighteenth-Century England, Berkeley, California, 1980, 146–7, 210.
120 'Lincoln's Inn Fields: the French Prophets', *Notes & Queries*, 6th series, 11, 10 Jan. 1885, 21–2.
121 Schwartz, *Opposition to French Prophets*, 21–4.
122 Ibid., 31–65.
123 *Enthusiastick imposters no divinely inspir'd prophets*, 1707, 68.

CONCLUSION

1 Caroline Walker Bynum, Introduction, in Caroline Walker Bynum, Stevan Harrell and Paula Richman (eds), *Gender and Religion: On the Complexity of Symbols*, Boston, 1986, 8–16.
2 *To the supreme authority*, [5 May 1649].

Index